*Dedicated to
the people of Kansas*

The Capper/MRI
Quick-Fact Book of
KANSAS

Compiled by
Midwest Research Institute
and Capper Press

Capper Press
Topeka, Kansas

Published by	Capper Press
Copyright	Copyright © 1990 by Capper Press
All rights reserved	No part of this book may be used or reproduced in any manner whatsoever without written permission except in the case of brief quotations embodied in critical articles and reviews, or for non-commercial, educational uses in the classroom.
Compiled by	Midwest Research Institute 425 Volker Boulevard, Kansas City, Missouri 64110 Capper Press 616 Jefferson, Topeka, Kansas 66607
Acknowledgment	We at Capper Press and Midwest Research Institute would like to thank the state agencies, chambers of commerce, organizations and individuals who graciously provided so much information and assistance in the publication of this book.
Midwest Research Institute	Linda W. Thornton, *Project Director* Gary Sage, *Business Manager* Robert E. Gustafson, *Creative Director* LaDene Morton, *Researcher* James P. Becker, *Researcher*
Capper Press	Diana J. Edwardson Persell, *Project Director* Michele R. Webb, *Editor* Tammy R. Dodson, *Editor — First Printing*
Book Design by	The Amundson Group 1100 W. Cambridge Circle, Suite 550 Kansas City, Kansas 66103
The Amundson Group	Jerry Amundson, *Designer* Eric Amundson, *Production Manager* Beverly Amundson, *Production Coordinator*
Cover Photo by	John Schlageck, Kansas Farm Bureau
Original Art by	Diana J. Edwardson Persell
Softcover Edition	ISBN 0-941678-21-0 Softcover Edition
First Printing	September 1990
Second Printing & Update	August 1992

preface

Many people know that Kansas is associated with wheat fields and sunflowers, but did you also know that the first motion picture theater west of the Mississippi River was built in Lawrence? Or that the famous circus clown Emmett Kelly was born in Sedan? Or that approximately 1.3 million people are currently employed in Kansas, which is more than twice as many as in 1940?

With *The Capper/MRI Quick-Fact Book of Kansas*, you don't have to dig through 50 different volumes to find the facts you need and want to know – we've already done the research for you! *The Capper/MRI Quick-Fact Book of Kansas* is a compilation of key information, statistics, charts, and fun facts presented in one reference volume.

This fact book features an easy-to-read format, and the chapter title and subject area are clearly marked at the top of each page for handy reference. The sidebars allow you to thumb through the pages to scan for quick facts. Major topics are highlighted in color on each page so you can easily locate information without having to pore over chapters of text.

The Capper/MRI Quick-Fact Book of Kansas is perfect for educators, students, librarians, business executives, tourists, residents of the state, and individuals who want the facts about Kansas in one convenient edition. This fact book includes: state symbols, chronology of historical events, list of county seats and county abbreviations, population figures, vital statistics, tourist attractions, arts programs, crop and livestock data, maps, charts, and more. Whether life-long residents of the state or visitors, readers will enjoy discovering the many surprises that Kansas has to offer.

Educators will find *The Capper/MRI Quick-Fact Book of Kansas* to be a beneficial teaching supplement for history, English, geography, geology, social studies, and other classroom subjects. Students will find the graphs and data especially useful for researching and writing reports. And all Kansans, regardless of age or profession, will enjoy learning more about their state.

The Capper/MRI Quick-Fact Book of Kansas is the result of a team project between Capper Press and the Midwest Research Institute.

Capper Press, owned by Stauffer Communications, Inc., in Topeka, Kansas, is the book publishing division of *Capper's* magazine (formerly *Capper's Weekly*), one of the oldest and most-loved publications in America. *Capper's* has been printed for more than 110 years and reaches a subscriber base of nearly 400,000 readers throughout the Midwest and the United States.

Midwest Research Institute, headquartered in Kansas City, Missouri, is an independent, not-for-profit organization that has become one of the nation's leading independent research institutes. Founded in 1944 by a group of Midwestern civic, business, and technical leaders, Midwest Research Institute performs and manages

preface

research and development programs for clients in business, industry, government, and for other public and private sector groups.

In doing the research for this book, we were fortunate to have talked with people from many organizations throughout Kansas. We would like to say a heartfelt thank you to the many representatives and officials at the state agencies and organizations who so graciously took time out to provide us with assistance and information. The Kansas Secretary of State's Office, the Kansas Historical Society, the Kansas Department of Commerce, and the Kansas Farm Bureau deserve recognition and thanks for their valuable assistance.

Thanks also goes to the numerous chamber of commerce representatives whom we spoke to about their hometowns. With their help we were able to pass along to the readers a flavor of the delightful attractions, festivals, and historical sites across the state. Whether a small town or metropolitan area, the sense of hometown pride is strong in Kansas.

The Capper/MRI Quick-Fact Book of Kansas is an almanac you will enjoy referring to again and again. We're sure you will always find some interesting tidbit of information about Kansas and that you will often say (as we did many times in the making of this book), "I didn't know that!"

Diana J. Edwardson Persell
Capper Press

To order additional copies of The Capper/MRI Quick-Fact Book of Kansas, please call toll-free 1-800-777-7171 ext. 107. Also available from Capper Press are The Missouri Quick-Fact Book, The Iowa Quick-Fact Book, and The Colorado Quick-Fact Book.

table of contents

Chapter 1
Introduction
1-18

The cornerstone of the east wing of the State Capitol, located in Topeka, was laid Oct. 17, 1866. Construction was completed in 1903.

Chapter 2
History
19-52

More than 1,000,000 head of Texas cattle were driven along the Chisholm Trail to the great shipping center of Abilene.

Chapter 3
Government
53-78

Kansas has 125 representatives and 40 senators in state government. The Legislature convenes in January.

Chapter 4
People
79-106

The urban population of Kansas has grown steadily since 1860, while the rural population has declined since 1910.

Chapter 5
Culture
107-136

Ethnic foods, crafts, and a parade highlight the annual Wilson Czech Festival, held the last Friday and Saturday in July.

Chapter 6
Business
137-154

Approximately 1.3 million people are currently employed in Kansas, which is more than twice as many as in 1940.

Chapter 7
Places
155-182

The Cathedral of the Plains in Victoria was completed in 1911 by industrious German-Russian immigrant settlers.

Chapter 8
Land
183-204

The Flint Hills in the east-central part of the state is the only extensive, unplowed tract of bluestem or true prairie remaining in the United States.

Index
205-211

The Capper/MRI
Quick-Fact Book of
KANSAS

CHAPTER 1
INTRODUCTION

KANSAS

State Symbols • County Seats
County Map • Mileage Chart
Highway Map • Trivia

INTRODUCTION

Photo courtesy of Kansas Department of Commerce / Tourism Division.

overview

This is Kansas
5

The majority of the state is located within the Central Time Zone.

State Symbols
6-9

The cottonwood, often called the pioneer tree of Kansas because of its abundance on the plains, was adopted as the state tree in 1937.

County Seats
10

Cimarron is the county seat of Gray County, located in the southwest part of the state.

County Map
11

Kansas is divided into 105 counties.

Mileage Chart
12

The distance from Kansas City to Liberal is 403 miles.

Highway Map
13

Kansas has one of the most extensive road systems in the nation.

Trivia
14-17

Abraham Lincoln visited Kansas before he became president and gave speeches at Atchison, Elwood, Troy, Doniphan, and Leavenworth.

CHAPTER OPENER PHOTO: Spring on the Kansas prairie is a remarkable time. Flowers emerge out of their dormant state to greet the warm Kansas sunshine. This fence post which stood alone throughout the winter months now stands in a field suddenly bursting with life.

introduction

Kansas is a land of contrasts from the wheat fields to the Flint
Hills to the urban areas; from the rural farms to the factories to
the corporations. It's difficult to use just one word to describe
the variations that the state offers. Sunflowers, wheat fields, and, yes,
Dorothy and Toto from "The Wizard of Oz" are certainly easily
identifiable symbols of the state. But to truly appreciate what Kansas
is all about, one must consider many different aspects. Whether it's the
miles of gently rolling prairie land as far as the eye can see or a
windmill turning slowly in the gentle breeze, the land, people, and
places intertwine with the rich cultural heritage that defines Kansas.

The main component of any state is its people. Citizens of Kansas
have been proud and hard working in their quest to create a better life
for the next generation. Kansas is a blend of various ethnic backgrounds. From the Native Americans who first occupied this land to
the pioneers and emigrants who poured into the area seeking a better
way of life, Kansas has become a home for people from all walks of life.

There is always something fascinating happening in Kansas.
Towns and cities alike hold festivals throughout the year and there are
always local attractions to see. The diverse heritage of a community
comes alive during the active festival season.

Small town living is a vital part of Kansas lifestyle. Only 13 cities
in Kansas have a population greater than 25,000. A hometown
atmosphere is special to Kansans and all those who visit the state.
There is nothing like the feeling of coming home to an old-fashioned
cookout in a rural community. The small towns of Kansas are gracious
hosts to all those who want to get away from the hustle of the cities.

Kansas is more than wheat fields and pasture land. Major
corporations have chosen to locate their headquarters in Kansas. The
state's central location is one of the key factors in enticing businesses to
the area. The transportation and communication links allow
businesses to maintain rapid access to customers. Industries have
expanded in Kansas making the state economically sound.

Certain images come to mind when thinking about Kansas. A soft
breeze blowing across a golden wheat field, a youngster clutching
balloons on a carnival ride or at a festival, a tail-gate party at one of
the area football games, or going for sleigh rides on a winter evening.
The sleek, modern office complexes and the huge industrial buildings
create the skyline of the business districts. Kansas is all of this and
much more, including its history, people, places, land, business,
government, and education. To Kansans it is a state to be proud of and
to visitors it is a place of wonder and surprise. There is always
something new to be discovered in Kansas. In 1910, Carl Lotus Becker
said of Kansas: "To understand why people say 'Dear old Kansas!' is to
understand that Kansas is no mere geographical expression, but a state
of mind, a religion, and a philosophy in one." ❏

fun facts

Border Line Decision	When Kansas was formed as a territory, it had 126,283 square miles in 1854. The original Kansas Territory included portions of what is now Colorado west to the Continental Divide, and Pike's Peak was in Kansas at that time. Today the state encompasses 82,264 square miles.
Flying Colors	The Kansas state flag was first displayed in 1927 at Fort Riley by Gov. Ben Paulen in the presence of troops from Fort Riley and the Kansas National Guard.
A State by Any Other Name	There are 54 different spellings for "Kansas" other than the one used today, including "Konza," "Kaw," and "Kanzas."
Spoils of War	The Memorial Building at 120 W. 10th in Topeka was completed in 1914 at a cost of more than $600,000. Most of the money came from the federal government in settlement of Civil War claims.
A Ton of Bricks	Brick factories were once common in Kansas. Bricks were made at the old Shawnee Indian Mission in what is now Johnson County as early as the 1830s. Manufacturers included the town's name on the bricks, and road building crews would reach a county line and then switch to using bricks made in the next county.
Low Spirits	From 1880 to 1949, the Kansas Constitution prohibited the manufacture, sale, or gift of all forms of intoxicating liquor.
State Holliday	The state capitol stands on 20 acres of ground donated to the state by Cyrus K. Holliday. The Legislature accepted the block of land by a joint resolution approved Feb. 7, 1862.
Hogging Space	In the 1870s, a "five-board, pig-tight fence" was constructed around the Capitol Square.
Check Mate	In September 1908, five men were arrested in Topeka for playing checkers on Sunday.

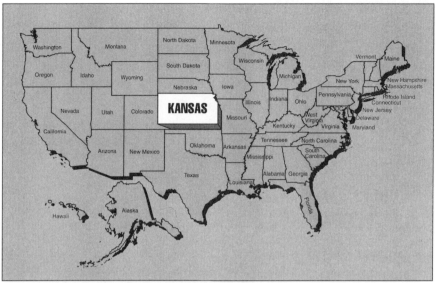

Kansas is located in the heart of the United States and includes the geographic center of the Continental United States. Kansas is bordered by Nebraska, Missouri, Oklahoma, and Colorado.

Date Admitted into the Union: Jan. 29, 1861, as the 34th state.
Capital City: Topeka.
Population: 2,477,574 (1990).
Major Cities: Wichita, Kansas City, Topeka, Overland Park.
Major Businesses and Industries: Manufacturing, agriculture, food processing, printing and publishing, services, minerals and fuels.
Geographic Size: 82,282 square miles. Kansas ranks 15th among states in geographic size.
Geographic Center of the United States: Near Lebanon in Smith County, Kansas.
Highest Point: Mount Sunflower in western Kansas at 4,039 feet.

Lowest Point: The Verdigris River in southeast Kansas at 680 feet.
Time Zones: The majority of the state is located in the Central Time Zone. A small portion of western Kansas is in the Mountain Standard Time Zone.
Area Codes: The northern half of the state is located in the 913 Area Code while the southern half is in the 316 Area Code.
Nickname: Sunflower State.
State motto: "Ad Astra Per Aspera," Latin for "To the stars through difficulties."
State song: "Home on the Range."
State tree: Cottonwood.
State flower: Native sunflower.
State bird: Western meadowlark.

state symbols

QUICK FACTS:

Twelve types of sunflowers grow in Kansas. The tallest species is the wild native sunflower, Helianthus, which is the official state flower.

Kansas Day is celebrated annually on January 29 in recognition of the state's heritage.

The Kansas state banner featured a sunflower and the state seal on a blue field.

The Great Seal of the State of Kansas was adopted on May 25, 1861, and represents elements of Kansas life. On a prairie landscape, buffalo are pursued by Indian hunters, representing the history of the state. Commerce is represented by a steamboat on a river. A farmer plowing and a settler's cabin represent agriculture and future prosperity. The train of ox-wagons represents westward expansion. A banner bearing the state motto flies above a cluster of 34 stars representing Kansas' admittance as the 34th state in the Union.

Nicknames:

Sunflower State. Wheat State. Jayhawker State.

State Name:

Kansas means "People of the South Wind."

Kansas State Banner:

In 1925, the Legislature passed a law providing for the adoption of an official state banner. The banner is solid blue with a sunflower in the center.

Flag:

In 1927, the state Legislature determined that the state flag should consist of a sunflower (the state flower) atop the state seal on a blue background. Directly beneath the sunflower is a blue and gold bar signifying Kansas as part of the Louisiana Purchase. The word "Kansas" in gold block letters was added to the flag in 1961.

Motto:

The state motto, "Ad Astra Per Aspera," is Latin for "To the stars through difficulties."

Illustration by Diana J. Edwardson.

QUICK FACTS:

The wild native sunflower, "Helianthus," was adopted in 1903 as the official state flower.

The election for the state bird, in which 120,000 votes were cast, was sponsored by the Audubon Society of Kansas. The closest competitors to the Western meadowlark in the voting were the quail, cardinal, and robin.

The Western meadow-lark is the official state bird. It was designated by the Legislature in 1937 after Kansas school children selected it in an election on Kansas Day, 1925.

Song:

"Home on the Range" became the state song in 1947. The words to the song were written by Dr. Brewster Higley, a pioneer Kansas physician. Dr. Higley did his writing in his cabin on Beaver Creek near Smith Center in 1871 or 1872. The song was originally titled "My Western Home," and Dan Kelly, a local druggist and friend of Dr. Higley, composed the music. There are few differences in the song as first written and as it is commonly sung today. The most often used verse of the song is: "Oh, give me a home where the buffalo roam, Where the deer and the antelope play, Where seldom is heard a discouraging word, And the sky is not clouded all day."

March:

"The Kansas March," composed by Duff E. Middleton, was established as the official state march of Kansas in 1935 by the Legislature.

Illustration by Diana J. Edwardson.

state symbols

QUICK FACTS:

The honeybee was chosen to be the state insect in 1976, following a campaign by Kansas school children.

Kansas became the 34th state on Jan. 29, 1861. An election was held to decide on a capital city and Topeka was selected over Lawrence and several other towns.

Illustration by Diana J. Edwardson.

Tree:

The cottonwood, often called the "pioneer tree of Kansas" because of its abundance on the plains, was adopted as the state tree in 1937.

The American Buffalo, or Bison, ranging on early Kansas prairies in great herds, was adopted as the official state animal in 1955.

Reptile:

Kansas school children launched a successful campaign in 1986 to name the ornate box turtle the state reptile.

Illustration by Diana J. Edwardson.

The State Capitol:

The cornerstone of the east wing of the State Capitol was laid Oct. 17, 1866. It was yellow limestone placed in the northeast corner of the building (now east wing). The sandstone foundation, which had crumbled to a mass of mud by 1867, was replaced by limestone from Geary County, Kansas. The east wing was completed in 1873.

The west wing is architecturally similar to the east wing, except it is four feet wider and six feet longer. The limestone used was from Cottonwood Falls, Kansas. By 1880 this wing was enclosed.

The 1881 Legislature authorized the construction of the central portion of the Capitol and appropriated additional funds for the completion of the west wing. The exterior of the central portion was completed by the turn of the century.

The Capitol building was completed in 1903. The interior consists of a basement and five floors in the central portion of the building and a basement and four floors in the east and west wings.

QUICK FACTS:

The excavations for the Capitol's foundations extend more than 25 feet into the ground. Workmen doing the excavation discovered a spring in the rock, and the spring still flows beneath the Capitol.

Ornate marble and hand-hammered copper columns decorate the Senate chamber in the State Capitol.

Photo courtesy of Kansas Department of Commerce.

The murals on the second floor of the Capitol were painted by the artist John Steuart Curry, (1897-1945) who was born near Dunavant, Kan., in Jefferson County. Centered on the north wall is the most famous of Curry's murals, the gigantic figure of John Brown. In his outstretched left hand is the word of God and in his right hand a "Beecher Bible" (rifle). Flanking him facing each other, are contending free soil and proslavery forces, and at their feet, two figures symbolic of the Civil War dead.

9

county seats

KANSAS

Abbr.	County	County Seat	Abbr.	County	County Seat
AL	Allen	Iola	LN	Linn	Mound City
AN	Anderson	Garnett	LG	Logan	Oakley
AT	Atchison	Atchison	LY	Lyon	Emporia
BA	Barber	Medicine Lodge	MN	Marion	Marion
BT	Barton	Great Bend	MS	Marshall	Marysville
BB	Bourbon	Fort Scott	MP	McPherson	McPherson
BR	Brown	Hiawatha	ME	Meade	Meade
BU	Butler	El Dorado	MI	Miami	Paola
CS	Chase	Cottonwood Falls	MC	Mitchell	Beloit
CQ	Chautauqua	Sedan	MG	Montgomery	Independence
CK	Cherokee	Columbus	MR	Morris	Council Grove
CN	Cheyenne	St. Francis	MT	Morton	Elkhart
CA	Clark	Ashland	NM	Nemaha	Seneca
CY	Clay	Clay Center	NO	Neosho	Erie
CD	Cloud	Concordia	NS	Ness	Ness City
CF	Coffey	Burlington	NT	Norton	Norton
CM	Comanche	Coldwater	OS	Osage	Lyndon
CL	Cowley	Winfield	OB	Osborne	Osborne
CR	Crawford	Girard	OT	Ottawa	Minneapolis
DC	Decatur	Oberlin	PN	Pawnee	Larned
DK	Dickinson	Abilene	PL	Phillips	Phillipsburg
DP	Doniphan	Troy	PT	Pottawatomie	Westmoreland
DG	Douglas	Lawrence	PR	Pratt	Pratt
ED	Edwards	Kinsley	RA	Rawlins	Atwood
EK	Elk	Howard	RN	Reno	Hutchinson
EL	Ellis	Hays	RP	Republic	Belleville
EW	Ellsworth	Ellsworth	RC	Rice	Lyons
FI	Finney	Garden City	RL	Riley	Manhattan
FO	Ford	Dodge City	RO	Rooks	Stockton
FR	Franklin	Ottawa	RH	Rush	LaCrosse
GE	Geary	Junction City	RS	Russell	Russell
GO	Gove	Gove	SA	Saline	Salina
GH	Graham	Hill City	SC	Scott	Scott City
GT	Grant	Ulysses	SG	Sedgwick	Wichita
GY	Gray	Cimarron	SW	Seward	Liberal
GL	Greeley	Tribune	SN	Shawnee	Topeka
GW	Greenwood	Eureka	SD	Sheridan	Hoxie
HM	Hamilton	Syracuse	SH	Sherman	Goodland
HP	Harper	Anthony	SM	Smith	Smith Center
HV	Harvey	Newton	SF	Stafford	St. John
HS	Haskell	Sublette	ST	Stanton	Johnson City
HG	Hodgeman	Jetmore	SV	Stevens	Hugoton
JA	Jackson	Holton	SU	Sumner	Wellington
JF	Jefferson	Oskaloosa	TH	Thomas	Colby
JW	Jewell	Mankato	TR	Trego	Wakeeney
JO	Johnson	Olathe	WB	Wabaunsee	Alma
KE	Kearny	Lakin	WA	Wallace	Sharon Springs
KM	Kingman	Kingman	WS	Washington	Washington
KW	Kiowa	Greensburg	WH	Wichita	Leoti
LB	Labette	Oswego	WL	Wilson	Fredonia
LE	Lane	Dighton	WO	Woodson	Yates Center
LV	Leavenworth	Leavenworth	WY	Wyandotte	Kansas City
LC	Lincoln	Lincoln			

(Source: Kansas Dept. of Transportation.)

KANSAS COUNTIES

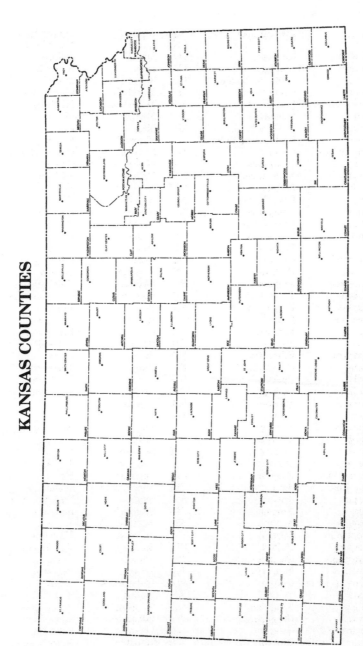

Source: Kansas Department of Transportation.

	HUTCHINSON	KANSAS CITY	SALINA	TOPEKA	WICHITA
Abilene	89	149	27	89	94
Arkansas City	106	224	143	168	55
Atchison	212	54	163	53	188
Chanute	159	123	192	109	108
Coffeyville	187	170	223	152	136
Concordia	112	199	52	137	139
Dodge City	124	335	160	272	154
El Dorado	70	163	102	107	28
Emporia	108	107	115	57	84
Fort Scott	193	92	224	133	150
Garden City	175	376	201	313	206
Goodland	267	410	238	345	318
Great Bend	64	251	76	188	114
Hays	124	266	98	205	175
Hutchinson	X	216	63	159	54
Kansas City	216	X	177	62	191
Lawrence	188	41	141	30	159
Leavenworth	218	29	171	61	193
Liberal	192	403	243	347	212
Manhattan	131	116	68	55	132
Oakley	211	354	181	289	262
Ottawa	163	54	147	52	138
Parsons	185	148	218	143	134
Pittsburg	211	122	244	162	160
Pratt	57	269	121	213	78
Salina	63	177	X	112	90
Topeka	159	62	112	X	135
Wichita	54	191	90	135	X

Example: To determine the number of miles between Salina and Coffeyville, find Coffeyville on the left side of the chart and read across to find the number listed under the Salina column. The distance is 223 miles.

Source: Kansas Department of Transportation.

12

KANSAS HIGHWAYS

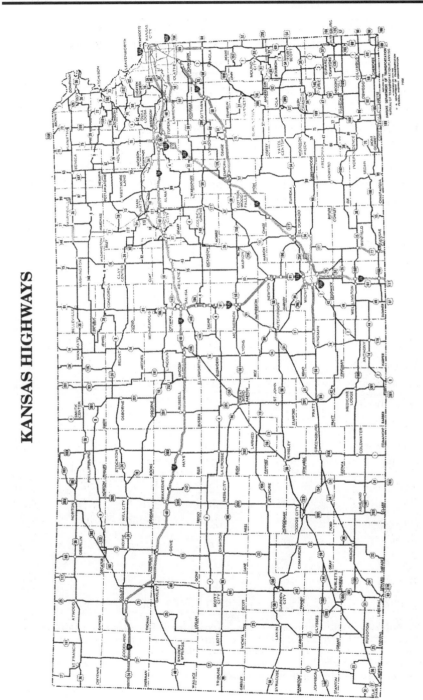

The **"Jayhawker"** state is another nickname for Kansas. Legend says a pioneer once started across Kansas with a bare minimum of provisions, saying he would complete his journey by "jayhawking" his way. The term's origin is hard to determine. It has been used to define horse thieves and abolitionists, but has come to define a tough, resilient individual illustrated now by a mythical bird with a proud appearance.

Abraham Lincoln visited Kansas before he became president. He gave speeches at Atchison, Elwood, Troy, Doniphan and Leavenworth.

The Smoky Hill Trail was the quickest route to the Denver goldfields discovered in 1859. The trail paralleled the Smoky Hill River. David Butterfield's stage line, the Butterfield Overland Dispatch, traveled the route during the line's existence.

Kansas had at least four automobile factories in the early 1900s. They were in Topeka, Parsons, Hutchison, and Wichita. One of the largest was the Jones Company in Wichita. These automobiles cost from $1,000 to $3,000.

Photo courtesy of Kansas Department of Commerce / Tourism Division.

A peaceful back road in Douglas County reflects the beauty of a Kansas autumn. Colorful foliage can be seen statewide during the fall months.

Photo by John Schlageck, Kansas Farm Bureau.

Kansas is known for its farmlands. This rooster weather vane symbolizes the family farm and the down-home atmosphere found in Kansas.

The first forward pass in football history was thrown in December 1905 in a football game between Washburn University and Fairmount College.

Buffalo Bill Cody moved to Leavenworth in 1854 at the age of nine. At age 13 he worked for the Russell, Major and Waddell Freight Line in downtown Leavenworth and later became a Pony Express rider for the same company.

Belle Plaine, incorporated in 1884, is the oldest town in Sumner County. Belle Plaine was once famous for its apple orchards.

The largest recorded earthquake in the history of Kansas came in 1867 near Manhattan and caused some minor damage. The earthquake was felt as far east as Dubuque, Iowa, and would have registered about 5.5 on the Richter Scale.

Hunters may use the more than 9,000 acres of public hunting lands available at Clinton Lake, near Lawrence.

The worst infestation of grasshoppers came in August 1874 when practically all of the grass and vegetation in the state was destroyed.

The first newspaper in Kansas was written in the Shawnee Indian language.

Dodge City has approximately 16 miles of brick streets. At intersections, the cross-diagonal weave prevents heavy vehicles from tearing up the street when making turns.

In 1987, Overland Park set a record in the state of Kansas with more than $300 million in new construction. Retail sales in the city jumped from $180 million in 1970 to approximately $938 million in 1982.

A 350-acre Carey Salt mine in Hutchinson is the home of Underground Vaults and Storage where documents, records, and other items are stored. The salt mine has a constant temperature of 68 degrees and a relative-humidity of 50% making it a good storage facility. Metro-Goldwyn-Mayer stores all of its fine-grain masters, including "Gone With the Wind," in the old mine.

Gasoline sold for 16¢ a gallon in 1932.

Photo courtesy of Kansas Department of Commerce / Tourism Division.

The State Capitol in Topeka is a striking sight at sunset.

Photo courtesy of Emporia / Lyon County Convention & Visitors Bureau.

Soden's Bridge in Emporia offers beautiful scenery and great fishing.

The Grassland of the Great Plains was a natural habitat for buffalo, whose numbers in early historic times have been estimated at 60 to 75 million. By 1830, after gunpowder had begun to take its toll, an estimated 40 million buffaloes remained. Early explorers reported sighting herds containing as many as three or four million buffaloes. In 1871, Major Richard Irving Dodge reported traveling at least 25 miles through one immense herd of buffaloes. The great herd "was about five days passing a given point, or not less than fifty miles deep," Dodge said.

Invertebrate fossils can be easily found throughout the state, especially in the limestone layers in eastern Kansas. The chalk beds and limestones in the western part of the state have an abundance of clam and oyster fossils.

Kate Bender, head of the notorious and violent Bender clan who settled near Parsons in 1871, once served as commentator of women's affairs for the *Altoona Tribune*.

In 1988, the University of Kansas men's basketball team won the NCAA tournament by beating Big-Eight rival University of Oklahoma in Kansas City's Kemper Arena.

sources

Emporia/Lyon County Convention and Visitors Bureau, P.O. Box 417, Emporia 66801.

Greater Hutchinson Chamber of Commerce, P.O. Box 519, Hutchinson 67504-0519.

Howes, Charles C. **This Place Called Kansas**. Norman, Okla.: University of Oklahoma Press, 1984.

"Kansas Capitol Square," Kansas Secretary of State, 2nd floor Statehouse, Topeka 66612.

Kansas Department of Commerce, 400 W. 8th St., 5th floor, Topeka 66603-3957.

Kansas Department of Transportation, Docking State Office Building, 4th floor, Topeka 66612.

Kansas Farm Bureau, 2627 Kansas Farm Bureau Plaza, Manhattan 66502.

Kansas Geological Survey, 1930 Constant Ave., Campus West, The University of Kansas, Lawrence 66046-2598.

Kansas Wildlife and Parks Department, Rt. 2, Box 54A, Pratt 67124-9599.

Larned Chamber of Commerce, P.O. Box 240, 502 Broadway, Larned 67550; "Larned is Your Kind of Town," 1988.

Office of the Governor, 2nd Floor, State Capitol, Topeka 66612-1504.

CHAPTER 2

HISTORY

KANSAS

HISTORY

Kansas History • Timeline
Trails • Forts • Museums
Historical Attractions
Historical Restaurants

Photo courtesy of Emporia / Lyon County Convention and Visitors Bureau.

**Kansas History
23-26** In May 1854, Kansas was organized as a territory, with boundaries that included the eastern half of Colorado.

**Timeline
27-30** In 1869 what is claimed to have been the first alfalfa in Kansas was planted on the present site of Kansas Wesleyan University.

**Trails
31-32** Meriwether Lewis and William Clark, while exploring the Louisiana Purchase, made camp at several points on the Kansas side of the Missouri River.

**Forts
33** Established in 1827, Fort Leavenworth is the oldest Army Fort in continuous existence west of the Mississippi River.

**Museums
34-47** The Pony Express Barn-Museum, in Marysville, is the only original home station along the Pony Express route that is still in its original location.

**Historical Attractions
48-49** At Post Office Oak in Council Grove, letters from passing caravans and pack trains on the Santa Fe Trail were left at the base of this oak tree from 1825-1847.

**Historical Restaurants
50-51** The Brookville Hotel in Brookville was built in 1870 and is famous for its family-style chicken dinners.

CHAPTER OPENER PHOTO: Many Kansans remember attending one-room schoolhouses. Today these abandoned buildings dot the countryside, but children can still learn from them, knowing this was the type of school their ancestors attended. This building, now on display at the Emporia State University campus, was constructed around 1880.

T he state's history reflects periods of struggles and triumphs. The area now known as Kansas was discovered and settled by explorers and pioneers who had a quest to find a better life. In 1540, Coronado came to Kansas in search of Quivira, but instead of finding gold, Coronado found the land to be abundantly rich and fertile. The first inhabitants of Kansas were the Indians and here they found rich hunting and farming lands. The nomadic tribes hunted the vast herds of buffalo, while other tribes made their homes along fertile waterways, where they could grow exceptional crops and live peacefully.

The Santa Fe and Oregon Trails opened the territory to settlement and established trade in the area. The pioneers who came across these trails were determined to fulfill their quest for a new life and to overcome hardships. Small towns began to emerge along the trails as travelers discovered they could start new lives in Kansas. Businesses opened and farmers broke ground. When more settlers began to use the trails and overflow in to the surrounding areas that belonged to the Indians, confrontations took place. As problems began to arise whether between Indians and settlers or among the settlers themselves, forts began to appear on the Kansas plains. These forts were used to settle disputes, survey the land, and protect travelers.

Kansas was organized as a territory in May 1854. Kansas became the site for skirmishes between proslavery and freestaters, which eventually led to the term "Bleeding Kansas." One of the most radical leaders of that time was John Brown, whose fiery speeches led the quest for Kansas to become a free state. The turbulent battle for statehood became a national issue, and Kansas finally became the 34th state on Jan. 29, 1861. By April 1861, the first call for troops was made and Kansas became involved in the Civil War.

After the Civil War, Kansas once again began to prosper. New riches were discovered that offered a new quest for the pioneer. Buffalo hunters depleted the great herds for hides and bones. After the buffalo hunters left, the cowboys moved in. The "cowtown" era was one of the most successful and memorable in Kansas. With the help of the railroads, towns such as Dodge City and Abilene sprang from the prairie. Millions of cattle were moved through the area.

Cowboys, outlaws, and lawmen often clashed, leading to gunfights and brawls. Some of the more famous characters of this time include Wyatt Earp, Wild Bill Hickok, Doc Holliday, and the Dalton Gang.

In 1875, Mennonites from Russia introduced turkey red wheat to the state, which eventually propelled Kansas to being an agriculture center and in the 20th century Kansas became known nationally as "The Wheat State."

Visitors will enjoy learning the history of Kansas at museums, historic sites, and unique historical restaurants throughout the state. ❑

fun facts

Rest Area	St. Mary's was originally a Jesuit Mission to the Potawatomi Indians and a site for trade and rest to the early settlers traveling west on the Oregon Trail.
Tough as a Post	Early day pioneers cut their fence posts from greenhorn limestone, known as post rock, because timber was scarce.
Where's the Beef?	In five years, from 1867-1872, nearly 3,000,000 head of cattle were driven up the Chisholm Trail from Texas to Abilene.
In a Rut	The ruts left by the Chisholm Trail can still be seen just north of Newton.
The Cream of the Crop	In the late 1890s the Chanute Creamery produced 14,000 pounds of milk daily that was marketed locally and in Chicago. The Neosho Valley Creamery produced butter that was shipped as far as New York and England.
Territorial Boundaries	Jefferson County was named for President Thomas Jefferson and the boundaries were set by the first territorial legislature that met in July 1855.
The Wrong Side of the Tracks	The first marshal was appointed in Dodge City after its incorporation in November 1875. The railroad tracks were known as the dead line. Respectable saloons and businesses were located north of the line. South of the line lawmen made little effort to enforce ordinances unless a complaint was made or an actual fight broke out.
River Crossing	Ford, Kansas, is located at the junction of the Arkansas River and Mulberry Creek, the site of a near confrontation on the Santa Fe Trail between Capt. Cook of the U.S. Army Dragoons and Col. Jacob Snively of the Republic of Texas.
How Sweet it is	In 1914, the beet sugar factory in Garden City made 13 million pounds of sugar from beets grown in Finney, Kearney, Hamilton, Pawnee, Lyon, Chase and Greenwood counties.

kansas history

Pioneering Spirit Reflected in State's History

(Reprinted with permission from the Kansas Secretary of State's office, Publications Division. Originally published in "Kansas Facts" publication, 1985.)

Kansas entered the Union Jan. 29, 1861, the culmination of the periods of exploration, territorial disputes, and the bloody days that had erupted over slavery. Ahead were the days of growth and development which contributed significantly to the strength and prosperity of the nation.

The region that is now Kansas had been inhabited by Indians for thousands of years before the first white man appeared. In 1540 the Spanish conquistador, Francisco Vasquez de Coronado, marched north from Mexico in search of the Seven Golden Cities of Cibola. In New Mexico he was told of the Land of Quivira, and he turned east and north in search of this fabled place of wealth. By the summer of 1541, 80 years before the Pilgrims landed at Plymouth Rock, he had reached the Arkansas River in Kansas, crossing it near present Dodge City. Coronado found no gold in Quivira, but he called the country, which is now part of Kansas, "the best that I have ever seen for producing all the products of Spain."

Coronado returned to New Mexico, but the following year a priest who had accompanied him returned to Kansas. Father Juan de Padilla hoped to bring Christianity to the Indians. He was killed, however, by those he tried to help. The exact place of his death is unknown, but it is presumed to have been in central Kansas. Father Padilla is said to have been the first Christian martyr in the United States.

During the years between 1682 and 1739, France sent several explorers to the Kansas area. Claude Charles du Tisne crossed southeastern Kansas in 1719, and Bourgmont arrived in 1724. The Mallet brothers, Paul and Pierre, crossed Kansas in 1739, as they sought to establish trade between the French and Spanish traders from Santa Fe.

For a time Spain, France, and England all had claims on the Kansas area. The English did nothing to further their claim. French claims were ceded to Spain in 1762, but in 1800 the title was returned to France, from whom the United States purchased the entire Louisiana Territory in 1803. This transaction ended the trading era for Kansas and brought forth the exploration of a new American settlement.

> *Coronado found no gold in Quivira, but he called the country "the best that I have ever seen for producing all the products of Spain."*

While exploring the Louisiana Purchase, Meriwether Lewis and William Clark made camp at several points on the Kansas side of the

kansas history

Missouri River in late June and early July, 1804. Two years later, Lt. Zebulon Pike of the United States Army crossed the Kansas area on an exploring expedition during which he met with the Indians and signed treaties with them as the representative of the new "White Father." He continued westward on this journey to discover the mountain that is now called Pike's Peak.

With the continued exploration of Kansas, trails were established by traders and immigrants. William Becknell, a Missouri trader, opened the Santa Fe Trail to trade with the Spanish in what is now New Mexico. Early in the 1820s wagon trains were being sent over this route from the Missouri River to Santa Fe. By 1825 the trail had become so important that Congress authorized a survey of the route. This survey, completed in 1826, provided a 775-mile route for the Union; two-thirds of it was in Kansas.

The Oregon Trail to the northwest was used during the middle decades of the 1800s. The route crossed the northeastern section of the state and impressed many of those who traveled the trail. Some stopped and made their homes in Kansas while others returned later to settle on the rich farmland.

The Territorial Period

In May 1854, Kansas was organized as a territory, with boundaries that included most of the eastern half of present-day Colorado. Conflict over the slavery question led to bloody battles between freestaters and proslavery forces. In May 1856, Lawrence was sacked by border ruffians led by Sheriff Jones. Many active freestaters lived there, and Lawrence became the mecca for escaped slaves. It was after this sacking that John Brown came into prominence. Brown, with his sons and a few other men, retaliated with a massacre. They dragged five proslavery neighbors out of their homes and killed them. This led to the Battle of Black Jack near Baldwin when Missourians came to avenge the massacre. In a later raid on Osawatomie in August, John Brown and 40 defenders were beaten back by about 400 Missourians, and all but four homes were burned.

Battle for Statehood

From 1855 to 1861 the battle for statehood was as intense as any fought in the state. The first attempt occurred in 1855 when a freestate constitution was framed in Topeka. It did not receive serious consideration in Congress. In 1857 a second constitution, which provided that Kansas be admitted as a slave state, was written at Lecompton. The constitution was adopted in an election in which freestate men refused to vote and later was rejected at a second election in which the proslavery men took no part. This constitution was sent to Washington, but while it was being debated by Congress, a third constitutional convention convened. The meeting was at Leavenworth, and the constitution drafted there was adopted by the people in 1858, but this too failed final acceptance.

The fourth and last convention assembled at Wyandotte, now part of Kansas City, in July 1859. This time freestate advocates were solidly in control, and the document they drafted barred slavery and fixed the present boundaries of the state. It was accepted by a vote of the people in October and in December a provisional state government was elected. In April 1860, the U.S. House of Representatives voted to admit Kansas, but the Senate, under proslavery domination, refused. Statehood for Kansas thus became a national issue, and the Republican platform of 1860 included a plank for immediate admittance. The victory of Abraham Lincoln in November was followed by secession of Southern states. The withdrawal of their senators and representatives gave control of Congress to the Republicans even before the change of administrations. In January 1861, the Kansas bill was passed by both houses of Congress and signed by President James Buchanan on January 29. Kansas thus became the 34th state of what at the time was a rapidly disintegrating union.

Kansans had known civil war since the territory was organized in 1854. Now large-scale rebellion faced the entire nation. In answer to President Lincoln's first call for troops in April 1861, Kansas supplied 650 men. Before the war ended in 1865, the state had furnished more than 20,000 men, a remarkable record in view of the fact that the population included less than 30,000 men of military age. Kansas also suffered the highest mortality rate of any of the Union states. Of the black troops in the Union army, 2,080 were credited to Kansas, though the 1860 census listed fewer than 300 blacks of military age in the state; most of them actually came from Arkansas and Missouri.

Although Kansas soldiers saw action in many of the important engagements of the war, only one major battle was fought within the state. This was the Battle of Mine Creek, which took place October 25, 1864, in Linn County. Some 25,000 men were involved. The Confederate army under Major Gen. Sterling Price was defeated, and the threat of a Southern invasion in Kansas was ended. Civil War action within the state consisted primarily of guerrilla skirmishes and raids. Of these, the most notorious was William C. Quantrill's surprise attack on Lawrence, August 21, 1863, in which 150 residents were slaughtered, and the city was looted and burned and about $1.5 million worth of property destroyed.

Late 19th Century Development

After the Civil War a series of Indian outbreaks threatened the western frontier. The tribes were alarmed by the steady encroachment of white settlers. Although undermanned military outposts did their best to protect settlers and travelers, and federal commissioners held peace talks with the chiefs, no permanent peace was obtained. Indian

25

attacks reached their height in Kansas in 1867, when nearly 130 settlers were killed. By the end of 1869 most of their troubles had shifted to other areas. However, western Kansas continued to have Indian problems until the last Indian raid in Decatur County in 1878.

Meanwhile, rapid settlement was being made. Towns were founded, schools established, businesses and small industries started, and railroads pushed westward across the state. By 1870 the Kansas (now Union) Pacific Railroad reached the Colorado line, and by the end of 1872, the Santa Fe Railroad had done the same. The era of the great cattle drives, which focused national attention on several Kansas towns, came in with the railroads. Abilene became a shipping center for Texas cattle in 1867 when Joseph McCoy persuaded Texas drovers to use the extended Chisholm Trail to bring their herds to the just arrived Union Pacific, Eastern Division (later the Kansas Pacific). Newton, Ellsworth, Caldwell, Wichita and Dodge City were other towns which became prominent as tracks were built south and west.

The introduction of Turkey Red wheat by Mennonites from Russia in 1874 was a milestone in Kansas agriculture. This hardy winter wheat was ideally suited to crop-growing conditions in the state and provided the early basis for the pre-eminence of Kansas as a producer of wheat.

Kansas in the 20th Century

Significant changes occurred in agriculture, industry, transportation and communication in the years after 1900. Mechanization became almost universal in farming; heavy industry began replacing individual shops and mills; transportation entered a new era which was to be characterized by diesel-powered trains, commercial air travel and multi-lane highways; and communication was revolutionized by radio and television which augmented the state's large publishing industry.

World War I brought an unprecedented boom in agriculture because of the demand for food from the warring nations of Europe. Thousands of previously uncultivated acres were planted in wheat, and this land, allowed to lie fallow during the recession of the 1920s, became part of the "dust bowl" of the 1930s. In the 1940s conditions improved. New industries came to Kansas and by the early 1950s industry for the first time surpassed agriculture as the state's largest source of income. Kansas became steadily more urbanized as industry concentrated more and more in the population centers around Kansas City, Wichita, Topeka and other major Kansas communities. ❏

1541 Francisco Coronado, Spanish explorer, was the first white man in present Saline County.

1724 M. Etienne Venyard de Bourgmont, a French Commandant, made contact with Indians in Doniphan.

1804-1806 Lewis and Clark expedition passed through the Leavenworth area. On July 4, 1804, at the location of present day Atchison the group celebrated what was probably Kansas' first Independence Day.

1821 The Santa Fe Trail was established to haul freight from Kansas City to Santa Fe.

1827 Fort Leavenworth was established.

1842 Fort Scott was established.

1853 Fort Riley was established.

1854 Kansas-Nebraska Act, opens territory to settlers.

1854 Topeka was founded by five antislavery activists.

1855 The first territorial capitol was built in Pawnee.

1855 Cholera raged at Fort Riley.

1856 Paola was the center of "Bloody Kansas" border wars.

1856 Olathe was founded.

1856 As of February 18, Kansas had 58 post offices.

1856 John Brown and his followers were attacked by several hundred pro-slavery men. In this "battle" of Osawatomie, the settlement was burned and Brown's son Frederick was killed.

1857 Abilene was founded.

1857 Emporia was founded.

1857 On October 31, the first court ever held in Lawrence was in session; Samuel N. Wood, Justice of the Peace.

1858 The Marais des Cygnes massacre took place.

1858 On December 11, poles for the telegraph were up as far as Leavenworth, Jefferson City, and Kansas City.

1859 Fort Larned was established.

1859 John Brown was hanged at Charles Town, Va., for his crimes.

1859 Junction City was incorporated due to a special act by the Kansas Territorial Legislature.

1860 The Pony Express was inaugurated in Kansas.

1860 On March 20, iron arrived in Kansas and track-laying began on the Elwood & Marysville Railroad. This was the first railroad iron laid down on Kansas soil.

1861 Topeka became the state capitol.

1861 Kansas entered the Union as the 34th state on January 29.

1861 Kansas women were given the right to vote in school elections, far earlier than in most states.

1863 Lawrence was sacked by Confederate guerrillas led by William C. Quantrill on August 21.

1863 Kansas State University in Manhattan was established as the nation's original land-grant university.

1863 Emporia State University at Emporia was established as the Kansas State Normal School.
1864 The only major Civil War battle fought in Kansas occurred at Mine Creek in Linn County on October 25. This battle, involving 25,000 men led by Generals Curtis, Blunt, and Pleasanton from the Union forces and Generals Marmaduke and Price from the Confederate Army resulted in the Southern troops being routed, ending the threat of a Confederate invasion of Kansas.
1866 The University of Kansas at Lawrence was opened as the first state university in the Great Plains area.
1867 Neodesha was founded.
1869 What is claimed to have been the first alfalfa in Kansas was planted on the present site of Kansas Wesleyan University.
1870 Concordia was established.
1870 Kansas population was 364,000.
1870 The Kansas Pacific reached through Kansas to the Colorado line, and by the end of 1872, the Santa Fe had done the same.
1870 The Old Dutch Mill in Wamego was constructed.
1871 Augusta was incorporated as a city.
1871 Parsons was incorporated as a city.
1871 Haysville was founded.
1871 Peter McVicar was elected President of Washburn College.
1871 The first railway in the state was in operation in Lawrence.
1872 Hutchinson was incorporated as a city of the third class on August 15.
1872 Dodge City was founded.
1872 The Santa Fe Railroad began.
1872 The Newton city council passed an ordinance prohibiting the running at large of buffalo and other wild animals.
1873 The first sidewalk in Hutchinson was a wooden one from the courthouse to a railway depot.
1874 Mennonites from Russia introduced Turkey Red wheat to Kansas.
1874 Four Kansas railroads shipped 122,914 head of Texas cattle in eight months.
1877 The first telephone in Kansas was installed in Lawrence.
1878 Chiefs Dull Knife and Little Wolf of the Northern Cheyennes led their people in a flight from starvation on the reservation in Oklahoma to their home lands in Yellowstone. The trek climaxed on Sept. 27, 1878, when 284 braves, women and children made their final stand on the bluffs of Ladder Creek, now Beaver Creek, just south of Scott County State Park. This encounter with the U.S. Cavalry was the last Indian battle in Kansas. The site — Squaws Den Battleground — drew its name from the pit in which the women and children were placed after helping to dig rifle pits for the warriors. The breastworks the Indians dug to withstand the attack by soldiers are still visible.

1878 Garden City was founded and later named after the beautiful garden of the founder's wife.

1879 The first telephone switchboard was used in Topeka.

1880 A Prohibition amendment to the Kansas Constitution was adopted. It remained in effect until 1948 when a system of licensed liquor sales was established.

1881 The first long distance connection was established between Wathena, Kansas, and St. Joseph, Missouri.

1884 First flour of Turkey wheat exported from Kansas.

1885 Kansas, at the New Orleans Exposition, took first prizes on wheat, corn, flour, sorghum sugar, apples and cattle; sixty-five first and second premiums, leading every state in the Union.

1889 The dial telephone was invented by Almon Strowger of El Dorado.

1889 Mentholatum was invented by Albert Alexander Hyde of Wichita.

1892 The Dalton gang rode into Coffeyville and robbed two banks of nearly $25,000 in 12 minutes on October 5. A shootout ensued and two of the three Dalton brothers were killed. The youngest brother was sentenced to life in the Kansas Penitentiary at Lansing.

1894 A brigade of "Coxey's Army" met its waterloo at Scott City when a train commandeered by miners at Cripple Creek, Colo., was halted in the area by a U.S. Marshal and his deputies — bringing to a close the "last invasion of Kansas soil by anybody's army."

1895 Wichita State University in Wichita was founded as Fairmount College.

1901 Fort Hays State University at Hays was established as the Western Branch of the State Normal School.

1903 Pittsburg State University at Pittsburg was established as the Auxiliary Manual Training Normal School.

1905 Charles Melvin tried to solve the "wet-dry" problem in Allen County by dynamiting the saloons on the Square. Three buildings were gone but the "wet" problem was not.

1906 The Federal Penitentiary in Leavenworth was completed.

1907 "The Vanderbuilt Cup" was the first opera shown in the new Brown Theater in Concordia.

1909-1910 America's first patented helicopter was invented by William Purvis and Charles Wilson of Goodland.

1911 On July 9, the Smoky Hill River was so low that farmers fished with pitchforks.

1911 Heavy snow over the state tied up railroad transportation on December 30.

1911 Housewives made fireless cookers from boxes and old trunks, insulating them with paper or hay. Food was partially cooked and quickly put in tight-fitting lard or syrup pails. This way the food was cooked without further heating the kitchen.

1912 Fresh eggs retailed for 40¢ a dozen at Topeka.

1912 When the first woman's jury in Kansas entered the jury room at El Dorado on Dec. 2, they paused, uncertain what to do. One said: "I believe we should pray." They bowed their heads in silent prayer, listened attentively to instructions, and returned a verdict in three hours.

1913 Kansas oil production was 24,083 barrels. Of 2,174 holes drilled, only 483 were dry.

1915 According to the automobile registrar, every sixth family had a car.

1915 Dwight D. Eisenhower graduated from the U.S. Military Academy at West Point with the rank of second lieutenant.

1917 Kansas had produced 25,402,521,000 cubic feet of natural gas in the past year, and 112 gas wells had been drilled.

1917 Over 15,000 children attended Governor Arthur Capper's birthday party at Garfield Park in Topeka on July 14.

1920 The O'Henry candy bar was invented by Tom Henry of Arkansas City. The candy bar was originally called "Tom Henry" but was changed later when Mr. Henry sold the rights to his candy bar to a candy factory.

1923 Amelia Earhart, a native of Atchison, became the first woman to be granted a pilot's license by the National Aeronautic Association.

1924 The handkerchief-dress craze hit Kansas. At Atchison over 250 dozen red and blue bandanas were sold to women who made dresses of them.

1925 Walter Anderson, Wichita, one of the founders of the White Castle eating houses and known as the "Hamburger King," operated 22 White Castles. He bought the first one in Wichita with a loan of $60.

1928 One-seventh of the world's wheat crop, 12,400,000 acres, was grown in Kansas.

1932 In Salina, sugar was 47¢ for 10 pounds, lard was 6¢ a pound, lettuce was 5¢ a head, frankfurters were 3 pounds for 25¢, coffee was 49¢ for 3 pounds, and cheese was 15¢ a pound.

1938 Brown County claimed what was said to be the first Kansas REA.

1942 A prisoner of war camp was built in Concordia.

1949 Paola was the first city in Kansas to authorize an industrial promotion levy.

1954 Autopilot was invented by David D. Blanton of Wichita.

1961 The ICEE machine, the first frozen carbonated drink machine, was invented by Omar Kneclik of Coffeyville.

1971 The first Electronic Switching System was installed at Kansas City, Kansas.

1986 Kansas produced 421,540,000 bushels of wheat.

1991 Kansans elect their first woman Governor, Joan Finney.

HISTORIC TRAILS IN KANSAS

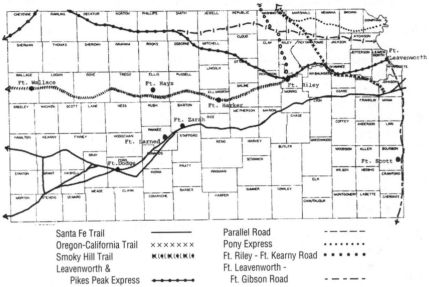

Santa Fe Trail	————	Parallel Road	― ― ― ―
Oregon-California Trail	× × × × × × ×	Pony Express	· · · · · · · ·
Smoky Hill Trail	(((((((((((	Ft. Riley - Ft. Kearny Road	• • • • • •
Leavenworth &		Ft. Leavenworth -	
Pikes Peak Express	•―•―•―•―•	Ft. Gibson Road	― ・ ― ・ ―

Photo courtesy of Kansas State Historical Society.

The Chisholm Trail

Indian trader Jesse Chisholm first marked this famous cattle drive trail for his wagons. More than 1,000,000 head of Texas cattle were driven along this trail to the great shipping center of Abilene. The Chisholm Trail ran north from the Red River Station across the Indian Territory, and entered Kansas near Caldwell. It crossed the Arkansas River at Wichita and continued past the present site of Newton to Abilene.

Lewis and Clark Route

Meriwether Lewis and William Clark, while exploring the Louisiana Purchase by order of President Thomas Jefferson, made camp at several points on the Kansas side of the Missouri River in late June and early July 1804 and again in 1806 upon their return. In 1804 the group celebrated the 4th of July in Kansas by firing a swivel gun. Later they named Independence Creek and closed the day with another cannon blast.

The Oregon Trail

This road to the West was known by many names and was called the Oregon Trail, the California Trail, the Platte Trail, and the Mormon Trail by people who traveled it. It was primarily an emigrant trail. However, the Oregon Trail was also used by the Army, and stagecoaches and the Pony Express followed part of the trail.

In 1830, William Sublette took the first wagons along the route to the Rocky Mountains. By the middle of the 1840s, traffic on the Oregon Trail was tremendous and the California gold rush increased its use even more in 1849 and 1850.

The trail continued to be heavily traveled during the Civil War, but as the Union Pacific railroad was built, the use of the trail declined. By 1870 parts of it were still used locally but the Oregon Trail was no longer the great throughway it had been.

Smoky Hill Trail

The Smoky Hill Trail was the quickest route to the Denver gold fields, discovered in 1859. The trail was named for the Smoky Hill River that it followed. David Butterfield's stage line, the Butterfield Dispatch, traveled the route during the line's existence.

Pony Express Route

From 1860 to 1862, Pony Express riders carried mail in relays from St. Joseph, Mo., to Sacramento, Calif. Riders out of "St. Joe" had only a brief gallop to the wide Missouri River where ferryboats conveyed them over the river. From St. Joseph the Pony Express followed the Oregon-California trail across several northeast Kansas counties, then ran north to the Platte River in Nebraska and west to Sacramento, California. The Kansas section of the route had 11 stations. The original station in Marysville still stands. Relay stations were established 10 to 15 miles apart where riders would change horses.

Santa Fe Trail

William Becknell, a Missouri trader, was the first to follow the general route and use wagons instead of pack mules or horses to take trade goods over the Santa Fe Trail.

The Santa Fe Trail was heavily used during the Mexican War because of the large volume of military supplies that were transported from the Missouri River towns to the Southwest. In the 1860s the trail was shortened at its eastern end, and with the coming of the railroad, the trail was no longer necessary. When the Santa Fe railroad was completed to the Colorado border in 1872, the days of the Santa Fe Trail as a main transportation route were over.

Fort Scott

Fort Scott was established in May 1842 to keep the peace between the native Indians of the area, as well as keep peace between white settlers and Indians. Normal daily activities included the general construction of the fort and drill by the Dragoons (horse soldiers). On occasion map making expeditions were made. The fort saw no major skirmishes. Trouble arose between slave activists and freestaters after the fort was abandoned in 1853. Fort Scott was one of nine forts originally planned to line the area between the Great Lakes and New Orleans to separate proposed Indian lands and white settlements.

Today visitors can see living history reenactments and take guided tours of the grounds. *For more information call 1-800-245-FORT.*

Fort Larned

Fort Larned National Historic Site commemorates the fort's significance as an important military post established to protect travelers and commerce on the Santa Fe Trail from 1859-1878. Fort Larned was also a key post during the Indian Wars of the late 1860s and the site of an Indian Agency from 1861-1868.

Visitors can see museum exhibits, a slide show, self-guided tours, and special events during the summer months. *For more information call (316) 285-6911.*

Fort Leavenworth

Established in 1827, Fort Leavenworth is the oldest Army Fort in continuous existence west of the Mississippi River. Branches of the Oregon and Santa Fe trails traversed the post carrying settlers further west. Some famous people who have resided at the fort were Douglas MacArthur, George Custer and Dwight D. Eisenhower.

Today visitors can go on a self-guided tour, see historic homes, and more. *For more information call (913) 684-5604.*

Fort Riley

Fort Riley was established in 1852 for the pacification of the territory and became known as the "Cradle of Cavalry." The Cavalry came to the fort in 1884. The infamous 7th Cavalry was located here as well as the 1st Division, otherwise known as the "Big Red One." Some famous residents were Wild Bill Hickok, who was a scout for the fort starting in 1867; the cavalry horse named Comanche, the sole survivor of Custer's Battalion of the 7th; George A. Custer; and General George S. Patton.

Visitors can go on a walking tour, visit the U.S. Cavalry museum, and see historical buildings. *For more information call (913) 239-6727.*

museums

Abilene

Abilene Library Doll Collection. Mamie Eisenhower, W.P.A., foreign doll collections. One of the few doll museums known in the United States.
Dickinson County Historical Society Museum. Museum depicts the pioneer life on the plains. Exhibits include Indian artifacts, pioneer living, railroad, cowtown period, and agriculture.
Eisenhower Center. The Center's Library and Museum depict the military and civilian careers of Dwight D. Eisenhower. Visitors can also see Eisenhower's boyhood home.
Greyhound Hall of Fame. Greyhound history dating back to 5,000 B.C., and famous racing greyhounds enshrined in the Hall of Fame.
Hall of Generals. Wax figures of famous World War II generals.
Museum of the Independent Telephony. Exhibits including antique telephones, insulators, switchboards, and pay stations.
Old Abilene Town & Western Museum. Re-creation of Texas Street in cowtown Abilene, including can-can girls, gunfights, and stagecoach rides.

Alma

Wabaunsee County Historical Museum. Turn-of-the-century farm exhibits as well as a blacksmith shop and an 1880 schoolroom.

Anthony

Historical Museum of Anthony. Housed in the old Santa Fe Depot, this museum has many artifacts including farm machinery as well as paintings by local artists.

Arkansas City

Cherokee Strip Land Rush Museum. Features exhibits, photographs, and documents of "run" pioneers as well as the Kansas Governor Robert Docking memorial and reference library.

Ashland

Clark County Pioneer Museum. Dedicated to the pioneer families who settled in the area, this museum displays items used by pioneer families.
Harold Krier Field Aerobatic Museum. Planes and other memorabilia from former National Aerobatic Champion Harold Krier are in this museum.
Lamkin Collection and Museum. A collection of Western Americana, Indian artifacts, Kansas rocks and minerals, and fossils.

Atchison

Atchison County Historical Museum. Includes memorabilia from Amelia Earhart.
Cray Historical Home. The 19th century, three-story Victorian mansion and carriage house includes a country store and period rooms.

Atwood
Rawlins County Museum. Pioneering history is depicted in a 28-foot mural painted by Rudolph Wendelin, creator of Smokey Bear.

Baldwin
Old Castle Museum Complex. The original home of Baker University, considered the oldest college building in Kansas.
Quayle Rare Bible Collection. Baker University. Rare Bibles, including a rare first edition King James Bible, books and manuscripts are in this collection that was started by Bishop Quayle, a president of Baker University.
Robert Hall Pearson Park. The park is the site of the first battle over slavery in the United States, in 1856. Federal troops and free-state militia commanded by John Brown clashed during the battle.

Belleville
Crossroads of Yesteryear Museum. Historical artifacts plus a Rock Island Railroad display.
Pawnee Indian Village. Features archeological diggings of the actual Indian village. This museum houses the relics of an Indian lodge and artifacts of the Pawnee Indians.
Republic County Museum. Emphasis on agriculture and the railroad plus the ethnic groups who settled in the area.

Beloit
Mitchell County Museum. Collection includes scrapbooks and antiques for each township found in Mitchell County.

Bonner Springs
The Agricultural Hall of Fame and the National Farmers Market. Features artifacts and historical relics depicting the important role of agriculture through the ages. Exhibits include farming implements, steam threshing engines, and a barbed wire collection. Three buildings house exhibits on the evolution of agriculture.

Caldwell
Border Queen Museum. Features a miniature replica of Caldwell when it was in its prime as a cowtown on the Chisholm Trail.

Cawker City
Hesperian Museum. This post rock limestone house is on the National Registry of Historic Places and includes a collection of military paraphernalia.

Chanute
The Martin and Osa Johnson Museum. The works of world-famous wildlife photographers Osa and Martin Johnson are on display in this museum. The pair traveled the world, including the South Seas and safaris in Africa, between 1917-1936.

Cheney
Souders Historical Farm Museum. A large collection of farm machinery and artifacts from Cheney's early days.

Cherryvale
Cherryvale Museum. The museum includes possessions of the infamous Bender family as well as antique dishes, including one of only three remaining Martha Washington plates on display.

Clyde
Clyde Museum. Housed in both the old jail and library.

Coffeyville
The Dalton Museum. Re-live the Dalton raid of Oct. 5, 1892. The Dalton brothers robbed two banks in Coffeyville. Four of the bandits were shot by citizens, but four citizens were also killed in the raid.

Colby
H.F. Davis Memorial Library. Special collections emphasize Kansas history and western Kansas heritage.
Prairie Museum of Art and History. Exhibits include china, porcelain collection, large doll collection, sod house, educational room, and collection of artifacts.
Thomas County Museum. Features the famous Kuska Collection, including dolls, porcelains, furniture and other antiques.

Coldwater
Comanche County Museum. Emphasis on the Comanche Pool, early cattle cartel.
Fort Dodge. Built in 1864 as one of the Army forts guarding the old Santa Fe Trail. Now the Kansas Soldiers Home.

Columbus
Big Brutus. One of the three tallest coal shovels in the world.

Concordia
Cloud County Museum. Built in 1908, this museum has a collection of clothes, dolls, flags and agricultural machinery.
Frank Carlson Library. Visitors can see the furniture, photographs, books, awards, and letters of the late Sen. Carlson. Carlson is the only Kansan in state history to serve in the U.S. House of Representatives and the U.S. Senate as well as governor of Kansas.

Cottonwood Falls
Chase County Historical Society Museum & Library. Eight rooms full of history. Permanent exhibits include photos and outdoor exhibits.
Roniger Memorial Museum. A private collection of Indian artifacts and hunting trophies donated by the Roniger Family, plus an extensive collection of Indian arrowheads.

Council Grove
Kaw Methodist Mission and Museum. The Mission was established in 1851 as a school for Indians and also served as the first Kansas school for white children.

Dodge City
Boot Hill Museum. Village museum where exhibits re-create life in 19th century Dodge City. Exhibits include photographs, documents, medicine shows, gunfights, and stage entertainment.
Famous Gunfighter's Wax Museum. Life-size replicas of famous gunfighters who were in and around Dodge City during the Old West are featured in this museum.
Kansas Teachers Hall of Fame. The first teachers' hall of fame in the United States. It honors individuals in the teaching profession.

El Dorado
Butler County Historical Museum. Reflects Kansas' oil history and includes exhibits such as equipment used during the oil boom, drill bits, drilling rig, a tank car, and a 100-foot steel derrick is adjacent to the museum.
Kansas Oil Museum. Big oil in Kansas began with the discovery of the El Dorado field in 1915. Indoor and outdoor exhibits trace Kansas oil through 500 million years of history.

Ellis
Ellis County Historical Society Museum. The museum has a large collection of historical photos.
Walter Chrysler Boyhood Home. The museum is open daily May through September.

Ellsworth
Ellsworth County Museum. The museum is housed in what was the Hodgden House and includes a livery barn, old schoolhouse, and 19th century church.
Hodgden House & Museum. The building was erected in 1875 and reflects the early "cowtown" beginnings of Ellsworth's history.
Rogers House Art Museum. Charles Rogers earned the nickname "The Kansan" during his studying and teaching. His technique was built upon the Japanese use of egg-white. The museum itself was an old hotel.

Emporia
Lyon County Historical Museum. Includes a unique Gilson Scrapbooks collection that covers nearly a century of information.

Eureka
Greenwood County Museum. A collection of genealogical and historical research material can be found here.

Florence
Harvey House Museum. The first restaurant/hotel in Florence was opened by Fred Harvey in 1876. The hotel was the center of all gala affairs and the famous "Harvey Girls" who served here.

Garden City
Finney County Historical Museum. Information about Garden City's founding fathers, local industries and rodeo. The Leola Howard Blanchard Research Library offers a large collection of genealogical records and state history.

Garfield
Fort Larned National Historic Site. Restored original buildings with period furnishings.

Girard
Museum of Crawford County. Formerly the St. John's Episcopal Church built in the late 1800s and offers exhibits featuring 1800s clothing and dishes, farming equipment as well as the Lindburg Scroll.

Goessel
Mennonite Heritage Museum. Guests can experience the Mennonite way of life and learn about their contributions. Displays include the Mennonite immigrant house and full scale Liberty Bell replica made from "Turkey Red" wheat, which was displayed at the Smithsonian Institute from 1976-78.

Goodland
High Plains Museum. Displays pioneer and Indian artifacts and an automated replica of America's first patented helicopter.

Gove
Gove County Historical Museum. Historical items of area interest.
Yesterday House Museum. One of the largest barbed wire collections in the world.

Great Bend
Barton County Historical Village and Museum. Eight buildings are included in this village consisting of 1871 pioneer rock home, 1915 schoolhouse, 1898 church, 1910 depot; also included is a doll collection, Santa Fe Trail and Indian artifacts, and a wedding dress collection.

Halstead
Kansas Health Museum. Exhibits show medical artifacts through the years.

Hanover
Hollenberg Pony Express Station & Museum. The only remaining unaltered station still standing in its original location.

Hays
Ellis County Historical Museum. More than 10,000 artifacts dealing with Ellis County history, including household antiques, farm machinery, musical instruments, furniture and a restored 1873 church. **Historical Sternberg Museum.** Houses the unique "fish within a fish" fossil and emphasizes area and natural history.

Herington
Tri-County Historical Society Museum. Located in the basement of the Herington Post Office where many historic items are displayed. Early-day newspapers are also on microfilm.

Highland
Iowa, Sac, and Fox Presbyterian Mission. Missionaries were sent to the location to educate the Indian tribes, and lessons were taught in the Iowa language and English.

Hill City
Historical Oil Museum. Numerous exhibits and displays show past and present day methods used in the oil industry.

Hillsboro
Pioneer Mennonite Adobe House Museum. A seven room whitewashed adobe house built in 1876 with attached barn and shed depicting a pioneer Mennonite farmstead of central Kansas. **Schaeffler House Museum.** A 1909 Lutheran immigrant's home.

Holton
Jackson County Historical Museum. Includes a unique display on Holton's Campbell College (1882-1917) where C.F. and Flo Menninger taught prior to establishing the Menninger Foundation in Topeka.

Hugoton
Stevens County Gas and Historical Museum. Features gas equipment, Indian artifacts, farming tools, and six rooms furnished in early 1900s style.

Hutchinson
Reno County Museum. Exhibits on local history and early pioneer days as well as traveling exhibits. The museum offers a wide selection of educational programs, meetings, lectures and other special events.

Independence
Independence Museum. Rooms feature a particular subject and include the Oil and Gas Room, the Country Kitchen, Country Store, and the Indian Room.

Jetmore
Haun Museum. Displays showing pioneer family life, many relics and items from early settlers.

Junction City
Geary County Historical Museum. This museum, housed in the old Junction City High School, is filled with relics and innovative displays from the frontier days.
U.S. Cavalry Museum. Authentic cavalry uniforms and artifacts, plus original paintings by Frederic Remington are housed in this building, which was constructed in 1855.

Kanopolis
Fort Harker Guardhouse & Museum. This 1867 building of Dakota sandstone is on the National Registry of Historic Places. Artifacts and photos help describe life at the fort.

Kansas City
Rosedale Memorial Arch. The Arch was modeled after the Arc de Triomphe in Paris and is dedicated to the men who gave their lives in service to our country.

Kinsley
Edwards County Historical Museum & Sod House. Furniture and kitchen, plus tools and implements.
Half-Way Park. A sign at the park proclaims that San Francisco is 1,526 miles west and New York City is 1,526 miles east.

La Crosse
Barbed Wire Museum. This museum highlights the many uses and types of barbed wire on the prairie. LaCrosse has been referred to as "The Barbed Wire Capital of the World."
Post Rock Museum. The museum describes how post rock was obtained from stone outcroppings and the uses of post rock, including stone posts and buildings.
Rush County Historical Museum. The museum is located in the Sante Fe depot.

Lakin
Kearny County Historical Society & Museum. Features a Santa Fe Depot and a country school.

Larned
Fort Larned National Historic Site. From 1860 to 1878 the fort served as a major military post protecting travelers and commerce on the eastern portion of the Santa Fe Trail. Exhibits include nine original sandstone buildings that were constructed during the military period and a portion of the park includes 44 acres of "virgin prairie" with prominent Santa Fe Trail ruts traversing the area.
Santa Fe Trail Center & Museum. The museum traces the Santa Fe Trail. Exhibits include pre-historic Indian artifacts, Wichita Indian grass lodge, sod house, dugout home, and Santa Fe Railroad depot.

Lawrence

Dyche Museum of Natural History. Located on the University of
Kansas campus, this museum features one of the largest collections of
fossils and mounted animals in natural habitats.
Museum of Anthropology. University of Kansas. The oldest
building on the KU campus, known as Spooner Hall, houses ethnic
objects from around the world.
Watkins Community Museum. The building that was once the
Watkins Bank, constructed in 1888. It now houses the Kansas All
Sports Hall of Fame with memorabilia of outstanding Kansas sports
figures.

Leavenworth

Fort Leavenworth. The fort, established in 1827, is the oldest Army
Fort in continuous existence west of the Mississippi River. Exhibits
include the National Cemetery, the Main Post Chapel, and many
historic buildings.
Frontier Army Museum. At Fort Leavenworth. Focuses on the
theme of "Fort Leavenworth's Role in Westward Expansion" and
includes an extensive collection of horse-drawn carriages.
Leavenworth County Historical Society Museum. The museum is
located in a 16-room mansion built in 1867, and now includes heirlooms
and period furnishings.

Lecompton

Constitution Hall. A pro-slavery constitution was drafted here
during Lecompton's reign as the pro-slavery capital of Kansas.
Lane University Museum. This building was constructed on the
foundation of the proposed capitol of Kansas in 1865 and served as a
university until 1902. Pres. Eisenhower's parents met while attending
Lane University and they married in Lecompton in 1855.

Lenexa

Legler Barn Museum. The 1864 Legler homestead and barn is a
unique museum. Jesse James and William Quantrill reportedly stayed
with their horses in the barn.

Liberal

Coronado Museum. Remnants of the Wild West are housed and
catalogued in this museum, which was originally the old Lee Larrabee
mansion built in 1917-1918.
Liberal Air Museum. Commemorates Liberal's history of aviation.
Nearly 50 aircraft are on display as well as photo displays, memorabilia
and period aviation items.

Lincoln

Kyne House Museum. The post rock house was built in the late
1800s and was donated as a museum in 1978.

Lindsborg
Old Mill Museum. A restored flour mill, historic and natural history exhibits are featured in this museum at the south end of town. An adjacent park features the restored Swedish Pavilion from the St. Louis World's Fair, a one-room schoolhouse, log cabin, and maypole.

Logan
Dane G. Hansen Museum. Exhibits of oriental art, guns and coins, and Hansen memorabilia.

Lyons
Coronado-Quivira Museum. Artifacts from Coronado's trip to Kansas in 1541 are featured along with relics from the Santa Fe Trail.

Macksville
Van Arsdale Antique Museum. Permanent displays of more than 25 automobiles are featured.

Manhattan
Pioneer Park. The location of three of Manhattan's historical attractions. The Goodnow House/Museum was home to Isaac Goodnow who was the major force in establishing the city of Manhattan and Kansas State University. The Riley County Historical Museum features historical exhibits and the Seaton Kansas History Library. The Hartford House is a re-creation of a prefabricated house brought on the Hartford Steamboat in 1855.

Mankato
Jewell County Historical Museum. Early settler years and numerous artifacts from the area are exhibited.

Marquette
Range School Museum. One-room country school museum.

Marysville
Koester House Museum. The home was built by a German immigrant in 1876 and was occupied by family members until 1964. The home is decorated with original furnishings.
Pony Express Barn-Museum. Built in 1859 by Joseph Cottrell, it is the oldest building in Marshall County and is the only original home station along the Pony Express route that is still at its original location.

McPherson
McPherson Museum. Exhibits include one of only five prehistoric giant ground sloths in the world, the largest collection of Arkansas Indian pottery outside the Smithsonian, rare snuff bottles from China, and the world's first man-made diamond.
Smokeys Car Museum. More than 45 restored antique and collectable cars are on exhibit.

Meade
Dalton Gang Hideout & Museum. The infamous Dalton Gang "holed up" here between robberies. Exhibits include the original escape tunnel and a gun collection.
Mead County Historical Society Museum. A blacksmith shop, general store, church, school, Indian artifacts and maps are on display.

Medicine Lodge
Stockade Museum. A replica of a frontier stockade surrounds an 1874 log house and a house made of native gypsum.

Minneapolis
Ottawa County Historical Museum. A new building that has exhibits on a rotating basis.

Mulvane
The Mulvane Historical Museum. Located in the original Santa Fe Depot. A one-of-a-kind 1940s Santa Fe caboose and original jail built in the 1870s are on display.

Neodesha
Norman #1 Oil Well & Museum. The oil well is a replica of the first successful commercial oil well west of the Mississippi that opened the Mid-Continent Oil Field.

Ness City
Ness County Historical Society & Museum. This museum is housed in a limestone school house built in 1881. It is open afternoons, the last Sunday of each month, and by appointment.

Newton
Harvey County Historical Library & Museum. Visitors can find an excellent research library plus exhibits of old fire equipment, Civil War memorabilia, guns, clothing, and cameras.
Kauffman Museum. Visitors can trace the development of prairie life and the influences of the Mennonites and other immigrants.

Norton
Adobe House. The adobe house, now a museum, was made of mud and straw in the 1890s and is the only adobe house in Kansas that is still in its original location.
Presidential Also Ran Gallery & Doll Collection. The gallery includes biographies of presidential candidates who were unsuccessful in their bid for the presidency.

Oakley
Fick Fossil & History Museum. Fossils including more than 10,000 petrified sharks' teeth discovered in the Monument Rock area. In the museum visitors can see a sod house, a railroad depot and minerals.

Oberlin
Last Indian Raid & Sod House. A look at prairie life with exhibits that include a sod house, an 1885 jail, and general store.
Decatur County Museum. Exhibits include Indian artifacts, sod house, country store, quilt/doll collection, stagecoach and machinery.

Olathe
Esnor Museum. A preservation of the 1880s includes a stately home, several barns built in the 1890s, plus Civil War items, handmade furniture, and early radio equipment.
Mahaffie Farmstead & Stagecoach Stop Historic Site. The farmstead served as a stagecoach stop from 1865 to 1869 with three main lines running through the land.

Osawatomie
John Brown Museum. The 1854 log cabin that John Brown used as his headquarters.

Osborne
Osborne County Museum. Located in one of two old train depots.

Oswego
Historical Museum. Features relics from early-day railroads, 19th century clothing and furnishings.

Ottawa
Franklin County Courthouse. A beautifully preserved brick courthouse with stone accents.
The Downtown Ottawa Historic District. Built between 1872 and 1900 this block offers buildings of Victorian styling with Renaissance Eclectic and some Classical features. All offer a look at the past. Many magnificent homes have been restored in the area.
Old Depot Station. The museum is housed in a former railroad depot built in 1888. The museum includes artifacts from "Bleeding Kansas" days, Civil War displays, an old general store, toys and dolls, period rooms, a 1918 steam locomotive and an H-O scale model railroad.

Peabody
Peabody Museum. The first free library in Kansas was at Peabody and the museum was erected here.

Phillipsburg
Fort Bissell Museum. The restored stockade contains two original log cabins, an 1885 store building, the 1879 Glade depot, sod house, gun collection, and one-room schoolhouse.

Pittsburg
Crawford County Historical Museum. Features coal mining artifacts, farming items, printing exhibits and horsedrawn vehicles.

44

Pratt
Kansas Fish and Game Museum. One of the world's largest
freshwater fish hatcheries plus a natural history museum and
freshwater aquarium.
Pratt County Historical Museum. Features an "Old-Time Main
Street," library and research area containing genealogical information,
old land patents and cemetery records.

Republic
Pawnee Indian Village Museum. Modern museum that is constructed around the floor of a Pawnee earthlodge occupied in the early 1800s.

Russell
Fossil Station Museum. The building was erected in 1907 and was
originally used as a county jail. The museum features the early history
of Russell County from 1871-1930.
Oil Patch Museum. An outdoor display of historical oil field artifacts
and equipment.

Russell Springs
Butterfield Trail Historical Museum. The building was made of
native limestone in 1887 and sits on a portion of the Smoky Hill Trail
and the Butterfield Dispatch Stagecoach Line, known in the 1860s as
the shortest and most dangerous of the routes to the West. Exhibits
reflect the struggles of western Kansas pioneers.

Salina
Graves Truck & Auto Museum. A glimpse of how America has
traveled in automobiles since the turn of the century featuring 50
antique cars, trucks, and farm equipment.
Smoky Hill Museum. Collection was started in 1879 by Col. Wm. A.
Phillips and has more than 30,000 artifacts and exhibits about
prehistoric man, the pioneer days, and tribal life of the Plains Indians.

Scandia
Scandia Museum & Carriage House. Depicts items of local history.

Sedgwick
Sedgwick Historical Society Museum. The city of Sedgwick was
named after U.S. Army Major John Sedgwick. This was the first city in
Sedgwick County and is the oldest city in Harvey County.

Shawnee
Old Shawnee Town. A re-creation of a pioneer town featuring a
collection of buildings from 1840-1880.
Shawnee Methodist Mission Museum. The Mission was established
in 1830 and was one of the earliest Indian missions in pre-territorial
Kansas. Three of the original structures remain where the first
territorial legislature met in 1855.

St. Marys
Indian Pay Station Museum. This building is where Pottawatomie Indians received their allotments. Displays include arrowheads and dishes from Union Pacific dining cars.

Stafford
Stafford County Museum & Historical Society. Features a steam engine and thresher as well as the Graves collection of glass negatives.

Sublette
Haskell County Historical Museum. Housed in the old depot, the museum includes 12 collections and special exhibits.

Topeka
Combat Air Museum. Combat aircraft and military artifacts dating back to 1939 are on display in the museum located at Forbes Field.
Kansas Museum of History. Exhibits trace the state's history from the Indian era to contemporary settings. Permanent exhibits include a full size locomotive, automobiles, a log cabin and more.
Menninger Foundation Museum. The museum traces the evolution of the mental health profession through artifacts and memorabilia.

Tribune
Horace Greeley Museum. This museum, in the 1880 old post rock courthouse, features a mammoth's skull and lower mandible.

Ulysses
Grant County Museum. Covering history from prehistoric mastodon tusks to gas wells.

Valley Falls
Valley Falls Historical Museum. Historical items from the Valley Falls area.

Wakeeney
Trego County Historical Society & Museum. Interesting artifacts from baby buggies to stoves and implements.

Wallace
Fort Wallace Memorial Museum. Visitors can see an original B.O.D. stage station.

Walton
The Walton Post Office Museum. The first building in Walton, the Walton Post Office Museum houses period pictures of Harvey County.

Wamego
Beecher Bible and Rifle Church. The church was built in 1862 by abolitionist settlers and was used to store and smuggle rifles during the pro-slavery/anti-slavery conflict in cartons marked "Bibles."

Wamego City Park, Museum Complex, and Dutch Mill. The complex includes an old log structure, jail and school building. The Dutch Mill is the only authentic operating Dutch mill in Kansas.

Washington
Washington County Historical Museum. Everyday items used by pioneers are displayed.

Wellington
Chisholm Trail Museum. Three floors and 42 rooms filled with scenes and relics of pioneer life in Sumner County.

Wichita
Children's Museum of Wichita. This museum is a "hands-on" facility for children and their families. Exhibits cover a wide range of topics including science, health, communications and the arts. The museum is ideal for children between the ages of 3 and 11; however, all children must be accompanied by an adult. Birthday parties and group rates are available and require reservations.
Coleman Museum. The Coleman Company was founded in Wichita in 1901 and still has its headquarters there. Coleman is one of the largest producers of outdoor products in the United States.
Fellow-Reeve Museum. Friends University campus. Contains a collection of mounted animals, rocks and minerals.
First National Black Historical Society of Kansas. Housed in a stately historical church (1917). Exhibits on Black heritage of early Wichita residents.
Great Plains Transportation Museum. Displays of railroad transportation equipment.
Mid-America Indian Center. A celebration of Wichita's Indian heritage that is exhibited through artifacts, pottery, and paintings.
Museum of Anthropology. Exhibits on human cultures around the world. The restored opera house is now used as a dance hall and community meeting center. The basement houses a museum filled with Czech memorabilia.
Old Cowtown Museum. The village museum features old west charm and includes buildings such as Wichita's first jail, Santa Fe Depot, and the J.P. Allen Drug Store. Visitors can see the "Dixie Lee" girls kicking out a can-can.
Sedgwick County Historical Museum. The building is listed on the National Register of Historic Places. Artifacts, historic photographs, film and slide shows provide a glimpse into the past.

Yates Center
Woodson County Historical Museum. The museum is housed in the old stone hatchery. An old authentic log cabin just west of the museum is also on display as well as the Yates Center town square.

historical attractions

Council Grove
Calaboose. This structure was the only jail on the Santa Fe Trail.
Council Oak Shrine. The birthplace of the Santa Fe Trail. A treaty
was signed with the Osage Indians in 1825, under a tree at the site.
Custer Elm. General Custer camped with his troops under this elm
shortly before his massacre by Sitting Bull.
Madonna of the Trail Monument. This monument, one of 12 in the
nation, commemorates the National Old Trails Road and pays tribute to
the Pioneer Mother.
Post Office Oak. Letters for passing caravans and pack trains on the
Santa Fe Trail were left at the base of this oak tree from 1825-1847.

Delphos
Letter to Abe Lincoln. This bronzed facsimile of a letter is honoring
Grace Bedell Billings. Ms. Billings, at age 11, wrote Abe Lincoln and
requested that he grow a beard. Mr. Lincoln wrote her back, thanked
her for her advice, and grew a beard.

Dodge City
Fort Dodge. An important military outpost on the western frontier,
this fort was established for the protection of wagon trains and the U.S.
mail. The fort was converted to the Kansas Soldiers Home in 1889 and
the original buildings, built in 1867, are still in use. Santa Fe Trail
wagon ruts can still be seen five miles east of here.

Fort Riley
First Territorial Capital. Two-story structure built of native stone
served briefly as the first territorial capitol of Kansas in July 1855 in
the town of Pawnee. Now it is operated as a museum.
Fort Riley. Sites include the Custer House, an historic officer's home
preserved in the 1860s style and the U.S. Cavalry Museum. Some of
the museum's exhibits include military equipment, uniforms, and
memorabilia from such men as J.E.B. Stuart and George S. Patton, Jr.
A life-size statue of Old Trooper and Chief stands on Fort Riley's Parade
Ground. Chief was the last cavalry mount on government rolls, and he
is buried in front of the monument.

Goodland
Kidder Massacre Site. Ten members of the Second Cavalry, an
Indian scout, Red Bead, and Lt. Lyman Kidder were killed at this site
while attempting to carry a message to Custer.

Hays
Old Fort Hays. The original stone blockhouse, guardhouse and
officers' quarters of the 1865 post have been renovated. Displays
through the historic site illustrate pioneer and military history. The
fort was built to protect military roads, guard the mail, and defend
construction gangs on the Union Pacific Railroad.

Kansas City, Kansas
The Grinter House. The house was built in 1856 by Moses R.
Grinter at the site of the first ferry crossing of the Kansas River. The
two-story house is the oldest unaltered building in Wyandotte County.
Huron Indian Cemetery. Located in the heart of downtown Kansas
City, Kan., this tribal burial ground of the Wyandot Indians was the
site of an estimated 400 burials from 1844 to 1859.
John Brown Statue. This life-sized statue was the first full
memorial to the martyred abolitionist. It was erected in 1910 on the
campus of Western University, the first all-black university west of
the Mississippi River.

Lecompton
Constitution Hall. A pro-slavery constitution was drafted here
during Lecompton's reign as the pro-slavery capital of Kansas.

Ness City
George Washington Carver Homestead. Listed on the National
Register. A historical marker gives directions to the homestead.
Ness County Bank Building. Built from 1888-1889, this imposing
four-story structure is constructed out of native stone. It was known
as the "Skyscraper of the Plains."

Nicodemus
Nicodemus. Nicodemus was the first black settlement in Kansas
and was established in 1877 by "Exodusters." This is the last survivor
of a dozen all black Kansas settlements and was declared a National
Historic Landmark in 1974.

Pawnee Rock
Pawnee Rock. A famous natural landmark on the Santa Fe Trail.
The attraction has been referred to as the "Citadel of the Prairie." It
was a strategic area for red and white men and was the most
dangerous point on the Santa Fe Trail. A monument and an overlook
tower are on top of the rock.

Pleasanton
Marais Des Cygnes Museum. The museum is located on the site of
a famous confrontation between pro-slavery and abolitionist forces on
May 19, 1858. The five victims of the massacre were immortalized as
martyrs in the cause for freedom.

Wamego
Louis Vieux Elm & Oregon Trail. This elm is the largest living
elm tree certified by the National Register of Big Trees of the
American Forestry Association. The tree is named after Louis Vieux
who operated an Oregon Trail toll ferry on the Vermillion River a few
yards from the tree.

historical restaurants

The Kirby House in Abilene.   *Photo courtesy of the Kirby House.*

Kirby House - Abilene
Thomas Kirby, an Abilene banker, built this grand Victorian mansion in 1855. The mansion has been restored and features eight dining rooms.

Hardesty House Hotel - Ashland
The hotel, built in the early 1900s, displays historic pictures, antiques, and furnishings. Lodging is available in rooms reflecting the early 1900s. The hotel serves meals six nights per week.

Brookville Hotel - Brookville
The Brookville Hotel, originally known as the Cowtown Cafe, was built in 1870. Only one dinner is served: family-style chicken dinner with all-you-can-eat fried chicken, mashed potatoes and gravy, cream-style corn, baking powder biscuits and dessert.

Bunker Hill Cafe - Bunker Hill
The native stone structure was built in 1916 and has been home to a drugstore, doctor, and dentist's office and now the Bunker Hill Cafe. The menu includes Kansas beef, seafood, and fresh baked raisin bread.

The Cimarron Hotel & Restaurant - Cimarron
The hotel has been a vital part of Cimarron since 1886 and continues to delight guests with its Old World charm. The restaurant features pan-fried chicken or roast beef. Lodging is available.

Van De Mark House - Clyde
Built in 1884 by Charles and Addie Van De Mark it served as the
center of Clyde's musical and cultural activities for many years.

The Hays House - Council Grove
The Hays House is the oldest continuously operating restaurant west of
the Mississippi. The Hays House was built in 1857 by Seth Hays,
great-grandson of Daniel Boone. The down-home style cuisine includes
Beulah's ham, homemade breads and fresh fruit pies.

The Castle Tea Room - Lawrence
The 17-room limestone mansion was built in 1894 and features
intricate woodwork. The carving was done by Englishman Sidney
Endicott, later knighted by Queen Victoria. The tea room was
established in 1947. Reservations required one day in advance.

The Eldridge Hotel - Lawrence
Three previous hotels were also located on the same site where the
present Eldridge Hotel now stands. The hotel has been restored to
early 1900s grandeur and includes banquet rooms and a restaurant.

The Hotel Brunswick Restaurant - Lindsborg
This hotel was built in 1877 and some of its notable guests included
Teddy Roosevelt and William Jennings Bryan. The restaurant features
Kansas beef, chicken, and homemade poppy seed and cheese breads.

The Wareham Hotel & Cotton Club Restaurant - Manhattan
Built in 1926 by H.P. Wareham and was the first high-rise hotel with
penthouse in Kansas. The hotel features custom-carved ceilings,
etched glass windows, marble staircase, and crystal chandelier. The
restaurant features Early Bird dinners, prime rib, and seafood.

Koester House - Marysville
This turn-of-the-century mansion was the home of Marysville banker
Charles J.D. Koester. The restaurant includes char-broiled steaks,
prime rib, roast duck, fried chicken and other complete dinners.

Old Mill Restaurant and Wine Bar - Newton
A recipient of the David E. Finley Award from the National Trust for
Historic Preservation. The Old Mill Restaurant and Wine Bar features
Continental and American cuisine.

Spring River Inn - Riverton
Known for its 35-foot smorgasbord of delicious food. The inn was built
in 1905 and is set on the picturesque banks of Spring River.

Ingleboro Restaurant - Smith Center
Located in a home originally built by J.R. Burrow, who later became
the Kansas Secretary of State. It has served as a hospital and rest
home as well as a private residence.

Annals of Kansas 1911-1925, Kansas State Historical Society, 120 W. 10th Topeka 66612.

Bonner Springs-Edwardsville Area Chamber of Commerce, P.O. Box 403, Bonner Springs 66012.

Brookville Hotel, P.O. Box 7, Brookville 67425; (913) 225-6666.

Bunker Hill Cafe, Bunker Hill 67626; (913) 483-6544.

Castle Tea Room, 13th and Massachusetts, Lawrence 66044; (913) 843-1151.

Chanute Area Chamber of Commerce, P.O. Box 747, Chanute 66720.

Cimarron Hotel and Restaurant, 203 N. Main, Cimarron 67835; (316) 855-2244.

Concordia Area Chamber of Commerce, 219 W. 6th, Concordia 66901.

Doniphan County Area Chamber of Commerce, P.O. Box 231, Troy 66087.

Eldridge Hotel, 7th and Massachusetts, Lawrence 66044; (913) 749-5011.

Fort Scott Chamber of Commerce, 231 E. Wall, Fort Scott 66701.

Hardesty House Hotel, 712 Main, Ashland 67831; (316) 635-2911.

Hays House, 112 W. Main, Council Grove 66846; (316) 767-5911.

Hotel Brunswick Restaurant, 202 S. Main, Lindsborg 67456.

Ingleboro Restaurant, Smith Center 66967; (913) 282-3798.

Junction City Convention and Visitors Bureau, 425 N. Washington, P.O. Box 5A, Junction City 66441.

Kansas Department of Commerce, Suite 500 Capitol Tower, 400 S.W. 8th, Topeka 66612.

"Kansas Facts" 1985, Secretary of State Department, 2nd Floor, Statehouse, Topeka 66612.

Kansas State Historical Society, 120 W. 10th St., Topeka 66612.

Koester House, Marysville 66508; (913) 562-3856.

Kirby House, 205 N.E. Third St., Abilene 67410; (913) 263-7336.

Larned Area Chamber of Commerce, P.O. Box 240, Larned 67440.

Leavenworth Convention and Visitors Bureau, 518 Shawnee St., P.O. Box 44, Leavenworth 66048.

Mattes, Merrill J. and Paul Henderson. **The Pony Express From St. Joseph to Fort Laramie.** St. Louis: The Patrice Press, 1989.

Ness County Bank Building Foundation, P.O. Box 1, Ness City 67560.

Newton Area Chamber of Commerce, P.O. Box 424, Newton 67114.

Nottage, James H. and Floyd R. Thomas, Jr. "There's No Place Like Home: Symbols and Images of Kansas," **Kansas History**: Kansas Historical Society, Volume 8, Autumn 1985.

Oakley Chamber of Commerce, P.O. Box 548, Oakley 67748.

Old Mill Restaurant; 3rd and Main, Newton 67114; (316) 283-3510.

Overland Park Convention and Visitors Bureau, 10975 Benson Drive, Suite 360, Bldg. 12, Overland Park 66210.

Richmond, Robert W. **Kansas, A Land of Contrasts.** St. Charles, Mo.: Forum Press, 1974.

"Smoky Hills: Land of the Post Rock," 1988, North Central Regional Planning Commission, 108 E. Main St., Box 565, Beloit 67420.

Spring River Inn, P.O. Box 177, Riverton 66770; (316) 848-3645.

Streeter, Floyd B. **Prairie Trails and Cow Towns**. New York: The Devin Adair Company, 1963.

Van DeMark House, 504 Washington, Clyde 66938; (913) 446-2245.

Wamego Area Chamber of Commerce, P.O. Box 34, Wamego 66547.

Wareham Hotel, 418 Poyntz, Manhattan 66502; (913) 539-9431.

Wilder, D.W. and T. Dwight Thatcher. **Annals of Kansas 1541-1815.** Kansas Publishing House, 1886.

CHAPTER 3

GOVERNMENT

KANSAS

GOVERNMENT

Federal Government • State Government • Local Government State Finances • Education

Photo courtesy of The Topeka Capital-Journal.

GOVERNMENT
overview
KANSAS

Federal Government 57-59
In 1986, Kansas received nearly $885 million in federal aid, or $359 for each Kansan.

State Government 60-69
The constitutional officers of the executive department are the governor, lieutenant governor, secretary of state, and attorney general and are elected for terms of four years.

Local Government 70
Kansas has 24 first-class cities, 88 second-class cities, and 515 third-class cities.

State Finances 71
Kansas, like most of its neighboring states, spends significant amounts of money on education, both at the state and local level.

Education 72-77
In the ten year period from 1979 through 1988, enrollment in Kansas public schools has increased about 1%.

CHAPTER OPENER PHOTO: The "Justice" sculpture located in the Judicial Center in Topeka stands 30 feet high, including the 8-foot base. The sculpture is a half-kneeling woman holding aloft a prairie falcon. A message on the north wall of the Hall of Justice area reads, "Within these walls the balance of justice weighs equal."

introduction

The early days of Kansas' government were difficult and trying times. From the organization of Kansas as a territory on May 30, 1854, to its admission into the Union on January 29, 1861, seven locations served as its capital.

Fort Leavenworth was the first territorial capital and Andrew Reeder served as the first territorial governor. Other capitals during the territorial period were Shawnee Mission, Pawnee, Lecompton, Minneola, Leavenworth, and Lawrence. Some towns served several times as the territorial capital.

Kansas became the 34th state in 1861 and later that year Topeka was chosen to be the capital. Charles Robinson of Lawrence was the state's first governor, serving two terms.

Through the years, Kansas has established a progressive government and was an active state in promoting the issue of women's rights. Kansas extended the right for women to vote in school elections in 1861, much earlier than in other states. The state's first constitution, adopted in 1861, gave women the right to acquire and possess property and to retain equal custody of their children.

Kansas has the traditional three branches of government: Executive Branch, which includes the elected state officers; Legislative Branch, composed of the State Senate and the House of Representatives; and the Judicial Branch, which includes the State Supreme Court, the Court of Appeals, plus district and municipal courts. The Senate and House chambers are located in the Capitol building in Topeka. The legislative session starts in January and ends in April, usually lasting for 90 days.

Throughout the state's history, there have been a number of notable political figures, including Dwight D. Eisenhower. The noble World War II general was raised in Abilene and later became President of the United States. Another important figure in national politics was Charles Curtis, Vice President under Herbert Hoover from 1929-1933. Alf Landon served as Governor of Kansas from 1933-1937 and was the Republican Presidential nominee in 1936. Landon lost the election to Franklin D. Roosevelt. Two prominent Senators from Kansas are Robert Dole and Nancy Landon Kassebaum. The famed orator John J. Ingalls was a U.S. Senator from Kansas. While Ingalls was a state senator, he submitted the design for the Great Seal of Kansas and also proposed the state motto.

Kansas is a leader in education and is home to several of the finest universities in the country. The state school system has emerged from the one-room schoolhouse to a more complex network of public schools. Undergraduate programs in several of the state's universities appear among the nation's most highly ranked. Kansas has a strong commitment to education, and is hopeful for the future of its younger generation. ❏

fun facts

Vote Getters Kansas pioneered the use of the direct primary election. Senator Joseph L. Bristow was the first U.S. Senator nominated in Kansas under that system. Senator Bristow introduced a resolution in Congress that put the direct election of U.S. Senators into the U.S. Constitution.

Hot Seat In the early days of statehood, "county seat wars" were hotly and sometimes violently contested. Being named a county seat could make or break a town so communities fiercely competed to earn the county seat designation.

First City Leavenworth, established in 1854, was the first city in Kansas.

Jockey for Position Charles Curtis, the only person of Indian descent ever to become Vice President of the United States, was a jockey before going to law school.

Oh, Susanna The historic Salter House, located in Argonia, was the home of the first woman mayor in the world, Susanna Madora Salter. In 1971, the Salter House was added to the National Registry of Historic Places.

Ladies Have Their Say In 1913, Haskell County women were the first women to vote in Kansas. Their votes helped make Sublette the county seat.

Safety First Hutchinson's first city ordinance, passed in 1872, prohibited stovepipes through walls without metal or other safe protection.

The Pits At one time it was against the law to serve ice cream on cherry pie in Kansas.

Whoa! In 1890, a Topekan was convicted of driving a horse faster than six miles an hour, which was the city speed limit.

Hide 'n' Seek A federal bill was introduced in January 1867 that would prevent the useless slaughter of buffalo.

Federal Government Employees

In 1988, there were 25,000 Kansans employed by the federal government, and nearly 27.5% of the total were employed in the defense sector. Only two of Kansas' neighbors, Nebraska and Iowa, employed fewer federal workers.

PAID CIVILIAN EMPLOYMENT IN THE FEDERAL GOVERNMENT: 1988		
State	**Total**	**Percent Defense**
Colorado	53,000	26.3
Iowa	19,000	8.1
KANSAS	25,000	27.5
Missouri	67,000	30.1
Nebraska	16,000	25.8
Oklahoma	47,000	52.1

Federal Aid to State/Local Governments

In 1989, Kansas received nearly $912 million in federal aid, or $363 for each Kansan. Kansas was ranked 47th nationally in the per capita amount of federal aid received.

Federal Dollars Spent in Kansas

Of the total federal dollars spent in Kansas, nearly 23% was spent for defense purposes. Nearly 67% of non-defense federal assistance payments are direct payments to individuals, such as pensions and social security.

FEDERAL FUND DISTRIBUTION BY TYPE
1991 – KANSAS & SELECTED STATES

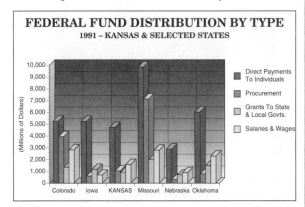

QUICK FACTS:

Kansans, with an adjusted gross income of more than $28 billion, paid nearly $3.9 billion in federal taxes in 1988. That year, 1,077,000 Kansans filed tax returns.

*Source: **Statistical Abstract of the United States**, 1991; U.S. Office of Personnel Management, Biennial Report of Employment by Geographic Area.*

Kansas received more than $2 billion in 1989 that was spent for defense purposes, which accounted for nearly 23% of the total federal dollars spent in the state. In 1989, over $1 Billion in federal funds were spent in Kansas on procurements.

The total federal fund distributed for Kansas in 1989 was $9.08 billion. Of Kansas' neighboring states, only Nebraska received less federal dollars.

*Source: **Statistical Abstract of the United States**, 1991, U.S. Bureau of the Census, Federal Expenditures by State.*

federal government

QUICK FACTS:

Federal Military Installations:

AIR FORCE

McConnell Air Force Base, Wichita, KS 67221. Phone: (316) 681-6100.

ARMY

Ft. Leavenworth, Leavenworth, KS 66027. Phone: (913) 684-4021.
• Command and General Staff College
• Combined Arms Center
• 35th Infantry Division

Ft. Riley, Junction City, KS 66442. Phone: (913) 239-3911.
• 1st Infantry Division
• 3rd ROTC Region

Federal Regional Offices:

Federal Information Center (Regional Office for Kansas), 1520 Market St., Room 2616, St. Louis, MO 63103. Toll-free number: 1-800-432-2934.

Federal Home Loan Bank Board: Three Townsite Plaza, P.O. Box 176, Topeka, KS 66601; (913) 233-0507.

Justice Department - U.S. Attorneys Office: 444 Quincy Street, Topeka, KS 66683; (913) 295-2850.

Department of Commerce - Bureau of the Census: Regional Director, One Gateway Center, Kansas City, KS 66101; (913) 236-3728.

Environmental Protection Agency: Regional Administrator, 726 Minnesota Avenue, Kansas City, KS 66101; (913) 236-2800.

National Labor Relations Board: Regional Director, Two Gateway Center, Room 616, Kansas City, KS 66101; (913) 236-3846.

The French cannons at Fort Leavenworth overlook the Missouri River. The cannons were cast in 1774 in Paris, but how or why they were brought to Fort Leavenworth is a mystery.

Photo courtesy of Department of the Army, Community Relations, Fort Leavenworth.

1992 KANSAS CONGRESSIONAL DISTRICTS

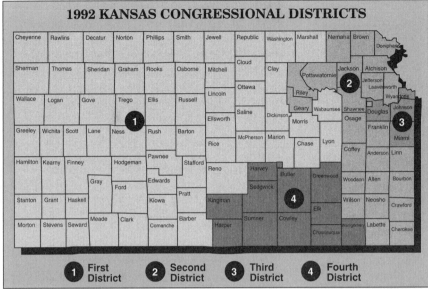

| ① First District | ② Second District | ③ Third District | ④ Fourth District |

Source: Kansas Legislative Research.

Congressional Delegation

Kansans elect two senators and four representatives to the United States Congress. Kansas is divided into four Congressional districts that generally follow county lines. Voters within those four districts elect one representative from each district.

U.S. senators serve for a six-year term. The two senatorial races in Kansas are staggered, with one Senatorial race being in 1990 and the next seat up for election in 1992.

Kansas has 6 electoral votes, which is the sum of the number of representatives (4) plus the number of senators (2) from the state.

Kansas Voter Requirements

To be eligible to vote in Kansas, a person must be: (1) United States citizen, (2) 18 years of age, (3) a resident of Kansas and the voting area, (4) registered to vote. Citizens who have moved or changed names are required to re-register to be eligible to vote in Kansas.

Due to redistricting in 1992, Douglas county shares the second and third districts and Marion county shares the first and the fourth districts.

The first woman elected to represent Kansas as a member of the U.S. Congress was Kathryn O'Loughlin, who served from 1933 to 1935.

Kansas had 1,101,982 registered voters as of August 1, 1991. Democrats numbered 330,562, Republicans 497,579, unaffiliated 273,192, and Libertarians 649.

state/executive

QUICK FACTS:

Photo courtesy of Kansas Secretary of State's Office.

The Kansas Capitol in Topeka is the symbol of state government in Kansas. Senate and House of Represen-tatives convene in their chambers in the Capitol building every January.

In 1937 a Democrat, Walter Huxman, was elected governor in Kansas. Over his protests the legislature enacted a 2% sales tax. At first the sales tax was paid with small, metal tokens, each worth one-tenth of a cent.

THE EXECUTIVE BRANCH IN KANSAS STATE GOVERNMENT

The constitutional officers of the executive branch of Kansas state government are the governor, lieutenant governor, secretary of state, and attorney general, who are elected for terms of four years at the regular general elections in even-numbered years, starting in 1974.

Governor

The governor serves as the supreme executive power of the state and is responsible for the enforcement of all state laws. The governor may not be elected to more than two successive terms as governor.

The governor may require information in writing from the officers of the executive departments upon any subject relating to their duties. The officers of the executive departments, and of all public state institutions, must, at least ten days preceding each regular session of the legislature, report to the governor who then presents these reports to the legislature.

On extraordinary occasions, the governor may call the legislature into special session by proclamation. At every session of the legislature the governor communicates in writing information regarding the condition of the state and the economy and issues his formal recommendations.

The governor also has the power to reorganize any state agency and its function, within the executive branch, when he considers it necessary for efficient administration. He must do so by an executive reorganization order, transmitted to both houses of the legislature. The governor also has the power of pardon.

The governor is responsible for keeping the official state seal, and issues all commissions.

In 1974, the length of term for governor increased from two to four years.

Lieutenant Governor

The lieutenant governor assists the governor and has other powers and duties as are prescribed by law.

When the office of governor is vacant, the lieutenant governor will become governor. In the event of the disability of the governor, the lieutenant governor will assume the powers and duties of governor until the disability is removed. Unlike some other states, the Kansas Supreme Court has held that the absence of the governor from the state does not entitle the lieutenant governor to act as governor. The lieutenant governor becomes governor whenever either the office becomes vacant or the governor becomes disabled. Should the office of the lieutenant governor become vacant, the president of the Senate would assume the place of the lieutenant governor on any statutory board or commission. Prior to 1972, the lieutenant governor served as president of the Senate, as is the practice in many states. A 1972 constitutional amendment deleted that provision, making the lieutenant governor's primary responsibilities to serve as an assistant to the governor.

Beginning in 1974, the candidates for the office of governor and lieutenant governor are nominated and elected jointly. No person may be elected to more than two successive terms as lieutenant governor.

Secretary of State

The secretary of state has been described as the chief housekeeper of state government. He is custodian of various important state papers, and he performs numerous ministerial tasks that are important for the successful administration of the affairs of the state. He is responsible for publishing the *Kansas Directory*; *Election Statistics*; *Legislative Directory*; *Directory of County Officers of Kansas*; *Kansas Facts*; *Kansas Election Laws*; *Trademarks and Service Marks*; and *Constitution of the State of Kansas with*

QUICK FACTS:

Democrat Robert Docking of Arkansas City became the only Kansas governor to be elected to a third term in 1970 and won an unheard of fourth term in 1972.

A plaque on the landing of the south Capitol steps marks the spot where Kansas Governor Alf M. Landon accepted the Republican Presidential nomination on July 23, 1936.

In February 1975, then-President Gerald R. Ford visited the Capitol in Topeka. A bronze plaque which commemorates his visit is mounted on the landing of the east steps, where he stood when he made his public address.

Major state agencies are headed by cabinet-level secretaries who are appointed by the Governor.

GOVERNMENT
state/executive

QUICK FACTS:

Kansas was one of the first states to ratify the Equal Rights Amendment to the United States Constitution, making ratification March 28, 1972.

The Fountain of Justice is in front of the Judicial Center in Topeka. The three towering plumes of water in the upper pool depict the three branches of government. The middle pool represents domestic tranquility when the spirit of Justice flows freely. The lower pool depicts the body of the Supreme Court with the seven Justices of the court being symbolized by the seven sprays through whom the spirit of Justice flows.

Barton County was named in honor of the famous Civil War nurse Clara Barton. This is the only Kansas county named for a woman.

Amendments. In addition, the secretary of state receives biennial reports from state agencies. He then edits the reports and publishes a consolidated biennial report that contains information about the operations, goals, and problems of the agencies.

The secretary of state's function as the administrator of election laws is particularly important. He receives the filings of various candidates, and he notifies the county clerks of these filings for district, state, and national offices. He receives the abstract of the votes cast for such offices in each of the counties. As a member of the State Board of Canvassers, he takes part in the counting of the election returns and declares the winners. He transmits to each house of the legislature a list of the members who have been officially elected.

Articles of incorporation are filed with the secretary of state. The maintenance of records for active and inactive corporations is one of the major duties of the office. The office receives the reports that are required concerning conflicts of interest under the State Governmental Ethics Act and the reports required by the Campaign Finance Act.

Lobbyists must register with the secretary of state. He is the custodian of all enrolled bills and resolutions. When the legislature adjourns, the secretary of state supervises the publication of *Session Laws* and concurrent resolutions, and he distributes copies of the laws to the officials who are entitled to receive copies. He has them, as well as *Kansas Statutes Annotated*, available for sale to the public.

Attorney General

The attorney general represents the state in all cases that come before the Kansas Supreme Court, and the governor or the legislature may require him to prosecute or defend the state in the courts of various other states or in the federal courts. He is required to advise and to assist all other state officers in all civil matters. The attorney general is also required to render advice and assistance to all county attorneys, and he may be asked to give opinions interpreting various provisions of the statutes.

The attorney general is an important law-enforcement official. In the event of any failure or alleged failure by a county attorney to enforce criminal laws locally, the attorney general may, on his own action, supersede the county attorney in the enforcement of such laws.

The attorney general is also charged with the prosecution of all ouster suits against public officials who are alleged to be guilty of not properly performing the duties of their offices. He represents the governor of the state in all proceedings for the extradition of fugitives from justice. The attorney general also exercises supervision over the Kansas Bureau of Investigation.

Whenever a resident of Kansas dies without a will and without any known heirs, the attorney general is required to represent the state of Kansas in the probate procedures. The attorney general is also required to pass judgment on the validity of all municipal bonds issued in the state of Kansas and upon the validity of all surety bonds required of various state officers and employees.

QUICK FACTS:

Source: "Constitution of the State of Kansas," published by the Secretary of State's Office, November 1987; Drury, James W., *The Government of Kansas*, Third Edition, Regents Press of Kansas, Lawrence, 1980.

Crawford County and the town of Crawfordville were named for Samuel J. Crawford, governor of Kansas from 1865 to 1868.

The Supreme Court Law Library, housed in the Kansas Judicial Center, has 225,000 volumes, including foreign and domestic law reports.

The Kansas Judicial Center, located in Topeka, houses the Kansas Supreme Court, the Court of Appeals, and the Attorney General's Office.

Photo courtesy of The Topeka Capital-Journal.

state/legislative

QUICK FACTS:

While the Kansas Supreme Court has held that the state government does not have inherent powers, the Kansas Constitution provides that "all powers not herein delegated remain with the people," and it is through the legislature that the people act.

Kansas has 125 representatives and 40 senators in state government. Senators serve four-year terms and representatives serve two-year terms.

State legislators must be qualified voters and residents of the district from which they are elected.

In the 1890s, the Populists installed porcelain bathtubs and white marble wash basins in most offices in the Capitol; all the bathtubs have since been removed.

THE LEGISLATIVE BRANCH IN KANSAS STATE GOVERNMENT

Qualifications and Election

The constitution of the State of Kansas requires that all state legislators be qualified voters and residents of the district from which they are elected. Representatives are elected for two-year terms and senators for four-year terms. There is no overlapping of terms in either house. Representation in the legislature is based on a system of districts that largely follows county lines.

Organization of the Legislature

The formal organization of the legislature begins when the session convenes. The secretary of state or a deputy presides over the House and the Senate until each is organized.

After the certification of the members and the administering of the oath of office, each house moves to elect its officers. The Speaker of the House and the president of the Senate will officially appoint the chief administrative officers of the House and the Senate.

How Bills Become Laws

Introduction of a Bill: Any member or group of members, including a committee, may propose a bill. Either house may originate a bill on any subject, and there is no restriction on the number of bills that a member may introduce. While there is no constitutional or statutory limit on the time for the introduction of bills, each house usually determines by resolution near the beginning of each session a date after which only bills proposed by committees will be considered. By the same legislative custom, all bills pertaining to appropriations are introduced by the Committee on Ways and Means in each of the houses.

To introduce a bill, a member merely hands his written proposal to the reading clerk, who reads the title of the bill, assigns it a number, and records it. The clerk's reading of the title constitutes the first legal action on the bill. The numbered document is then dispatched to the state printer's office, where it is supplied to legislators, references services, and interested citizens.

Committee Actions: The bill is then referred to a standing committee, or to the Committee of the Whole, which is the entire membership of the chamber meeting as a committee. The sponsor of the bill may tell the presiding officer of the particular house what committee he wishes to have consider the proposal. The Speaker of the House or the president of the Senate then assigns the bill to the committee he considers appropriate.

The bill is given to the committee chairman. Rules of both houses require committees to report on each bill. On the basis of its hearing and deliberations the committee makes a report to the full chamber. The committee may report the bill adversely or it may recommend that it be passed or passed as amended. It may report the bill without recommendations or ask that the bill be referred to another committee.

Final Action by the First House: If the committee reports the bill favorably for passage and the chamber accepts the report, the bill is sent to the secretary of state for engrossment prior to final action. Engrossment consists of making a new, corrected, typed copy of the bill, which contains all amendments and has been checked for accuracy.

When the engrossed bill is returned to the house of its origin, the bill is placed on the calendar under Bills on Final Action. A roll-call vote is taken on each measure, although several bills may be grouped together for "bulk voting." For a bill to pass it must have 63 affirmative votes in the House, and 21 affirmative votes in the Senate.

Action by the Second House: The processes discussed above are repeated in the second house. If the bill is passed in exactly the same form as by the first house, it is sent to the governor for his consideration. Should the bill

QUICK FACTS:

The stained glass windows above the south doors of the Capitol depict the contributions of the military to historical and contemporary Kansas life. The stained glass windows were a gift to the State from the Kansas Chapter of the Veterans of Foreign Wars for the 1976 U.S. Bicentennial.

The dome murals upward from the rotunda in the Capitol are allegorical in composition. The four paintings have a mosaic background and depict knowledge (east panel); power (south panel); plenty (north panel); and peace (west panel).

"The Great White Buffalo," a statue by the late Lumen Martin Winter, was dedicated at the entrance to the Kansas Museum of History in Topeka on Oct. 18, 1983.

state/legislative

QUICK FACTS:

The first Kansas legislature in 1861 gave women the right to vote in school elections. Universal suffrage was granted in Kansas in 1912 by constitutional amendment.

Kansas was the first state to create a Legislative Council to carry on legislative functions when the lawmaking body is not in session.

Haskell County was named after politician Dudley Chase Haskell, who served in the Kansas House of Representatives in 1872 and from 1875 to 1876 and was a U.S. representative from 1877 to 1883.

The "Kansas Day" celebration originated in Paola in 1877.

Source: "Constitution of the State of Kansas," published by the Secretary of State's Office, November, 1987; Drury, James W., **The Government of Kansas**, Third Edition, Regents Press of Kansas, Lawrence, 1980.

be rejected by the second chamber, the bill dies and does not become a law. If the bill is amended and passed, it is then returned to the first house for concurrence on any amendments. Should the first house not concur, a conference committee that is composed of members of both houses is appointed to meet and settle the differences.

Effective Dates of Laws: According to the Kansas Constitution, the legislature may determine the time when a law is to become effective. Normally, laws are made effective upon their appearance in the *Session Laws*, a bound volume that is prepared by the secretary of state. The volume contains indexed copies of all laws that were passed during the legislative session.

Legislative Coordinating Council

In 1933, Kansas became one of the first states to establish a Legislative Council. The council was "to prepare a legislative program in the form of bills or otherwise, as in its opinion the welfare of the state may require, to be presented at the next session of the legislature."

In 1971, after review and recommendations by the council, the system that provided for interim legislative activities and for the supervising of legislative staff services was revised. The Legislative Coordinating Council was established as the central management group for the legislative leaders.

The council appoints the revisor of statutes, the director of the Legislative Research Department, the director of Legislative Administrative Services, and the legislative counsel. The Legislative Coordinating Council also approves the budgets for and gives general administrative direction to these legislative staff offices. The council is authorized to speak for the legislature in certain matters between sessions. It approves the budget estimates for the legislature in advance of the session.

The Kansas Capitol building was constructed over a period of 37 years, from 1866 to 1903, at a total cost of $3.2 million. The Capitol is 339 feet north and south and 386 feet east and west, and 304 feet from the ground to the top of the cupola. The ornamentally finished House of Representatives and Senate chambers are located on the third floor. The murals on the second floor, including the dramatic "John Brown" mural, were painted by John Steuart Curry. Four statues of famous Kansans Dwight D. Eisenhower, William Allen White, Arthur Capper, and Amelia Earhart are located in the rotunda. The Kansas Capitol was declared a National Historic Site on September 3, 1971.

Photo by Paul Beaver, The Topeka Capital-Journal.

THE JUDICIAL BRANCH OF STATE GOVERNMENT IN KANSAS

In 1972 the voters of Kansas approved a new judicial article that vests the judicial power of the state in one court of justice. This marked the official adoption of the concept of a unified court system. It called for one court of justice to consist of a supreme court, district courts, and such other courts as would be provided for by law.

Supreme Court

The legislature has established as minimum qualifications for justices that they have been admitted to practice law in the state and have at least 10 years experience as a practicing lawyer or judge or as a teacher in an accredited law school. Supreme Court justices are selected through a nonpartisan process. The governor appoints persons to fill vacancies on the Supreme Court from lists of three persons nominated by the Supreme Court Nominating Commission. After having been appointed by the governor, the justice serves for at least a one-year period. At the first general election after the completion of one year's service, the name of the new justice is submitted on a nonpartisan ballot, and voters indicate whether the justice should be retained in office.

The Kansas Constitution requires that the Supreme Court hold one term each year in Topeka. By statute, the first Tuesdays in January and July are fixed for its convening. The Supreme Court has both original and appellate jurisdiction. The original jurisdiction includes three extraordinary remedies of quo warranto, mandamus, and habeas corpus. Statutes define the court's appellate jurisdiction. It now includes, as a matter or right, all class-A and class-B felony cases and cases in which a law has been declared unconstitutional. The Supreme Court can grant a petition to review the decision of the Court of Appeals.

Court of Appeals

The basic function of this court is to relieve the workload of the Kansas Supreme Court and to make for a more expeditious hearing and disposition of cases. The Court of Appeals is a middle court between the Supreme Court and the District Courts. The Court of Appeals has a chief judge and six associate judges.

The Court of Appeals may hear cases as a full court or in panels of three judges. It is based in Topeka, but it may hear cases in any part of the state. All appellate cases beyond the explicit jurisdiction of the Supreme Court will be appealed to the Court of Appeals. The Supreme Court may grant a petition to review the decision of the Court of Appeals; otherwise a decision handed down by this court is final.

District Courts

The district court in Kansas has long been the general trial court, with broad civil and criminal jurisdiction. Civil actions of divorce may be begun in it, as may claims involving any amount of money. Prosecutions of both felonies and misdemeanors may also be heard. The district court has acted as appellate court for the probate and county courts, justice-of-the-peace courts, city courts, and municipal courts.

Today the state is divided into 31 judicial districts, with jurisdictions ranging from one to seven counties. Districts that have more than one judge are said to have divisions. The typical arrangement is for the district judge to visit the county-seat towns in his district and hold court. A clerk of the court is appointed in each county to handle records and serve as a local representative for the district judge.

Each judicial district in Kansas has an administrative judge who may assign judges from one court to another within the district. The administrative judge is required to develop a plan for the equal distribution of work within the district.

QUICK FACTS:

The Court of Appeals has a chief judge and six associate judges. The Court of Appeals is based in Topeka but may hear cases in any part of the state.

Federal Courts Serving Kansas
U.S. Court of Appeals, 10th Circuit:
Clerk, C-404 U.S. Courthouse, 1929 Stout St., Denver, CO 80294; (303) 837-3157.

U.S. District Court - Kansas District:
Clerk, 204 U.S. Courthouse, 401 N. Market St., Wichita, KS 67202; (316) 269-6491.

U.S. Bankruptcy Court:
Clerk, 303 U.S. Courthouse, 401 N. Market St., Wichita, KS 67202; (316) 269-6486.

Source: "Constitution of the State of Kansas," published by the Secretary of State's Office, November, 1987; Drury, James W., *The Government of Kansas*, Third Edition, Lawrence: Regents Press of Kansas, 1980.

local government

QUICK FACTS:

The town of Haddam in Washington County has an unusual Haddam City Jail. The jail was built in 1901 by an all-woman city council and mayor to keep the men in line.

On the south lawn of the Johnson County Courthouse in Olathe is a bandstand built in 1982. It is a replica of a bandstand that stood on the site from 1907 to the 1940s and was used for the Olathe Civic Band.

Kansas includes several forms of local government: the commission form; the mayor-council-manager system; the commission-manager system; and the mayor-council plan.

Greeley County was the last of the 105 counties in Kansas to be created.

Incorporated Cities

Kansas has 24 first-class cities; 88 second-class cities; and 515 third-class cities. The first-class cities are: Atchison, Coffeyville, Dodge City, Emporia, Fort Scott, Garden City, Hutchinson, Junction City, Kansas City, Lawrence, Leavenworth, Lenexa, Liberal, Manhattan, Newton, Olathe, Overland Park, Parsons, Pittsburg, Prairie Village, Salina, Shawnee, Topeka, and Wichita.

Local Jurisdictions

Kansas had a network of 3,803 local government jurisdictions in 1987, including county, municipal, township, school district, and various special districts (natural resource, fire protection, and housing/community development). There were 1,360 townships and 627 municipal governments that provided the primary leadership for local government in Kansas.

Sources of Revenue

In 1988, local governments in Kansas generated most of their revenues from local taxes and other local sources. Federal sources accounted for only about 4% of revenue to Kansas communities. Of the $3.97 billion in revenue collected by local governments in 1988, 74% was generated locally, and 26% was collected from intergovernmental sources (state and federal).

Source: *Statistical Abstract of the United States,* 1991; *U.S. Bureau of the Census, Census of Governments 1982, Historical Statistics on Governmental Finances and Employment, and Governmental Finances.*

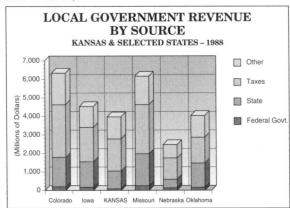

LOCAL GOVERNMENT REVENUE BY SOURCE
KANSAS & SELECTED STATES – 1988

The State Budget

The 1993 State Budget for Kansas shows that most of the state's General Fund revenues (91%) are generated through taxes, and the largest share comes from individual income taxes, which accounts for more than 39% of all revenue. The second largest revenue source — sales and use tax — accounts for 36% of all revenue. By far the greatest single appropriation is to the education agency, which accounts for 58% of all expected expenditures. The total 1993 General Fund Budget is expected to be $2.5 billion.

QUICK FACTS:

In 1988, Kansas was ranked 44th in terms of per capita general state expenditures with slightly less than $1,400.

Source: "The Governor's Budget Report;" State of Kansas; Fiscal Year 1993; Vol. 1.

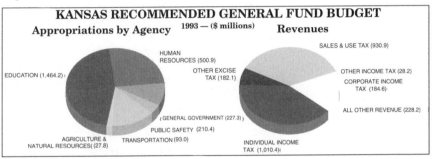

KANSAS RECOMMENDED GENERAL FUND BUDGET
Appropriations by Agency 1993 — ($ millions) **Revenues**

HUMAN RESOURCES (500.9)
OTHER EXCISE TAX (182.1)
EDUCATION (1,464.2)
(GENERAL GOVERNMENT (227.3)
PUBLIC SAFETY (210.4)
AGRICULTURE & NATURAL RESOURCES(27.8)
TRANSPORTATION (93.0)

SALES & USE TAX (930.9)
OTHER INCOME TAX (28.2)
CORPORATE INCOME TAX (184.6)
ALL OTHER REVENUE (228.2)
INDIVIDUAL INCOME TAX (1,010.4)

Tax Collections

In 1989, Kansas' state tax collections amounted to $2.5 billion. About 46% of the tax collections were derived from sales receipts and approximately 34% came from individual income tax payments.

Kansas, like most of its neighboring states, spends significant amounts of money on education, both at the state and local level.

In 1988, state and local governments in Kansas generated revenue totaling nearly $6.9 billion, 40% of which came from non-property taxes.

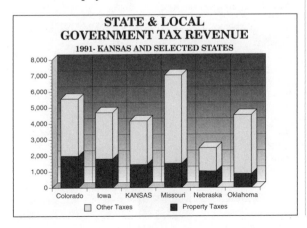

STATE & LOCAL GOVERNMENT TAX REVENUE
1991- KANSAS AND SELECTED STATES

8,000
7,000
6,000
5,000
4,000
3,000
2,000
1,000
0

Colorado   Iowa   KANSAS   Missouri   Nebraska   Oklahoma

☐ Other Taxes   ■ Property Taxes

Source: Statistical Abstract of the United States, 1991; U.S. Bureau of the Census, Governmental Finances, Series GF, No. 5 annual.

education

QUICK FACTS:

In 1991, the total number of students in non-public schools (grades K-12, special education and non-graded) was 28,447.

Women comprise a majority of the teachers in Kansas (71.6%) as compared with their male counterparts (28.4%). However, principals are predominantly male (81.6%) as compared with females (18.4%).

Student/teacher ratios in public elementary and secondary schools have remained nearly constant during the last 11 years, ranging from 13.2 students per teacher in 1979-80 to 13.6 in 1991-92.

In 1991 the head count enrollment for Kansas public schools, including grades K-12, special education, and non-graded students was 445,390 students.

Source: Gary Watson, Kansas Board of Education.

Public School Enrollment

In the 13-year period from 1979 to 1991, enrollment in Kansas public schools increased about 1%. Within the different grade levels, there was an increase of nearly 25% in the number of 1st graders, and a nearly 11% decrease in the number of 10th graders.

Private School Enrollment

In the 13-year period between 1979 and 1991, enrollment in Kansas non-public schools has declined by slightly less than 1%. Within the different grade levels, there has been a 73% increase in the number of kindergartners, and a nearly 24% decrease in the number of 9th graders.

Average Teachers' Salaries

During the 1991-92 school year, the average teacher's salary was $30,731, an increase of 24.5% over the 1988-89 year. The average principal's salary was $48,344, an increase of 27.1% during the same period. As of 1991, average salaries for Kansas classroom teachers were below national averages at all levels.

PUBLIC SCHOOLS STUDENT-TEACHER RATIOS: 1979-1992

YEAR	NUMBER OF CERTIFIED EMPLOYEES	ENROLLMENT K-12	STUDENTS PER TEACHER
1979-80	30,703	422,924	13.2
1980-81	30,899	415,291	12.8
1981-82	30,631	409,909	12.8
1982-83	30,504	407,074	12.7
1983-84	30,545	405,222	12.6
1984-85	30,859	405,347	12.5
1985-86	31,294	410,229	12.4
1986-87	31.668	416.091	12.5
1987-88	31,971	421,112	12.5
1988-89	32,955	426,596	12.3
1989-90	33,694	430,864	12.3
1990-91	34,324	437,034	13.3
1991-92	34,568	445,390	13.6

High School Graduates

The number of public high school graduates in Kansas declined during the 1979-1991 period, from 30,890 to 24,414. However, persons graduating increased to 27,036 in the 1987-88 school year.

QUICK FACTS:

In the 1989-90 school year the drop out rate was highest among white students with 3,799 drop outs, which was 79.2% of all dropouts that year.

In 1990-91, Kansas ranked 27th among states in current expenditures per pupil.

TOTAL NUMBER OF KANSAS HIGH SCHOOL GRADUATES

YEAR	TOTAL	% CHANGE PREVIOUS YEAR
1979-80	30,890	—
1980-81	29,397	-4.8%
1981-82	28,298	-3.7%
1982-83	28,316	0.1%
1983-84	26,730	-5.6%
1984-85	25,983	-2.8%
1985-86	25,587	-1.5%
1986-87	26,933	5.3%
1987-88	27,036	0.4%
1988-89	26,848	-0.7%
1989-90	25,367	-5.5%
1990-91	24,414	3.8%

Source: Gary Watson, Kansas Board of Education.

High School Dropout Rate

During the period from 1979-1980 to 1990-91, over 64,000 students in secondary schools dropped out of Kansas' public schools. Students most oftened dropped out in the 11th grade. The largest decline in the dropout rate during this period occurred between the 1979-80 and 1980-81 and the 1981-82 and 1982-83 academic years. The largest increase in dropouts during this period occurred during the most recent period, 1987-88 and 1988-89, with an increase of 0.2%.

During the 1990-91 school year, a total of 48,927,122 lunches and 2,414,500 breakfasts were served to students in Kansas.

Source: Gary Watson, Kansas Board of Education.

NUMBER OF KANSAS HIGH SCHOOL DROPOUTS BY GRADE: 1981-1991

YEAR	GRADE				Total	Average %
	9th	10th	11th	12th		
1981-82	623	1,598	1,969	1,504	5,694	4.6%
1982-83	763	1,439	1,724	1,174	5,100	4.2%
1983-84	629	1,425	1,722	1,359	5,135	4.3%
1984-85	619	1,280	1,648	1,346	4,893	4.0%
1985-86	712	1,392	1,539	1,283	4,926	4.0%
1986-87	735	1,359	1,468	1,127	4,934	4.1%
1987-88	753	1,460	1,605	1,287	5,105	4.3%
1988-89	707	1,447	1,703	1,368	5,225	4.5%
1989-90	767	1,349	1,549	1,130	4,795	4.2%
1990-91	918	1,334	1,551	1,192	4,995	4.3%

QUICK FACTS:

The Kansas educational system received national attention during the *Brown v. Board of Education of Topeka* case. The U.S. Supreme Court handed down its landmark decision on May 17, 1954, which held that the "separate but equal" school facilities were inherently unequal and that school segregation violated the U.S. Constitution's guarantee of equal protection under the Fourteenth Amendment.

Topeka High School, which was designed by Topeka architect Thomas Williamson, was completed in 1931 at a cost of over $1 million.

During the 1991-92 school year, 48.6% of the students attending Kansas schools were female and 51.4% were male.

EDUCATION FACILITIES IN KANSAS
1991-92

Public Schools	Number
Unified School Districts	304
High Schools	352
Junior High Schools	176

(Middle Schools, 105 are accredited as Junior High or Elementary)

Elementary Schools	935

Accredited Private Schools

High Schools	24
Middle Schools	1
Elementary Schools	138
Community Colleges	19
Area Vo-Tech Schools	16
Adult Education Centers	37
GED Testing Centers	38

Average Age of Public Elementary and Secondary School Buildings *(in years)* 34

Size of Unified School Districts *(Square Miles)*

Smallest:	10.0
Median Size:	228.5
Largest:	992.0

Source: Gary Watson, Kansas Board of Education.

Public School System

The school system in Kansas has emerged from the one-room schoolhouses (none of which are in use today) to the more complex network of public schools. The State Board of Education supervises all public elementary, secondary, vocational-technical schools, and community colleges.

Kansas is divided into unified school districts, and each district is controlled by a board of education with the members being elected by the district residents. The state provides basic finance and guidelines, but the policies and day-to-day operations are left up to local school districts. The length of the school year 1992-93, which must be at least 181 days or 1,086 hours taught, is mandated by Kansas regulations.

QUICK FACTS:

Kansas averages were significantly higher than national averages in SAT scores in 1990; however, this could be anticipated because of the fact that only 10% or less of the Kansas seniors took the SAT as compared to about 43% of the national college bound seniors who took the test.

TRENDS IN AVERAGE ACT COMPOSITE SCORES: 1987-1991

Year	Number	Kansas	Number	National
1987	18,324	21.2	777,424	20.8
1988	19,053	21.1	841,322	20.8
1989	19,104	21.0	855,322	20.6
1990	182,000	20.9	817,096	20.6
1990	176,689	21.1	796,983	20.6

TRENDS IN AVERAGE SAT COMPOSIT SCORES: 1987-1990*

Year	Verbal Kansas	Means National	Math Kansas	Means National
1984-85	504	431	550	475
1985-86	498	431	544	475
1996-87	498	430	547	476
1987-88	494	428	541	476
1988-89	495	427	545	476
1989-90	492	424	548	476
1990-91	493	422	546	474

* Approximately 10% of seniors took the SAT

Source: "What's Happening in Kansas Education, May 1991," Kansas Board of Education.

The Alfred M. Landon Lecture Series at Kansas State University was established in 1966 and attracts politicians, journalists, and prominent personalities to speak at K-State.

Source: Kansas Board of Regents; Secretary of State, "Kansas Facts."

Regents' Institutions

Higher education in Kansas is the responsibility of the State Board of Regents, a nine-member board whose members are appointed by the governor. The Board coordinates programs of the state institutions and provides certain assistance for students enrolled in higher education in Kansas. Six state universities and one technical institute are in the Regents System in Kansas.

THE REGENTS' INSTITUTIONS

INSTITUTION	CONFERENCE	MASCOT
1. University of Kansas, Lawrence	Big Eight	Jayhawks
2. Kansas State University, Manhattan	Big Eight	Wildcats
3. Wichita State University, Wichita	Missouri Valley	Shockers
4. Emporia State University, Emporia	M.I.A.A.*	Hornets
5. Fort Hays State University, Hays	Independent	Tigers
6. Pittsburg State University, Pittsburg	M.I.A.A.	Gorillas
7. Kansas College of Technology, Salina	—	—

*M.I.A.A. is the Missouri Intercollegiate Athletic Association.

education

QUICK FACTS:

Kansas ranks 5th in the U.S. in number of institutions of higher learning per capita, and 8th among the states in the number of public institutions of higher learning per capita.

The first Mennonite college in the nation was Bethel College in Newton.

Fort Hays State University won the NAIA basketball championship in 1984 and 1985.

Haskell Indian College in Lawrence is a federally operated two-year college for Indians.

Source: Kansas Legislative Research Department.

A ridge of land in Douglas County was originally called Hog Back Point and Hog Back Ridge. It was later renamed Mt. Oread and became the site of the University of Kansas.

College Enrollment

Overall, enrollment in higher education institutions in Kansas has increased more than 6.5% between 1988 and 1991. Enrollment has increased for two-year public community colleges by 13%, but decreased for Regents and other four-year public institutions, by 11.2%

In 1991, there were 163,202 students enrolled at Kansas colleges and universities. Kansas has total of 47 private colleges, public universities and community colleges that offer a variety of degrees.

SPRING ENROLLMENT AT KANSAS COLLEGES AND UNIVERSITIES: 1991

Four year institutions:

Regents Institutions & other Public Institutions 78,684

Private Colleges and Universities 13,202

Total: *(Four year institutions)* 91,886

Two year institutions:

Public Community Colleges 56,951

Private Two Year Colleges 1,163

Total: *(Two Year Institutions)* 58,114

Combined Total: *(All Colleges and Institutions)* 163,202

Top Undergraduate Programs

Undergraduate programs at the University of Kansas, Kansas State University, and Wichita State University appear among the nation's most highly ranked, according to the Gourman Report. KU's highest ranking undergraduate program is in architectural engineering (3rd); Kansas State's is in landscape architecture (3rd); and Wichita State's is in physical therapy (70th).

Top Graduate Programs

Graduate programs at four Kansas Universities appear among the nations' most highly ranked, according to the Gourman Report. KU and KSU rankings are for their programs, except for KU's overall graduate school rank. KU's highest ranking graduate programs are in entomology and petroleum engineering (9th), and Spanish (12); Kansas State's are in landscape architecture (8th), and veterinary medicine (10th); Wichita State's is in the School of Engineering (123rd); and Washburn's is in the School of Law (102nd). The University of Kansas appears on Gourman's list of top graduate schools overall in the nation, ranked 42nd.

College Degrees

In 1987, Kansas institutions of higher education conferred 53,103 degrees and diplomas. In 1988, the number of degrees and diplomas was 49,956. In 1990-91, 13,759 bachelor and advanced degrees were conferred from post secondary schools in Kansas. Community and junior colleges conferred more than 6,456 associate degrees and the area vocational schools gave 24,376 diplomas or certificates of training.

QUICK FACTS:

Aggieville is a popular business district adjacent to the Kansas State University campus in Manhattan. The area has been known as "Aggieville" since the time the college was known as the Kansas State Agricultural College and its students were called "Aggies."

The high point of any student's career is college graduation. Here the students at Kansas State University eagerly await the moment when they can throw their caps aloft in celebration.

Photo courtesy of Kansas State University Photo Services.

The College Blue Book, Narrative Descriptions, 21st Edition, New York: Macmillan
Publishing Company, 1987.

"The Constitution of the State of Kansas," Secretary of State's Office, November 1987.

Director of the Budget, Kansas Department of Administration, Capitol Building,
Topeka 66612.

Drury, James W. **The Government of Kansas**, Third Edition, Lawrence: Regents Press
of Kansas, Lawrence, 1980.

Federal Yellow Book, New York: Monitor Publishing Co., Fall 1987.

**The Gourman Report: A Rating of Graduate and Professional Programs in
American and International Universities,** 5th ed., Gourman, National
Education Standards.

**The Gourman Report, A Rating of Undergraduate Programs in American and
International Colleges and Universities,** 7th ed., Dr. Jack Gourman, National
Education Standards.

Kansas Board of Education, Gary Watson, researcher, 120 E. 10th St., Topeka 66612.

Kansas Department of Commerce, 400 W. 8th, 5th Floor, Topeka 66603-3957.

"Kansas Directory 1988," Kansas Secretary of State, 2nd floor, Statehouse,
Topeka 66612.

"Kansas Higher Education Enrollment Report," Kansas Legislative Research
Department, Capitol Building, Topeka 66612.

Kansas Statistical Abstract, 1990-91, Institute for Public Policy and Business Research,
The University of Kansas.

State Information Book, INFAX Corporation, Rockville, MD, 1987.

Statistical Abstract of the United States, 108th edition, U.S. Department of
Commerce, Bureau of the Census, 1988.

"What's Happening in Kansas Education," Kansas Board of Education, 120 S.E. 10th,
Topeka, 66612.

CHAPTER 4
PEOPLE

KANSAS

PEOPLE

Population • Vital Statistics
Employment • Housing
Famous Kansans

Photo courtesy of Emporia Twin Rivers Festival Inc.

79

PEOPLE

overview

KANSAS

Population Characteristics 83-86 — Kansas has both a rural/small town and a metropolitan focus. The metropolitan areas are located in south central and eastern regions of the state, while the western and north central regions are primarily rural.

Vital Statistics 87-90 — The average life expectancy for Kansans in recent years is slightly more than 75 years, which is nearly two years more than the average American.

Employment 91 — The increase of the effective buying income of the average Kansan has nearly matched that of the average American, increasing about 300% since 1970.

Households and Housing 92-93 — Since 1950, the total number of households in Kansas has grown 56%. The average size of the Kansas household has declined slightly since 1950.

Famous Kansans 94-105 — Silent film comedian Buster Keaton was born in Piqua, Kan., on October 4, 1895, during a cyclone. Other famous Kansans include Dwight D. Eisenhower and Amelia Earhart.

CHAPTER OPENER PHOTO: This youngster finds a splashing way to cool off during the Water Fun activity at the annual Twin Rivers Festival in Emporia.

D uring his speech in Emporia in 1883, Henry Ward Beecher said, "There is no monument under heaven on which I would rather have my name inscribed than on this goodly state of Kansas." Those sentimental words reflect the special feeling that many Kansans have about their state. The early pioneers who settled this land had grit and determination to create a better life despite harsh conditions on the plains. The tradition of pride and courage is shared by Kansans today.

Kansans are good-hearted and caring people. Stop in at a local diner, have a cup of coffee, and talk with the people of Kansas. Conversations can vary from local politics, to the economy, to a much-discussed topic in Kansas — the weather.

While many people think Kansans live only in rural locations, Kansas has a blend of metropolitan and rural areas. The family farm has been an important part of the state, and small towns dominate the landscape even today. The western and northern sections of the state have primarily rural and small town populations. However, more than half of the state's total population resides in counties that include the four metropolitan areas of Kansas City, Lawrence, and Topeka, located in the eastern section of the state, and Wichita, which is located in the south central region.

Kansas has a diverse ethnic background. The original inhabitants of the state were Native American Indians. As white settlers came into the state, many were of English, German, Irish, and Polish ancestral heritage. Lindsborg has a strong Swedish tradition, Pittsburg is known as "Little Balkans," and Wilson is known as the "Czech Capital of Kansas." Topeka has grown around various ethnic settlements, including Little Russia in the northern part of the city and a large Hispanic population. These communities and ethnic groups celebrate their heritage and maintain strong ties with their native culture and traditions through annual festivals and celebrations.

Keeping an eye on their past, Kansans are not afraid of progress. They have achieved strides in literature, government, the arts and sciences, sports and many other areas. Out of the state's rich past has emerged success stories such as William Allen White, President Dwight D. Eisenhower, Amelia Earhart, Jim Ryun, Bradbury Thompson, and Walter Chrysler. Dwight D. Eisenhower, perhaps Kansas' most famous son, said as a tribute about his home state, "The proudest thing I can claim is that I am from Abilene." Many Kansans have shared Ike's sentiments about the Sunflower state.

The heart and soul of Kansas can be found in its people. Strength and perseverance are characteristics Kansans have relied on to endure times of adversity and prosperity. Generations of Kansans have grown up being taught the down-to-earth values that were such an important part of their pioneer heritage. ❏

fun facts

Boxing Champ | Jess Willard, a native of Emmett, won the heavyweight boxing championship of the world in 1915.

Presidential Candidate | In 1940, Wendell Wilkie opened his campaign as the Republican candidate for President of the United States, 27 years after he taught history in Coffeyville.

Batter Up | Baseball great Walter "Big Train" Johnson of the Washington Senators resided in Coffeyville for many years during the off-season. He was one of the first inductees into the Baseball Hall of Fame.

Dance Hall Queen | Alice Chambers was a dance hall queen who was the last person — and the only woman — to be buried on Boot Hill in Dodge City.

Boone's Boy | Napoleon Boone, son of Daniel Boone, was the first white male child born in Kansas.

First Martyr | Father Juan de Padilla, the first Christian martyr in the United States, was killed in Kansas after accompanying Coronado into the area in 1541.

Scientific Plot | George Washington Carver owned land at the northeast corner of Rock and Chestnut Streets in Minneapolis.

Fast Draw | National figure Tom Smith was hired as the first city marshal in Abilene. He was replaced by Wild Bill Hickok, a "fast draw" two-gun expert.

Picture Perfect | Western artist Frederic Remington operated a sheep ranch near Peabody in 1883.

Reporting White's Way | The journalism school at the University of Kansas is named after the famous Emporia editor William Allen White.

Capper Connection | Arthur Capper, the first native Kansan to be elected governor of the state, was inaugurated in 1915.

population

Population Density

Most counties in Kansas (93) have a low population density of less than 50 persons per square mile. Only four counties have a total population exceeding 100,000. In 1990, Sedgwick County (Wichita) had the largest population (403,662), and Greeley County had the smallest population (1,774). Population densities in these two counties ranged from 404 persons per square mile to 2 persons per square mile, respectively.

QUICK FACTS:

The most densely populated county is Wyandotte (Kansas City), with 1,070 persons per square mile.

Source: "Kansas Statistical Abstract, 1990-91," Institute for Public Policy and Business Research, The University of Kansas.

KANSAS POPULATION BY COUNTY: 1990

10 Largest Populated Counties	COUNTY	POPULATION	LAND AREA	DENSITY
	1. Sedgwick	403,662	1,000	404
	2. Johnson	355,054	477	745
	3. Wyandotte	161,993	151	1,070
	4. Shawnee	160,976	550	293
	5. Douglas	81,798	457	179
	6. Riley	67,139	610	110
	7. Leavenworth	64,371	463	139
	8. Reno	62,389	1,254	50
	9. Butler	50,580	1,428	35
	10. Saline	49,301	720	69

10 Smallest Populated Counties	COUNTY	POPULATION	LAND AREA	DENSITY
	1. Greeley	1,774	778	2
	2. Wallace	1,821	914	2
	3. Hodgeman	2.177	860	3
	4. Comanche	2,313	788	3
	5. Stanton	2,333	680	3
	6. Lane	2,375	717	3
	7. Hamilton	2,388	996	2
	8. Clark	2,418	975	3
	9. Wichita	2,758	717	4
	10. Chase	3,021	776	4

Land area figures are per square mile.
Density figures are based on persons per square mile.

PEOPLE
population
KANSAS

QUICK FACTS:

Kansas has an aging
population, and there
are more females
(51.0%) living in the
state than males
(49.0%). In 1900, about
51.8% of the population
was under 25 years of
age. Today, only about
36.9% of the population
is under 25 years of
age.

In 1860, the Kansas
population was
107,000.

*Source: Kansas Statistical
Abstract, 1990-91, various
issues; U.S. Bureau of the
Census, 1990 Census of
Population and Housing.*

Population Trends

Between 1900-1990, Kansas recorded moderate
but sustained population growth, increasing
68.6%. During the 1980-1990 period, total
state population has increased 4.8%.

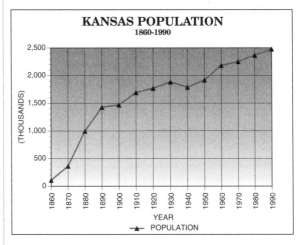

Douglas, Johnson, and
Finney counties had
the largest percentage
increases in population
from 1980 to 1990.
Osborne, Jewell, and
Washington counties
had the largest
percentage decreases.

*In 1880, nearly 90% of
the population in
Kansas lived in rural
areas. By 1990, the
rural population had
declined to 30.9% while
the urban population
had increased to 69.1%.*

Urban and Rural Population Trends

The urban population of Kansas has grown
steadily since 1860, while the rural population
has declined since 1910. The shift in the rural
to urban majority of the population occurred
sometime between 1950 and 1960, where for
the first time more Kansans lived in urban
areas than rural.

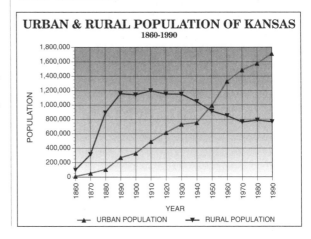

*Source: 1980 Census of
Population, Number of
Inhabitants; 1990 Census of
Population and Housing.*

84

KANSAS

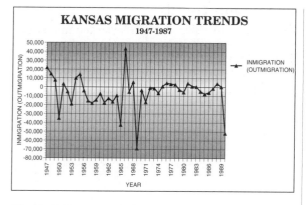

KANSAS MIGRATION TRENDS
1947-1987

INMIGRATION
(OUTMIGRATION)

YEAR

QUICK FACTS:

It would appear from the migration table that almost 52,000 Kansans migrated out of the state in 1990. However, this statistic is more a result of over-estimates of population in the years between Census counts, and possible under-counting of the Census, than an actual migration of 52,000 out of the state.

Source: Kansas Statistical Abstract, 1990-91; Kansas Division of the Budget; and Annual Summary of Vital Statistics, 1990.

Lenexa, in Johnson County, was named for the wife of Black Hoof, a Shawnee Indian Chief.

Racial Composition

The racial composition of Kansas is more diverse today than at the beginning of the century; however, the state is still predominantly white. Today, more than 90.1% of the population is white, compared to 96.3% in 1900. Since the turn of the century, the white population has increased by about 816,000, while non-white groups increased by approximately 191,000.

KANSAS POPULATION BY RACE: 1900-1990

YEAR	TOTAL	WHITE	BLACK	AMERICAN INDIAN	JAPANESE	CHINESE	FILIPINO	OTHER RACES
1900	1,470,495	1,416,319	52,003	2,130	4	39	—	—
1910	1,690,949	1,634,352	54,030	2,444	107	16	—	—
1920	1,769,257	1,708,906	57,925	2,276	52	68	*	30
1930	1,880,999	1,811,997	66,344	2,454	37	60	95	12
1940	1,801,028	1,734,496	65,138	1,165	19	133	*	77
1950	1,905,299	1,828,961	73,158	2,381	116	315	*	368
1960	2,178,611	2,078,666	91,445	5,069	1,362	537	372	1,160
1970	2,246,578	2,122,068	106,977	8,672	1,584	1,233	758	5,286
1980	2,363,679	2,168,221	126,127	15,256	1,585	2,425	1,662	48,403
1990	2,477,574	2,231,986	143,076	21,767	2,037	5,330	2,548	70,830

(*) - Included with Other Races

Indian Reservations in Kansas

Kansas has a diverse Indian culture background. Four Indian reservations are located in Kansas: the Iowa reservation (part) in Brown and Doniphan Counties; the Sac and Fox reservation in Brown County; the Kickapoo reservation, also in Brown County; and the Pottawatomi reservation in Jackson County.

Source: 1990 Census Summary Tape File 1A.

QUICK FACTS:

Small town living is typical in Kansas. Approximately 614 incorporated cities with less than 25,000 inhabitants are in the state.

Kansas has 105 counties and 627 cities.

Dean Mc Gee, founder of Kerr Mc Gee Oil, was from Humbolt.

Source: 1990 Census of Population and Housing, "Thank You America" data.

In 1887, the largest city in the state was Leavenworth with the population listed at 29,150.

Lewis Lindsay Dyche is remembered as one of the leaders in wildlife conservation. Lewis came to Kansas with his family after the Civil War and later became a professor at the University of Kansas. In 1910, he was hired by the state to work with the fish and game department. Lewis Dyche died in Topeka in 1915. The natural history museum at K.U. was renamed for him.

Source: 1990 Census of Population and Housing, "Thank You America" data.

10 SMALLEST COMMUNITIES IN KANSAS

City	Population
Freeport	8
Oak Hill	13
Benedict	16
Frederick	18
Waldron	19
Bassett	20
Latimer	20
Penalosa	21
Cedar	25
Scottsville	26

Metropolitan Living

Small towns dominate the Kansas landscape. Only 13 cities in Kansas have a population greater than 25,000, and only four (Wichita, Kansas City, Overland Park and Topeka) have a population of more than 100,000.

COMMUNITIES WITH POPULATIONS GREATER THAN 25,000

CITY	POPULATION
Wichita	304,011
Kansas City	149,767
Topeka	119,883
Overland Park	111,790
Lawrence	65,608
Olathe	63,352
Salina	42,303
Hutchinson	39,308
Leavenworth	38,495
Shawnee	37,993
Manhattan	37,712
Lenexa	34,034
Emporia	25,512

Ethnic Populations

The majority of Kansans have either German, English, or Irish ancestral heritage.

POPULATION OF SELECTED ANCESTRY GROUPS IN KANSAS: 1980	
ANCESTRY GROUP	**POPULATION**
Dutch	99,645
English	405,709
French (except Basque)	110,045
German	986,820
Irish	436,115
Italian	44,638
Polish	34,844
Scotch-Irish	74,643
Scottish	57,460
Swedish	79,188

Religious Affiliations

The majority of Kansans who have religious affiliations are Protestant. However, the largest single religious denomination is the Roman Catholic church, followed by the United Methodist church and Baptist groups.

Source: Churches and Church Memberships in the United States, 1980, Glenmary Research Center, Atlanta, Ga.

QUICK FACTS:

Wilson is known as the "Czech Capital of Kansas." The annual Czech Festival is held in Wilson the last Saturday in July.

Rick Mears, four-time Indianapolis 500 winner, is a Wichita native.

Source: 1980 Census, General Social and Economic Characteristics, Table 105, General Characteristics of Selected Ancestry Groups: 1980.

SELECTED COMMON CHURCHES AND CHURCH MEMBERSHIPS IN KANSAS: 1980

CHURCH NAME	NUMBER OF CHURCHES	NUMBER OF ADHERENTS*
African Methodist Episcopal Zion Church	2	189
American Baptist Churches in the U.S.A.	255	72,789
American Lutheran Church, The	52	14,370
Assemblies of God	154	24,735
Catholic Church	396	337,077
Christian Church (Disciples of Christ)	178	68,858
Christian Churches and Churches of Christ	208	45,276
Church of Jesus Christ of Latter-Day Saints, The	48	10,492
Church of the Nazarene	138	31,322
Churches of Christ	183	17,258
Episcopal Church, The	82	21,763
Reform Judaism	4	1,173
Lutheran Church in America	83	29,621
Lutheran Church - Missouri Synod, The	162	58,218
Mennonite Church, The General Conference	44	14,478
Presbyterian Church in the United States	50	18,917
Southern Baptist Church	184	73,306
United Church of Christ	86	20,934
United Methodist Church, The	775	262,082
United Presbyterian Church in the U.S.A., The	215	58,683

* Adherents: All members, including full members, their children, and the estimated number of other regular participants who are not considered as communicant, confirmed or full members.

vital statistics

QUICK FACTS:

The birth rate in Kansas in 1955 was 25.8 births per thousand.

Birth and Death Rates

The death rate in Kansas in 1989 was nearly as low as it had been at any point since 1947, equalling the rate of 8.9 deaths per thousand. Birth rates had been declining since 1955 until 1988, when the birth rate increased slightly.

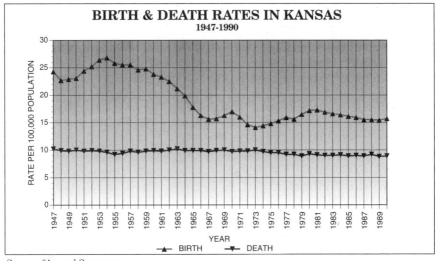

BIRTH & DEATH RATES IN KANSAS
1947-1990

Source: "Annual Summary of Vital Statistics," 1990; Kansas Department of Health and Environment.

Kansas has a lower overall crime rate than many of its neighboring states, with the exception of Nebraska, Iowa, and Missouri. Kansas is below the national average for all violent and property crime rates given. In 1990, there was a total of 11,129 violent crimes committed in Kansas.

Average Life Expectancy

The average life expectancy for Kansans in 1979-1981 was slightly more than 75 years, third only to Iowa and Nebraska among neighboring states, and nearly two years more than the average American (73.88 years). The average life expectancy for males in Kansas was 71.6 years and the average for females was 78.99 years. While women on average have a longer life than men in all areas, Kansas males have a greater life expectancy than males in neighboring states, with the exception of Colorado and Iowa.

Only 60 years ago, the average life expectancy for an American was 57.1 years, more than 17 years less than it was in 1986. Females have a greater life expectancy than males in all categories, and whites have a greater life expectancy than blacks or all other races combined.

KANSAS

Leading Causes of Death

Heart disease and cancer lead the list of causes of death in Kansas, and together account for nearly 59.8% of all Kansas deaths. Among causes of accidental death, motor vehicle accidents account for more than 51.4% of all deaths.

QUICK FACTS:
The average age of death in Kansas is 73.2 years.

Source: "Annual Summary of Vital Statistics, 1990," Kansas Department of Health and Environment.

LEADING CAUSES OF DEATH IN KANSAS: 1990

CAUSE OF DEATH	DEATHS	PERCENT
Heart Disease	7,634	16.9
Malignant Neoplasms	5,018	21.9
Cerebrovascular Disease	1,701	2.8
Accidents	919	2.4
Chronic Obstructive Pulmonary Diseases	962	16.7
Pneumonia and Influenza	943	1.4
Diabetes Mellitus	454	1.6
Suicides	296	5.5
Arteriosclerosis	245	0.2
Nephritis, Nephrotic Syndrome, and Nephrosis	219	0.5
All Other Causes	3,219	30.1
TOTAL	**21,173**	**100.0**

CAUSE OF ACCIDENTAL DEATH	DEATHS	PERCENT
Motor Vehicle Accidents	472	51.4
Accidental Falls	147	16.0
Inhalation and Ingestion of Food Causing Obstruction/Suffocation	43	4.7
Accidents Caused by Fire and Flames	37	4.0
Accidental Poisonings	28	3.0
Accidental Drowning and Submersion	27	2.9
Accidents Caused by Machinery	25	2.7
Accidents Due to Natural and Environmental Factors	24	2.6
Air and Space Transport Accidents	14	1.5
Accidents Caused by Firearm Missile	13	1.4
Accidents Caused by Electricity	8	0.9
All Other Causes	75	8.2
TOTAL	**919**	**100.0**

MARRIAGES & DIVORCES IN KANSAS: 1956-1990

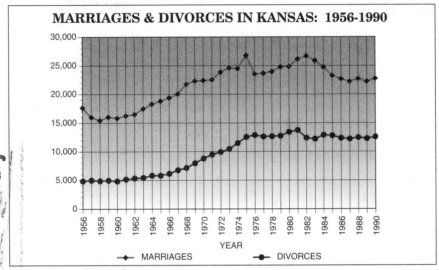

Source: "Kansas Statistical Abstract," 1990-91; Kansas Department of Health and Environment.

In 1990 there were 22,720 marriages occurred in Kansas, an increase of 2.3% from 1989.

The greatest number of marriages (4,229) occurred in Sedgwick county, but Geary county had the highest marriage rate of 25.9 marriages per 1,000 population. The least number of marriages (9) occurred in Hodgeman county, with Hodgeman having the lowest marriage rate of 4.1 marriages per 1,000 population.

Source: "Annual Summary of Vital Statistics 1990," Kansas Department of Health and Environment.

Marriage and Divorce Rates

The number of marriages in Kansas has increased almost 29% since 1956, while the number of divorces has nearly tripled. The lowest overall marriage rate since 1956 occurred in 1958, and the highest in 1975. The high point for the Kansas divorce rate was in 1981 with 5.8 divorces per thousand, and the low point was in 1960, with 2.2 divorces per thousand.

MARRIAGE IN KANSAS BY AGE & SEX: 1990

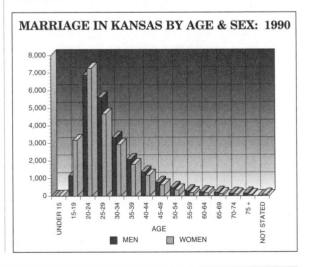

Unemployment Rates

The unemployment rate in Kansas during the Depression years was nearly 13% in 1940, but 10 years later was down to 2.5%. In recent years the state's unemployment rate rose again to 5.5% in December 1985, but by 1991, the rate was back down to less than 4.4%.

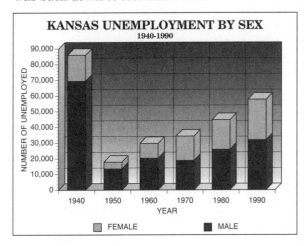

KANSAS UNEMPLOYMENT BY SEX
1940-1990

FEMALE ■ MALE

Average Income

The increase of the effective buying income of the average Kansan has nearly matched that of the average American, increasing about 300% since 1970. The Topeka SMSA has shown the greatest increase in buying income, with more than a 335% increase since 1970. The median household income in Kansas in 1970 was $10,127, but in 1987 that figure had increased to $25,291.

QUICK FACTS:

Jim Porter, of Galena, holds the world record for the largest whittled chain. He began his chain in 1983. Each link takes about 30 minutes to complete. In 1989, Porter and his chain appeared on "The Tonight Show." At that time, the chain stretched 705 feet and had 3,525 links. Today it reaches nearly 900 feet.

During 1989 the highest average annual wage in Kansas by county was Sedgwick at $22,086; the lowest was Chase at $10,546.

Source: U.S. Bureau of the Census.

The annual average wage in Kansas during 1969 was $6,145. By 1989 that figure had increased to $19,016.

Source: Sales & Marketing Research Magazine: "Survey of Buying Power," annual, years 1971, 1976, 1981, 1986; "Survey of Buying Power: Demographics USA, 1991."

PER CAPITA AND MEDIAN HOUSEHOLD INCOME: 1970-1987

	PER CAPITA INCOME					MEDIAN HOUSEHOLD INCOME				
	1970	1975	1980	1985	1990	1970	1975	1980	1985	1990
STATES	(EFFECTIVE BUYING INCOME *)					(EFFECTIVE BUYING INCOME *)				
U.S.	$3,308	$5,003	$7,940	$11,627	$13,952	$10,565	$12,824	$19,146	$23,680	$27,912
KANSAS	3,289	5,164	8,786	12,413	13,965	10,127	12,559	20,105	23,974	26,557
Lawrence	na	4,827	7,359	11,401	13,188	na	12,299	17,024	21,573	23,820
Topeka	3,459	5,119	8,526	14,095	15,573	10,759	13,124	19,896	27,502	29,723
Wichita	3,254	5,471	9,869	14,573	15,533	10,098	13,877	23,043	28,884	30,264

* Effective Buying Income: A term used by Sales & Marketing Management magazine which is defined as total income less taxes, penalties, social insurance, and payments to military & government personnel overseas.

household/housing

QUICK FACTS:

The median size of houses in Kansas is 5.3 rooms. Rural homes are usually larger than their urban counterparts, 5.5 rooms to 5.2 rooms respectively.

In 1950 the total number of households was 606,783. By 1990 that number had increased to 944,726.

Source: Census of the Population, General Population Characteristics, "Summary of General Characteristics," U.S. Department of Commerce, Bureau of the Census, years 1950, 1960, 1970, and 1980.

Two person households made up 33.5% of the total Kansas households in 1990.

Large households are on the decline. In 1990 only 3.1% of the households in Kansas had six or more persons.

As of the 1990 Census, 90.5% of the 1.05 million housing units in Kansas were occupied. Sixty-eight percent of occupied units were owned, as opposed to rented.

Source: Sales and Marketing Managment's "Survey of Buying Power, Demographics USA, 1991."

Urban & Rural Households

Since 1950, the total number of households in Kansas has grown by 56%. From 1950 to 1980 (1990 breakdowns were not yet available) the number of urban households increased 82%, rural farm households increased 68%, and the number of households in rural nonfarm areas declined more than 57%.

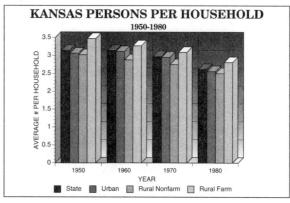

KANSAS PERSONS PER HOUSEHOLD
1950-1980

Household Size

The average size of the Kansas household has declined slightly since 1950, from 3.14 persons to 2.62 persons in 1990. The majority of Kansans live in comparatively small family groups. About 59% of all the 944,723 households in Kansas are composed of one or two persons. One-person households make up about 25.9% of this total.

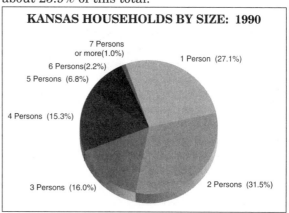

KANSAS HOUSEHOLDS BY SIZE: 1990

7 Persons or more(1.0%)
6 Persons(2.2%)
5 Persons (6.8%)
4 Persons (15.3%)
3 Persons (16.0%)
2 Persons (31.5%)
1 Person (27.1%)

Value of Households

In 1990, the average value of occupied housing units in Kansas was about $52,200, compared to $37,800 for housing units in 1980. In 1980 (the latest census year available) the value for urban housing was approximately 29.9% higher than in rural areas, while condominiums were valued about 46.4% higher in rural areas than in urban areas.

VALUE & PRICE ASKED OF KANSAS HOUSING
1980 STATE AND SELECTED CITIES

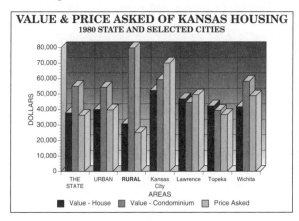

Source: 1980 Census of Housing, General Housing Characteristics, U.S. Bureau of the Census.

Household Characteristics

About one-third of Kansas' householders are under 35 years of age, while nearly 23% of all householders are over age 65. About 13% of all women of marriage age are widowed, compared to only 2.4% of the men. Only 3.1% of the men and 7% of the women are divorced.

AVERAGE HOUSEHOLD INCOMES (1) IN KANSAS & SELECTED STATES: 1990

STATE	MEDIAN EBI(2)	AVERAGE EBI(3)
Colorado	28,558	35,927
Iowa	24,699	33,163
KANSAS	26,557	36,633
Missouri	25,574	34,544
Nebraska	24,959	34,359
Oklahoma	20,869	28,472

(1) Average Household Income measured in terms of Effective Buying Income (EBI). EBI is a classification exclusively developed by Sales & Marketing Management magazine.
(2) Divides the income distribution into two equal parts, one-half the households above it, the other half below it.
(3) Total EBI divided by the number of households.

QUICK FACTS:

The state average for housing rent was $285 in 1990. The median value of owner-occupied housing units was $52,200 in 1990.

In Chanute, a four-room house rented for $5 a month in 1910.

The average number of persons per family in Kansas in 1990 was 3.08 persons.

The average household income ($36,633) of Kansans is higher than any of its comparative states, and the median household income ($26,557) in Kansas is higher than any neighboring states except Colorado.

Source: Sales and Marketing Management's "Survey of Buying Power, Demographics USA, 1991."

The Early Days

John Brown — Osawatomie. Abolitionist who was one of the principal characters in the "Bleeding Kansas" period.

William "Buffalo Bill" Cody — Leavenworth. Pony Express rider, sharpshooter, and Indian scout who lived much of his life in Kansas.

Thomas R. Boston Corbett — Concordia. The man who shot Abraham Lincoln's assassin, John Wilkes Booth, moved to Cloud County just south of Concordia in 1878. A monument stands south of Concordia marking the spot where Corbett lived in his dugout.

Dalton Gang — Meade and Coffeyville. The Daltons had a hideout in Meade in 1887. They also tried to rob two banks in Coffeyville at one time in 1892.

Wyatt Earp — Marshal of Wichita and Dodge City in the 1870s.

Colonel Nathaniel S. Goss — A resident of Neosho Falls; founder of the Missouri-Kansas-Texas (Katy) Railway Company.

James Butler "Wild Bill" Hickok — Notorious gunfighter who became sheriff of Ellis County in the summer of 1869. He also served as marshal of Abilene.

Alvin "Creepy" Karpis — Topeka. Bank robber and bootlegger who began his life of crime in Topeka, where he spent his childhood. In 1936, Karpis replaced John Dillinger as "Public Enemy Number One."

William "Bat" Masterson — Sheriff of Ford County, Kansas, in the 1870s.

Carry Nation — Medicine Lodge. Symbol of the temperance movement who destroyed saloons with her hatchets.

Photo courtesy of The Topeka Capital-Journal.

William "Buffalo Bill" Cody

Politics & Government

Earl R. Browder — Wichita. Communist Party presidential candidate.

Frank Carlson — Concordia. The only Kansan to have served in the U.S. House of Representatives, the U.S. Senate and as Governor of Kansas.

Clifford Clark — Fort Scott. Served as Secretary of Defense.

Charles Curtis — Topeka. Served as Vice President of the United States under Herbert Hoover. He served in the U.S. Senate from 1907 until he was elected Vice President in 1929.

Robert Dole — Russell. U.S. Senator from Kansas. Graduated from the University of Kansas and Washburn University Law School. Served as Kansas state representative and U.S. Representative before being elected to be a U.S. Senator. He was the Republican candidate for Vice President in 1976; majority leader of the U.S. Senate in 1985; and a Presidential candidate in 1988.

Dwight D. Eisenhower — Raised in Abilene. A five-star U.S. Army General. He served as Commander-in-Chief of the Allied Armies in Europe during World War II. He later served as the 34th President of the United States from 1953-1961. He is buried in Abilene as is his wife, Mamie Doud Eisenhower.

Marlin Fitzwater — Born and raised in Abilene. Press secretary to President Ronald Reagan and President George Bush.

Georgia Neese Clark Gray – A Richland banker and businesswoman. Appointed by President Harry S. Truman, she was the first woman to serve as United States Treasurer (1949-53).

Photo courtesy of The Topeka Capital-Journal.

Dwight D. Eisenhower

Gary Hart — Ottawa. Served as U.S. Senator for the state of Colorado and was a Democratic party hopeful in the 1988 presidential campaign.

John J. Ingalls — U.S. Senator from Kansas who gained fame in the 1870s and 1880s as an orator. While a state senator, he submitted the design for the Great Seal of Kansas. He also proposed the state motto.

Nancy Landon Kassebaum — Topeka. In 1978, Kassebaum was elected the first woman U.S. Senator from Kansas. She is the first woman in history to be elected to a full term in the Senate in her own right. She is the daughter of former Kansas Governor Alf Landon.

Mary Alice Lair — Piqua. The first woman to become Vice-chairman of the state Republican Committee.

famous kansans

Alf M. Landon — Topeka. Kansas governor from 1933 to 1937 and was the Republican Presidential nominee in 1936. Landon lost the election to Franklin D. Roosevelt.

Photo courtesy of The Topeka Capital-Journal.

Alf Landon

Kay McFarland — First woman to serve on the state's high court. She was appointed to the Kansas Supreme Court in Sept. 1977. In 1973 she became the first woman ever elected district judge in Kansas.

Kathryn O'Loughlin — First woman elected to represent Kansas as a member of the U.S. Congress. She served from 1933 to 1935 for the Democratic Party.

Edmund G. Ross — U.S. Senator from 1866 to 1871; best remembered for his part in the impeachment trial of Andrew Johnson.

Susanna Madora Salter — Argonia. In 1887 she was selected as mayor of Argonia, the first woman mayor in the country.

Wendell Wilkie — Coffeyville. Wilkie was the Republican presidential candidate who ran against Franklin D. Roosevelt in 1940. He lived in and taught school in Coffeyville from 1913 to 1914.

The Media - Radio, Television, Newspapers

Arthur Capper — Born in Garnett. Well-known politician and publisher who edited the *Topeka Daily Capital, Capper's Weekly,* and several farm journals. Capper served two terms as governor of Kansas before being elected to the U.S. Senate for four terms.

Ben Hibbs — Born in Fontana and grew up in Pretty Prairie. He was editor of the *Saturday Evening Post* from 1942 to 1961 and *Reader's Digest* from 1962-72.

William "Bill" Kurtis — Independence and Topeka. Television news anchor who attended the University of Kansas and Washburn University, where he received a law degree. He was an anchorman for WIBW-TV in Topeka and later co-anchored the CBS "Morning News."

Clyde M. Reed — Parsons. Newspaper publisher of the *Parsons Sun* and later elected to serve as Governor of Kansas in 1928.

John Cameron Swayze — Born in Wichita, April 4, 1906. Attended University of Kansas. NBC radio and television commentator who began "News Caravan" (1949-1956) and later served as Timex spokesman.

William Allen White — Emporia. Editor and publisher of the *Emporia Gazette*; he was awarded a Pulitzer Prize in 1923 for his editorial "To An Anxious Friend."

Photo courtesy of The Topeka Capital-Journal.

William Allen White

The Visual Arts, Performing Arts and Film

Kirstie Alley — Wichita. Actress who co-stars in the television comedy series "Cheers."

"Fatty" Arbuckle — Smith Center. Silent film actor.

Edward Asner — Kansas City, Kan., native. Television actor who played in the popular television comedy "The Mary Tyler Moore Show" and the long-running drama series "Lou Grant."

Hugh Beaumont — Born in Lawrence. Actor who played the part of Ward Cleaver in the television show "Leave it to Beaver."

Carla Burns — Wichita. Actress who was a 1983 nominee for a Tony Award for Best Featured Actress for the role of Queenie in the Broadway musical "Show Boat."

Jean Harlow — Known at the time as Harlean Carpenter, she attended elementary school from 1921-1922 in Seneca.

Dennis Hopper — Dodge City. Actor, director. Credits include co-starring in the motion picture "Hoosiers."

Don Johnson — Wichita and Galena. Actor who co-starred in the television series "Miami Vice."

Osa and Martin Johnson — Chanute. Photographers and explorers who traveled the South Seas and Africa in the early 1900s.

Gordon Jump — Manhattan. Actor who starred in the television series "WKRP in Cincinnati."

Buster Keaton — Piqua. Silent film comedian was born in Piqua on Oct. 4, 1895, during a cyclone.

famous kansans

Emmett Kelly — Sedan. Circus clown known as "Weary Willie." A museum featuring circus exhibits and special bottle and plate displays has been established in his honor in his hometown of Sedan.
Hattie McDaniel — Wichita. Actress who received the 1939 Academy Award for Best Supporting Actress in "Gone With the Wind."
Vera Miles — Wichita. Television and Broadway actress.
Gordon Parks — Fort Scott. Photographer, writer, and motion picture director who won the Pulitzer Prize for photography in 1973.
Larry Parks — Olathe. Actor who was nominated for the 1946 Academy Award for Best Actor in "The Jolson Story."
ZaSu Pitts — Parsons. Actress who made her film debut in 1917 in "The Little Princess." Her long film career spanned several decades and her last film was "It's a Mad, Mad, Mad, Mad World" in 1963.
Charles "Buddy" Rogers — Olathe. Actor. Attended University of Kansas.
Marilyn Schreffler — Topeka. Voice of Olive Oyl in "Popeye." She attended Topeka West High School and Washburn University and later was a member of Second City, a Chicago improvisational comedy group.
Milburn Stone — Burrton. Actor who played "Doc" on the television series "Gunsmoke."
Dee Wallace Stone — Kansas City. Actress who played Elliott's mother in the movie "E.T. The Extra-Terrestrial."
Vivian Vance — Cherryvale. Actress who played Ethel in the successful television comedy series "I Love Lucy."
Lyle Waggoner — Kansas City. Actor known for his role on the television series "The Carol Burnett Show."

Music

Stan Kenton — Wichita. 1950's Big Band leader.
Kathleen Kersting — Wichita. Opera singer.
Mike Love — Hutchinson. A member of the Beach Boys rock group.
Charlie "Yardbird" Parker — Kansas City. Jazz saxophonist.
Samuel Ramey — Colby. Opera singer with the Metropolitan Opera and the New York City Opera.

Photo courtesy of The Topeka Capital-Journal.
Vivian Vance

Marion Talley — Colby. Opera star who debuted at the Metropolitan on Feb. 17, 1926 and sang four seasons at the Met. She owned land in Colby and visited frequently.

Literature

Zula Bennington Greene — Topeka. Author known for her column "Peggy of the Flint Hills."

William Inge — Independence. Pulitzer Prize-winning playwright whose works included *Picnic, Bus Stop*, and *Come Back, Little Sheba*.

Emanuel Haldeman-Julius — Girard. Famous for his literary *Little Blue Books*.

Edgar Lee Masters — Garnett. Poet, biographer. Known for *Spoon River Anthology*.

Margaret Hill McCarter — Topeka. Novelist whose works included *The Price of the Prairie*. She was the first woman to address a Republican National Convention (1920).

Lawrence Van Cott Niven — Topeka. Washburn University graduate. Hugo Award Winner in Science Fiction Writing.

Zula Bennington Greene   *Photo courtesy of The Topeka Capital-Journal.*

Damon Runyon – Born in Manhattan. Short-story writer and journalist whose works include "Guys and Dolls."
Charles M. Sheldon – Topeka. Congregational minister who wrote the best-selling book *In His Steps.*
Rex Stout — Grew up in Topeka. Mystery writer who created the character Nero Wolfe.

The Arts

John Steuart Curry — Jefferson County (Dunavant). Artist whose works include the murals in the east and west wings of the Kansas State Capitol in Topeka.
Peter F. Felten, Jr. — Hays. Sculptor.
Robert Merrell Gage — Native Topekan. His sculpture of Abraham Lincoln and the pioneer mother are exhibited at the Statehouse.
Marijana Grisnik — Kansas City. Artist known for her detailed paintings of the Strawberry Hill area.
Elizabeth "Grandma" Layton — Wellsville. Artist who has earned national recognition. Layton draws pictures of herself, reflecting the joys and pains of being a woman and the experience of growing older in a society that values youth.
Bruce Moore — Wichita. Sculptor.

Photo courtesy of The Topeka Capital-Journal.
Frederic Remington - self-portrait

Albert T. Reid — Concordia. American painter known for his paintings of horses and beautiful women.
Frederic Remington — Famous Western painter who operated a sheep ranch near Peabody in 1883.
Sven Birger Sandzen — Lindsborg. Artist who came to the United States from Sweden in 1894 to teach at Bethany College in Lindsborg. He painted bold paintings and block prints of Kansas and landscapes.
Bradbury Thompson — Topeka. Well-known graphic designer who graduated from Washburn University. He served as art director of *Mademoiselle* magazine for 14 years and has designed commemorative U.S. postage stamps.

Rudolph Wendelin — A native of Rawlins County who, as a U.S. Forest Service artist, is known as the caretaker of Smokey the Bear and has drawn Smokey numerous times.

Business and Industry

Henry Bloch — Mission Hills. Founder and owner of H&R Block.
Walter P. Chrysler — Born in Wamego and grew up in Ellis. Industrialist who established the Chrysler Corporation in 1925.
Nellie Cline — Larned. The first woman lawyer to appear before the U.S. Supreme Court, April 4, 1918.
Jim Halsey — Independence. Country music concert promoter and booking agency.
Robert H. Hazlett — El Dorado. By the 1930s Hazford Place, Hazlett's ranch north of El Dorado, produced hundreds of blue ribbon champions and earned Hazlett the title of America's premier Hereford breeder.
Miriam Loo — Washburn University graduate. Co-founder of Current Greeting Cards Company in Colorado Springs, Colorado.
Lutie Lytle — Topeka. The first black woman to be admitted to the practice of law in the United States (1897).
Jesse McCormack — Moran. The first woman in the United States to pass the examination for bank cashier, Dec. 21, 1912.

Photo courtesy of The Topeka Capital-Journal.

Walter P. Chrysler

The Sciences, Social Sciences, and Healing Arts

John Richard Romulus Brinkley — Milford. Famous for his goat gland transplants. Between 1918 and 1930, Brinkley performed as many as 16 transplants a day at his clinic in Milford. He operated the first radio station in Kansas and also ran for governor as a write-in candidate in 1930.
George Washington Carver — This agricultural scientist lived in Kansas during his youth. He mortgaged his homestead in Ness County in 1888 to go to college.

Dr. Samuel J. Crumbine — Dodge City. Became Secretary of the State Board of Health and was a leader in the campaign to stop the use of public drinking cups, roller towels, and other germ-spreading practices.

Amelia Earhart — Atchison. The first woman granted a pilot's license by the National Aeronautics Association and was the first woman to fly solo across the Atlantic Ocean. She disappeared during her 1937 flight around the world.

Photo courtesy of The Topeka Capital-Journal.

Joe Engle

Joe Engle — Chapman. Commander of the Space Shuttle Columbia's second mission.

Ron Evans — Graduate of Topeka schools and University of Kansas. Commander of the pilot ship during the flight of Apollo 17 to the moon.

Steve Hawley — Born in Ottawa and raised in Salina; graduated from the University of Kansas. He was a mission specialist aboard the maiden flight of the Space Shuttle Discovery.

Alvin Longren — Lenardville. Aviator and engineer. One of his inventions was the fold-up airplane wing that allowed a plane to be rolled into a barn. He was a popular performer as a stunt flyer at fairs throughout the Midwest.

Dr. C.F. Menninger and Menninger Family — Topeka. Psychiatrists. Established the well-known Menninger Foundation in Topeka. The non-profit organization is dedicated to the treatment and prevention of mental illness, research, and education of mental health professionals.

Earl Sutherland — Born in Burlingame. Winner of the Nobel Prize for physiology and medicine in 1971. He won his award for his discovery of the way hormones act.

Lucy Hobbs Taylor — Lawrence. The first fully-trained woman dentist in the world. She practiced dentistry in Lawrence from 1867-1907.

Clyde Tombaugh — Burdette astronomer. Discovered the planet Pluto in 1930.

Sports

Dr. Forrest C. "Phog" Allen — University of Kansas men's varsity basketball coach for more than 30 years. Allen Fieldhouse at the University of Kansas is named in honor of "Phog" Allen.

Wilt Chamberlain — Attended the University of Kansas. Chamberlain demonstrated his famous "dunk" shot in his first varsity basketball game for K.U. in 1956, scoring 52 points in that game against Northwestern University. He later became one of the great professional basketball stars.

Jim Colbert — Attended Kansas State University and placed second in the 1964 NCAA golf tournament. He has eight PGA tour victories.

Glenn Cunningham — Elkhart. In the 1930s, Cunningham held the world record in the mile run.

Lynn Dickey — Osawatomie. Green Bay Packers quarterback.

Walter "Big Train" Johnson — Born near Humboldt in 1887 and later lived in Coffeyville. Right-handed pitcher for the Washington Senators and member of the Baseball Hall of Fame.

Don Lock — Wichita. Major league baseball player.

Davy Lopes — Washburn University graduate. Baseball player with the Oakland A's.

Rudy May — Coffeyville. Major league baseball player.

Pete Mehringer — Kinsley. Won a gold medal at the 1932 Olympic games in light heavyweight wrestling.

Dr. James Naismith — Inventor of the game of basketball and a coach at the University of Kansas.

Steve Renko — Fort Scott. Pitcher for Montreal Expos, Chicago Cubs and Oakland A's.

John Riggins — Centralia. Played five seasons with the New York Jets and 10 seasons as a running back with the Washington Redskins. Riggins attended the University of Kansas and was named an All-American his senior season and was a three-time all-Big Eight selection.

Bill Russell — Pittsburg. Los Angeles Dodgers shortstop.

Photo courtesy of The Topeka Capital-Journal.

Dr. James Naismith

famous kansans

Jim Ryun — Wichita. Named World's Outstanding Athlete in 1966 - 1967, a three-time Olympian, and in the 1960s, set a new world's track record for the mile, the first American mile record holder in 30 years. He also held world records for 1500 meters and the half-mile.

Gale Sayers — Wichita. University of Kansas football star known as

Photo courtesy of The Topeka Capital-Journal.

Jim Ryun

"The Kansas Comet." He won the Rookie of the Year Award during his first season with the Chicago Bears.

Dean Smith — Emporia. Head basketball coach at the University of North Carolina since 1961. He played basketball at the University of Kansas and later coached the U.S. Olympic basketball team to a gold medal in 1971. In 1982 he lead the Tar Heels to a NCAA national title.

Marilyn Smith — Topeka. She has numerous career victories on the LPGA circuit. She was a founder and charter member of the LPGA.

Joe Tinker — Muscotah. Part of the double-play combination of Tinker to Evgers to Chance.

Mike Torrez — Topeka. Major league baseball player.

Tom Watson — Overland Park. Professional golfer.

Jess Willard — Emmett. World Heavyweight Boxing Champion during the World War I era. In 1915, Willard beat Jack Johnson at Havana, Cuba, in a highly publicized prizefight. He was later defeated by Jack Dempsey on July 4, 1919, in Toledo, Ohio.

Lynette Woodard — Wichita. Graduated from the University of Kansas. She was captain of the 1984 U.S. women's basketball team that won a gold medal in the Olympics and was the first female player for the Harlem Globetrotters.

The Military

General Frederick Funston — Iola. Became a hero while serving in the Filipino Insurrection and was commander of U.S. forces on the Mexican border in 1914-1916. He oversaw the rescue and clean-up following the San Francisco earthquake in 1906 and received the Congressional Medal of Honor.

Col. Frank E. Peterson, Jr. — Topeka. The first black Brigadier General in the U.S. Marine Corps. He was named NAACP "Man of the Year" in 1979.
General Bernard W. Rogers — Fairview. Served as commander of the NATO forces in Europe.
General Lewis Walt — Wabaunsee County. Former assistant commandant of the U.S. Marine Corps.
General Larry D. Welch — Liberal. Commander-in-chief of the Strategic Air Command and also served as vice chief of staff for the U.S. Air Force.

Miss Americas

Debra Barnes — Moran. Miss America 1968.
Deborah Bryant — Overland Park. Miss America 1966.
Kelli McCarty — Liberal. Miss U.S.A. 1991.

Debra Barnes and Deborah Bryant   *Photo courtesy of The Topeka Capital-Journal.*

Abilene Area Chamber of Commerce, P.O. Box 446, Abilene 67410.
Carruth, Gorton and Eugene Ehrlich. **The Harper Book of American
Quotations**. New York: Harper & Row, 1988.
Colby Area Chamber of Commerce, P.O. Box 572, Colby 67701.
Dodge City Area Chamber of Commerce, P.O. Box 939, Dodge City 67801.
El Dorado Chamber of Commerce, P.O. Box 509, El Dorado 67042.
Emporia Area Chamber of Commerce, P.O. Box 417, Emporia 66801.
Garnett Area Chamber of Commerce, 322 S. Oak, Garnett 66032.
Kansas Department of Health and Environment, Forbes Field, Topeka 66620.
Kansas Department of Human Resources, 401 Topeka Blvd., Topeka 66603.
Kansas Secretary of State, Publications Division, Capitol Building, 2nd Floor,
Topeka 66612.
Kansas Statistical Abstract, 1990-91, Institute of Public Policy and Business Research,
The University of Kansas.
Kansas State Data Center, State Library, 300 W. 10th, 3rd Floor, Topeka 66612-1593.
Leavenworth-Lansing Area Chamber of Commerce, P.O. Box 44,
Leavenworth 66048.
Parsons Chamber of Commerce, P.O. Box 737, Parsons 67357.
The Survey of Buying Power: Demographics USA, 1991, by Sales & Marketing
Management Magazine, Market Statistics, 633 Third Ave., New York, NY 10164-0615.
U.S. Department of Commerce, Bureau of the Census.
— **1990 Census of Population & Housing, State Tape 1 and 3,** and population counts;
— **County and City Data Book;**
— **Current Population Reports**, P-25 and P-26 Series,
— **Census of Population,** "General Social Characteristics," 1980 and prior years.
Washburn University Alumni Association, 1700 College Ave., Topeka 66621.
Wilson, Ray D. **Kansas Historical Tour Guide**. Carpentersville, Illinois:
Crossroads Communications, 1987.

CHAPTER 5
CULTURE

KANSAS
CULTURE

The Arts
Art Museums • Festivals

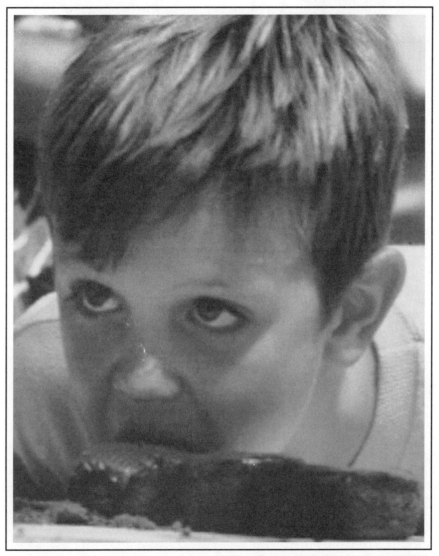

Photo courtesy of Twin Rivers Festival, Inc.

The Arts
111-117
Festivals, art centers, museums, and theaters enable the public to get hands-on training and knowledge as well as gain appreciation of a particular art.

Art Museums
118-119
The Spencer Art Museum in Lawrence displays a 25,000 piece collection and is known for its European Renaissance and Baroque period paintings.

Czech Folk Art
120
Born in Wilson, Kansas, The Czech Capital of Kansas, Kepka Belton learned *Kraslice* from her grandmother and because of her overpowering curiosity, pursued it.

Festivals
121-133
The Maple Leaf Festival in Hiawatha features arts and crafts with open booths around the courthouse square and the colorful setting of maple trees.

The Kansas State Fair
134
Following several different location sites and a heated legislative debate, the Fair finally found a permanent home in Hutchinson in 1913.

Hollywood Comes to Kansas
135
The high production costs in the traditional Southern California filmmaking area account for just one of the reasons filmmakers are expanding to other areas.

CHAPTER OPENER PHOTO: The Zinger eating contest at the Twin Rivers Festival in Emporia provides some wholesome fun for all participants.

introduction

K ansas has a rich and diverse culture that is reflected in events, programs, and people across the state. From festivals to sports, the arts to literature, Kansas has it all. Throughout the state, events occur regularly that promote Kansas culture, as well as educate and delight visitors. A range of ethnic backgrounds contributes to perhaps the most popular cultural activities in the state, the festivals and events. These events are rich in heritage and tradition and are the basis of what makes up Kansas. From Colby to Kansas City, visitors can enjoy the works of craftsmen and other artisans.

The arts are very important to Kansans. With the help of local and statewide organizations, the arts have been getting much needed exposure through education and exhibits. These organizations, located throughout the state, are introducing programs for the public and supporting local artists. The Kansas Arts Commission has a number of programs that have encouraged participation in the arts. Kansas has produced many famous artists in the past, and with this new interest in culture, the future looks bright for young artists. Aside from the visual arts, there are the theater arts, music, and dance as well. Museums dot the plains as a place to gather and enjoy Kansas culture and are found in the smallest towns and largest cities.

Communities statewide celebrate Kansas culture by hosting festivals. These casual gatherings are show places for Kansas artisans. Art shows and sales, craft making, and cultural demonstrations are generally featured at festivals. Live entertainment and a carnival atmosphere add sparkle to the Kansas landscape. Although most festivals are small they help promote the works of local artists and craftsmen and promote the state's heritage.

The Kansas State Fair in Hutchinson is one event in which everyone can take part. Visitors to the fair can see agricultural exhibits, taste a variety of foods, and enjoy some good old-fashioned fun. The fair is a celebration of all facets of Kansas culture and is a perfect gathering place for native Kansans as well as visitors from other states.

Kansas culture is not only attractive locally, but due in part to the Kansas Film Commission, Hollywood has come to the state. A number of films have been made in Kansas or about Kansas. The state's beautiful landscape has been a major factor in drawing filmmakers to Kansas.

Literature is also an important aspect of the Kansas culture. The state seems to fuel the imaginations of poets, playwrights, writers, and novelists. Kansas' own William Allen White and William Inge were both Pulitzer Prize winners, and new talent is constantly emerging.

Cultural events are abundant in Kansas. From nationally recognized community theater to festivals, museums, and concerts, Kansans are true patrons of the arts. ☐

Mighty Wurlitzer | The Wichita Pops hold several concerts each year in the "Wurlitzer Pop Series." The mighty Wurlitzer, which was formerly the New York Paramount Theatre organ, is now at home in Century II auditorium in Wichita.

The Silver Screen | The first motion picture theater west of the Mississippi River was in Lawrence.

Printer's Ink | From 1854 to 1936 more newspapers were published in Kansas than any other state.

Wild West Show | The movie "Dodge City," starring Errol Flynn and Olivia de Havilland, premiered in Dodge City, Kansas, in 1939.

And Toto Too | "The Wizard of Oz" premiered on the stage in 1902 in Chicago. In 1903 it moved to Broadway. Fred Stone, from Topeka, played the role of the Scarecrow. Metro-Goldwyn-Mayer's classic movie version of "The Wizard of Oz" premiered in 1939.

Eat Your Spinach | Lenexa is known as "The Spinach Capital of the World." The town hosts an annual Spinach Festival each September.

Where the Deer and the Antelope Play | The "Home on the Range" Cabin, located in Smith County, is where the internationally known song "Home on the Range" (and also state song of Kansas!) was written in 1873.

Past-A-Fair | In 1944, admission to the Kansas State Fair was $1.50, and for 16¢ fair-goers could buy a hamburger, glass of milk, or a bag of popcorn.

Putting on the Chips | Russell Springs sponsors the Cow Chip Throwing Contest every Labor Day weekend and is known as the "Cow Chip Capital of Kansas."

Classic Novel | The book **In Cold Blood**, written by Truman Capote, is the story of the Clutter Family murders at Holcomb in November 1959. Perry Smith and Richard Hickock were hanged on April 14, 1965 for those murders.

The Arts in Kansas

Kansas has celebrated the arts throughout its history and has contributed greatly to the nation as a whole with artists who have grown up in the state both past and present. The arts encompasses a wide range of medium. There are the visual arts such as sculpture, painting and drawing as well as the theater arts, dance and music.

Many Kansas organizations and communities take part in this celebration by providing facilities, introducing programs and grants, producing exhibitions and demonstrations, and much more. At festivals, art centers, museums and theaters the public can become involved with programs that enable them to get hands-on training and knowledge of a particular art. Here are some organizations and activities that promote the arts in Kansas:

Sandstone Theatre - Bonner Springs. A 16,000 seat outdoor amphitheater featuring concerts by current recording artists. *For information call (913) 721-3300.*

Western Plains Art Association - Colby. For 20 years, the Western Plains Arts Association has been able to promote and provide quality arts programming for the schools and communities in northwest Kansas. Some of the programs available to the public are Up With People, The National Theatre of the Deaf, The Wichita Symphony Orchestra, operas, dramas, and visual art exhibits. *For more information call (913) 462-3984.*

William Inge Festival - Independence. During four days in April, writers, actors, professors, and students attend workshops and seminars and celebrate William Inge. Inge was a Pulitzer Prize winning playwright with such works as **Picnic** and **Splendor in the Grass**. Plays by Inge are performed for visitors throughout the festival. *For more information call (316) 331-4100.*

QUICK FACTS:

Photo courtesy of Kansas State Historical Society.

The book The Wizard of Oz by Frank Baum projected an image of Kansas that generations have grown up with. This illustration by W.W. Denslow was the title page for The Wonderful Wizard of Oz, adapted by Ted Menten.

The William Inge Festival is held annually in Inge's hometown of Independence, Kan. The famous playwright once said about his hometown: "I've always been glad that I grew up in Independece, because it gave me a knowledge of people and a love of people."

111

the arts

QUICK FACTS:

The Frazier House, now a private residence in El Dorado, was used as a primary location in 1958 when the movie "The Gypsy Moths," starring Burt Lancaster and Deborah Kerr was filmed there.

The popular television series "Gunsmoke," which starred James Arness as Matt Dillon and Amanda Blake as Miss Kitty, was set in Dodge City and featured gunfighters on the Wild West frontier.

In the movie "Superman," the hero grows up on a farm near the Kansas town of Smallville. It is here that he develops his strong sense of "truth, justice, and the American way."

In 1928, it was reported that Kansas had more fairs, large and small, than any other state in the nation.

Accessible Arts Inc. - Kansas City, Kansas The mission of Accessible Arts Inc. is the advancement of the arts to all people including those with special needs. This program offers a unique blend of demonstrations and training to those who wish to become involved. Some services offered are the Arts Demonstration Center, Annual Forum on Arts, personnel training, Extensive Resource Library on Arts with Special Constituencies, and the distribution of free art supplies. *For more information contact Accessible Arts Inc. (913) 281-3308.*

Kansas Grassroots Art Association - Lawrence. A non-profit corporation founded in 1974 to preserve and document environmental folk art worldwide. The Association maintains a library of photographs and information on grassroots art and publishes a quarterly newsletter for members. It also maintains a museum and offers technical assistance to those preserving such sites. *For information about the Grassroots Arts Association call (913) 842-8242 or (913) 594-3801.*

The Lawrence Arts Center - Lawrence. The Center provides lively class schedules that run year-round. Experienced teachers offer inspiration and guidance for all ages in music, visual arts, writing, dance, dramatics, and much more. *For more information call (913-THE-ARTS.*
Arts-based preschool is a state licensed operation that provides a unique environment. Workshops, demonstrations, and master classes round out the education schedule. Outreach programs to public schools, regional community centers and arts councils are also offered.
The Arts Center Gallery sets off exhibited artwork. Visitors enjoy a continuously rotated schedule of individual and group presentations, juried shows, and traveling exhibits.
Performance Hall is filled daily with laughter, music, and applause.

The Seem-to-Be Players, an independent non-profit professional children's theater, present four productions annually. **The Popcorn, Peanut, and Pretzel Companies**, dance/drama troupes for children of different ages, perform five plays yearly. **Lawrence Barn Dance Association** holds monthly dances with caller and live band. **Summer Youth Theatre**, where teenagers can participate in energetic productions and learn every aspect of theater work. **Downtown Lawrence Sculpture Project.** Sculptures selected annually by a jury are displayed for one year along the streets of downtown Lawrence. **Team Carve Project and Stone Symposium** is organized for area sculptors to participate in a collaborative effort and make a single sculpture. The Symposium brings together both the beginner and accomplished carver to share secrets and learn new techniques. **Lawrence Indian Arts Show** is highlighted by a juried competition, the Lawrence Indian Market, a retrospective exhibit and an exhibit of contemporary American Indian art. **The Kansas Dance Network** was formed to unite the Kansas dance community, provide an information and support network, educate the Kansas public about dance, and promote dance artistry and excellence. *For more information about these and other programs contact the Lawrence Arts Center at (913) THE-ARTS.*

Lenexa's National 3-Dimensional Art Show - Lenexa. This juried art show brings together artists from throughout the United States, showing their best efforts in metal, glass, ceramic, fiber, jewelry, sculpture, wood and mixed media. The setting is outdoors in a beautiful tree-lined park. As in previous years, the show draws heavy local, regional and national publicity and is fast becoming one of the premier annual National 3-Dimensional art shows in the United States. *For more information call (913) 541-8592.*

QUICK FACTS:

In 1981, Kansas artist Stan Herd created a portrait of Kiowa Indian chief Santanta, using a tractor to etch the work on a 160-acre field of golden wheat. Since then Herd has created many crop art "paintings" featuring a variety of themes. These magnificent fields can be best appreciated by seeing aerial photos.

Wheat weaving is a craft that has become popular with many Kansas artists. Artists use wheat to create delicate shapes and designs.

Author Margaret Hill McCarter taught English at Topeka High School. Her novels include **The Price of the Prairie** and **The Peace of the Solomon Valley.**

QUICK FACTS:

Henry (Hawk) Maloy created the original Jayhawk cartoon character that appeared in the University of Kansas student newspaper, the *Daily Kansan*, beginning in 1912. The mythical Jayhawk bird later became the official mascot of the University, and the popular chant "Rock Chalk Jayhawk" can be heard at various KU sports events.

In 1926, one out of every seven Kansas families owned a radio.

During the 1940s, the famous Sally Rand performed her "Original Fan Dance" and "Glamorous Fan Dance" at the dance pavilion at the Kansas State Fair.

The first annual Ottawa County Fair was held in 1907.

Dane G. Hansen Museum and Memorial Plaza - Logan. The Memorial Plaza contains an all-purpose community room furnished with an organ, piano, and Kansas patchwork quilt from the Hansen family. The Plaza also houses a museum and art gallery. Some programs offered include performing arts, an arts and crafts festival, an artist of the month, and unique traveling exhibits from the Smithsonian Institution.

Manhattan Community Arts Programs - Manhattan. Visitors to Manhattan can enjoy a wide range of cultural activities. The arts in Manhattan are supported and encouraged by the Manhattan Arts Council. The Council sponsors and coordinates touring performances, exhibits, and guest artists to come to the city. *For more information call (913) 539-3276.*
The Manhattan Civic Theater has been successful with its theatrical productions and recently expanded its repertoire to include dinner theater and children's theater.
The Chamber Orchestra is a combined effort of Manhattan residents and Kansas State University students. Fall, spring, and Christmas productions are presented each year.
The Manhattan Chorale performs primarily classical and major choral works. The Chorale presents two major concerts each year.
The Youth Symphony encourages grade school through high school students to play string instruments. The group performs a "String Fling" each winter.
Arts in the Parks is sponsored by the Manhattan Recreation Commission to bring the performing arts to an open-air theater in City Park.

Overland Park, Kansas Arts Programs Barn Players. The community theater group performs a variety of plays during June, July, and August. This non-profit adult community theater uses local talent as well as professional actors for their productions. *For more information call (913) 381-4004.*

Theater for Young America has professional actors performing plays for children exclusively (and the young at heart). Delightful performances are held year-round. *For more information call (913) 648-4600.*

Paola Cultural Center - Paola. The Paola Cultural Center showcases a wide variety of cultural activities. The center's programs include everything from magic shows to debates, children's theater to visiting theater groups, art shows to talent shows, and more. *For more information about cultural events in the Paola area call (913) 294-2397.*

Salina Arts and Humanities Commission - Salina. The Commission coordinates a number of programs and services that serve the entire community and region. Some other programs offered in the Salina area are: The Salina Symphony, Children's Theatre, Spring Poetry Series, Arts Blitz, Resource Pool, newsletters and calendars, plus much more. *For more information contact the Salina Arts and Humanities Commission at (913) 827-4640.* **The Salina Art Center** offers visitors an exciting array of exhibitions, from photographers to sculpture to folk art to painting, in its rotating annual schedule. The exhibition concentrates on contemporary works by artists of national and regional stature. The Discovery Area at the Art Center is the only hands-on arts experience laboratory for children in a fine arts gallery in Kansas. The Salina Art Center provides visitors with the opportunity and tools to appreciate contemporary art, and to open up the exploration of personal creative expression. *For more information call (913) 827-1431.* **Arts in Education** is providing programs for local school children and teachers by allowing professionals to demonstrate and discuss their talents. Many projects expand the creative process through interaction with working artists. *For more information call (913) 827-4640.*

QUICK FACTS:
Topekan Charles M. Sheldon wrote the popular book **In His Steps** in the summer of 1896. Dr. Sheldon, who was pastor of Topeka's Central Congregational Church, read it chapter by chapter on Sunday evenings from his pulpit beginning Oct. 4, 1896. The book is one of the world's all-time best sellers.

Osa Johnson, who was born in Chanute, wrote about her extensive travels throughout the Pacific Islands and Africa in the book **I Married Adventure.**

Brian Lanker, a photographer for the Topeka Capital-Journal, won a Pulitzer Prize for photography in 1973.

the arts

QUICK FACTS:

The Fiscal 1988 Kansas appropriation for the Kansas Arts Commission, a state agency, was 0.0322 of 1% of the total state general fund budget. This percentage ranked Kansas 45th among the 50 states.

According to a University of Kansas study, the Kansas arts industry has combined primary and secondary impact upon the state's economy of more than $14 million annually.

Every dollar invested in the arts in Kansas returns at least three dollars to the Kansas economy.

In 1988, Kansas spent 43¢ per person for the arts.

The Smoky Hill River Festival. The three-day celebration of the arts is full of activities and events. There is a special day for regional artists to market both visual and performing art. *For more information call (913) 827-4640.*

Helen Hocker Performing Arts Center - Topeka. The goals of this group are to offer affordable, quality entertainment, stimulate volunteer arts involvement opportunities for all ages, offer affordable quality performing arts educational instruction, and to support and assist local arts entities whose goals reflect community needs. It is one of only five groups nationwide that provides and supports a program of this scope and diversity. *For more information call (913) 273-1191.*

The Kansas Arts Commission - Topeka. The duty of the Commission is to stimulate the growth, development, and appreciation of the arts in Kansas. Some of the ways that the Commission helps Kansas artists are by offering grants or fellowships, apprenticeships and visual arts programs, special projects in the recognition of art such as awards and exhibitions. In the Arts in Education program, professional artists are placed in residence in schools grades K-12 throughout the state. The artist then becomes a resource for students to explore and promote their artistic talents. *For more information call The Kansas Arts Commission (913) 296-3335.*

Rural Arts Initiative is a program that provides funding to rural Kansans. The program's basic theory is that every community, no matter how small, has a cultural life. Kansans can benefit by programs such as Local Initiative Programs that provide support for arts activities.

Rural Kansas Touring Program. The Kansas Arts Commission will provide up to 75% of fees for performances or workshops by artists including children's theater companies, dance groups, storytellers, folk, and bluegrass bands and more.

Kansas Committee for the Humanities - Topeka. The KCH offers various programs that bring scholars and the public together to discuss a wide range of topics. The KCH awards grants to non-profit groups to create their own community humanities projects. Through the KCH Research Center, speakers, exhibits, films, audio and visual cassettes, and more are made available as well as the traveling summer chautauquas. *For more information call (913) 357-0359.*

Kansas Folk Arts Apprenticeship Program - Topeka. The Kansas State Historical Society and the Kansas Arts Commission sponsor a statewide folk arts apprenticeship program. This folk arts apprenticeship program provides individuals experienced in a folk art with the opportunity to study with a master folk artist and learn new techniques. *For more information call (913) 296-3251.*

Association of Kansas Theatre - Wichita. AKT is also dedicated to the dual goals of accessibility and excellence in a wide range of theatrical experiences for all of the citizens of Kansas. *For information call (316) 685-9306.*

Children's Museum of Wichita. At this museum children are given the opportunity to understand the arts through hands-on exhibits, performances, concerts, and workshops. *For more information call (316) 267-3844.*

Very Special Arts - Wichita. The mission of Very Special Arts Kansas is to promote the arts by, with, and for individuals with disabilities to improve the quality of all our lives through programming, advocacy, training, and integration. *For more information call (316) 262-2828.*

The Wichita Symphony - Wichita. This group of talented musicians is the only professional symphony orchestra in Kansas. *For more information call (316) 267-5259.*

QUICK FACTS:

The fair of 1930 brought the term "free gate" to evening visitors. This was introduced in the midst of the Depression in deference to the many people unemployed at the time.

An improbable new invention, television ("in actual operation"), was an attraction at the State Fair in 1932. The gate fee was 35¢.

Governor Alf M. Landon and Senator Arthur Capper visited the fair on September 17, 1935, especially to dedicate a new $100,000 4-H Encampment Building.

In 1944 a child rode the Merry-Go-Round for 14¢ and explored "The Bughouse With Mirrors" for 21¢ at the State Fair. The Old Mill welcomed kids free while adults gladly paid the 14¢ to travel the dark waterways.

art museums

QUICK FACTS:

The May Masse Collection at Emporia State University features original works by some of the best loved illustrators of children's books, including works by Robert McCloskey, author and illustrator of the book **Make Way for Ducklings.**

The Mulvane Art Museum, located on the Washburn University campus in Topeka, has an extensive collection of rare prints and drawings.

The Helen Foresman Spencer Museum of Art on the University of Kansas campus in Lawrence has a permanent collection of works by Gainsborough and Rosetti, to name a few, plus the museum hosts traveling exhibits which in the past have contained pieces from artists such as Leonardo da Vinci.

Birger Sandzen Memorial Gallery — Lindsborg. Permanent displays of the work of renowned artist Birger Sandzen, located on the Bethany College campus.

Bow Studio and Gallery — Abilene. Kansas wheat and wild flowers are used to create unique designs in clay tiles and plates. Each handmade piece is an original made out of local clays deposited when Kansas was part of the Great Inland Sea over 96 million years ago.

Carnegie Center for the Art — Dodge City. This building was originally the Dodge City Library, built in 1907. It is now the headquarters for the Dodge City Area Arts Council and features artists' exhibits.

Edwin A. Ulrich Museum of Art — Wichita. Located on the campus of Wichita State University. Visitors should look for the huge Miro mosaic mural on its south facade.

Goodland Carnegie Arts Center — Goodland. Displays by area artists and sculptors, and performances by area musicians.

Hutchinson Community College Fine Arts Building. Includes a studio gallery and recital hall.

Mulvane Art Museum — Topeka. Washburn University campus. The museum hosts monthly exhibits, extensive art collections, and art education programs.

Pittsburg State University Art Gallery. Rotating exhibits include prints, posters, paintings, and sculpture.

Rogers House Museum and Gallery — Ellsworth. The works of Charles B. Rogers, noted western theme artist, are displayed in this former cowboy hotel built of native limestone. More than 300 works are displayed.

Salina Art Center. A modern facility with rotating exhibits by prominent artists.

Spencer Museum of Art — Lawrence. University of Kansas campus. Permanent exhibits plus special displays. One of the finest university museums in the country. It displays a 25,000 piece collection and is known for its European Renaissance and Baroque period paintings.

art museums

Stone House Gallery — Fredonia. This 1872 home was declared a Kansas Historical site and now provides a showcase for artists. The home is made of hand-hewn stone and is the site of nine monthly artists' exhibits during the gallery season of Sept.-May.

Ted Watts Sports Art Gallery — Oswego. Sports illustrator Ted Watts' works are on display in the gallery, which includes nearly 4,000 pieces of his artwork.

Warren Hall Coutts III Memorial Museum of Art — El Dorado. The museum houses over 500 paintings and 100 pieces of sculpture from artists all over the world, including Pablo Picasso and western artist Frederic Remington.

Wichita Art Association. The gallery features traveling shows and faculty work plus the Irene Vickers Baker Theater, one of the nation's largest children's theaters.

Wichita Art Museum. Exhibits include the famed Murdock collection of American art and a sculpture deck.

Pancake Race — In old England it was customary for the housewives to drop whatever they were doing and hurry to church at the tolling of the bell to be "shriven" of their sins. In 1445, a housewife in Olney, England, started baking her pancakes rather late. They were not quite finished when the church bell rang. Not wishing to leave her pancakes to burn she hurried to the "shriving" carrying her griddle and the pancakes with her. Thus an annual sporting event was born. Liberal, Kansas heard of this 500-year event of pancake racing over a 415-yard course from the "town pump" to the church, and in 1950 a challenge was accepted by Reverend R.C. Collins, Vicar of Olney. The International Pancake Race is held simultaneously in Liberal, Kan., and in Olney, England, each year at the start of Lent.

This buffalo was a team sculpture project of the Kansas Sculpture Association, Lawrence.

Photo by Jim Patti.

Belton Preserves Czech Culture

Kepka Belton has always done what she's wanted to do. She is an art teacher by trade, but it is the work she does in her spare time that makes her internationally known. Kepka is one of the few remaining artists who practice *Kraslice*, the Czechoslovakian folk art of decorating eggs using melted wax and dyes.

Dubbed the "Egg Lady" by an Associated Press writer in 1981, Kepka has practiced her art professionally since 1970, when she hesitatingly took 13 eggs to a Wichita art show at which she was displaying some of her paintings.

Born in Wilson, Kansas, the Czech Capital of Kansas, Kepka learned *Kraslice* from her grandmother and because of her overpowering curiosity, has pursued it.

The traditional method of decorating eggs was a painstaking process. Kepka devised a simpler method involving a wooden box that rests easily on her lap and an alcohol burner to heat wax. The "lap studio" is available at the Kansas Museum of History in Topeka.

Kepka uses chicken, duck, and goose eggs. Prices range from $4 to $150. The delicate task of blowing out the eggs was first taught by her grandmother. Two holes are punched in the egg and the contents are then blown out by mouth.

Over the years, Kepka has developed an international reputation for her authentic egg decorating. She was the first egg decorator in the United States to receive a National Heritage Fellowship from the National Endowment for the Arts in Washington, D.C., for preservation of the arts. In 1990 The International Folk Art Museum in Santa Fe, N.M., purchased some of her eggs for a permanent exhibition and an exhibit that will tour 12 museums across the country.

Photo by Kepka Belton.

An example of the Czech eggs made by Kepka Belton.

The art of *Kraslice* has a bright future through Kepka Belton. Her energy and devotion to preserving culture and tradition can be seen in her work. ❏

January

Interstate Classic Basketball Tournament — Coffeyville. Boy's high school basketball tournament held the third weekend in January.
Kansas Eagle Awareness Week — Salina. Held on a Saturday in January or early February. Urban Wildlife Project in Salina emphasizes eagle education classes.
Topeka Boat & Outdoor Show — Topeka. Kansas Expocentre. Exhibits show the latest fishing equipment, boats, and outdoor equipment.

February

Ground Hog Day Feed — Agra. Traditional celebration.
Kansas Flower, Lawn, and Garden Show — Topeka. Third weekend in February at the Kansas Expocentre. Exotic floral displays and landscaping information.

March

2-A and 5-A State High School Basketball Championship — Topeka. Usually the second weekend in March at Washburn University and Kansas Expocentre. The two championships are played simultaneously.
Big 8 Conference Women's Basketball Championship — Salina. Women's varsity playoffs.
Easter Sunrise Service — Abilene. Re-creation of events surrounding the Ascension performed on Easter morning by local youth in the outdoor theater in Brown's Park two miles south of Abilene.
International Pancake Day — Liberal. Always held the Tuesday before Ash Wednesday, the start of Lent. Activities include the International Pancake Day Race, dances, pancake eating contest, parade, and other events. The International Pancake Day Race is held over identical courses at the same time in Liberal, Kansas, and in Olney, England.
Kansas State High School 3A Basketball Championships (Boys and Girls) — Hutchinson. The tournaments are held every year in March.
National Junior College Athletic Association Men's Basketball Tournament — Hutchinson. The tournament is held in Hutchinson in March every year.
Spring Expo — Hutchinson. Second weekend in March at the fairgrounds. Emphasis is on the home, energy conservation, and recreational vehicles.
St. Patrick's Day Parade — Leavenworth. A truly Irish celebration.
St. Patrick's Day Parade — Topeka. A downtown parade and a "wee bit of Irish" highlight this annual celebration that includes food, music and entertainment.

festivals

St. Patrick's Day Parade — Wichita. A no-holds barred parade including unusual floats and parade participants of every age and inclination, all wearin' green, and Irish for the day.
Topeka Home Show. Kansas Expocentre. Booths and exhibits featuring redecorating, painting, papering, siding, building, and remodeling ideas for any home.

April

Art in the Park — Lawrence. Local artisans display their works in South Park.
City of Tulips — Smith Center. Spring-time celebration.
Designer's Showcase — Topeka. Usually last weekend of April through Mother's Day. One house is chosen to be completely redone on the interior by local decorators and furniture stores. A boutique and concessions are also offered.
Junior Miss Pageant — Oakley. First Saturday in April.
Kansas Relays — Lawrence. Track and field events at the University of Kansas campus.
Mennonite Relief Auction — Hutchinson. Held at the fairgrounds each year, this auction is popular because of the distinctive, quality handcrafted items that are available — from quilts to furniture. Authentic ethnic foods are also available.
Men's National AAU Basketball Tournament — Topeka. Second weekend in April at Washburn University. Features some of the finest amateur basketball in the nation. Teams from all over the United States compete for the title of National AAU Champion.
National Greyhound Association Spring Meet — Abilene. Five days of activities the last week of April including stake races, greyhound auction, and Hall of Fame induction ceremony.
New Beginning Festival — Coffeyville. Last weekend in April. Annual festival includes arts and crafts, cheese festival, chicken cook-off, and entertainment.
PEO Quilt Show — Oakley. Second weekend of April.
Renaissance Fair — Wichita. Kansas Newman College brings some of the spirit and flavor of the Renaissance. Crafts, dramatic and musical performances, games and activities are included.
Scott County Easter Pageant — Scott City. A religious program presented by volunteers that is staged outside on the evening of Good Friday.
Spring Festival — Olpe. Last Sunday in April. Includes food and activities held by the St. Joseph's Catholic Church.
Territorial Wagon Train — Caldwell. The wagon train begins in Caldwell and ends in Guthrie, Oklahoma.
Tulip Festival — Wamego. The third weekend in April. More than 18,000 Holland Tulips are in bloom during the festival. Features Dutch-style crafts, food and entertainment at the Old Dutch Mill.

Tulip Time — Belle Plaine. The Bartlett Arboretum, a 20-acre park, is the site of the Tulip Time event featuring music, arts and crafts, and tours of the arboretum. The arboretum is the only mature arboretum between the Mississippi River and the Rockies and features flowers, shrubs, trees and grasses from around the world. Each year 30,000 tulip bulbs are planted at the arboretum.

Washburn President's Open Regatta — Topeka. Rowing at Lake Shawnee on a marked 2,000 meter course and 400 meter course (the only one in the world). The regatta has men's and women's events. Colleges from all over the United States participate in the regatta.

Wichita Jazz Festival. A three-day educational and entertainment festival.

May

Barbecue Cook Off — Kansas City. Tasty and tangy barbecue concoctions.

Barbed Wire Swap and Sell Session — La Crosse. Collectors can find a variety of barbed wire at this annual event.

Celebrate Kansas Foods. Various locations. Sponsored by the Kansas Board of Agriculture, this event focuses on food products made in Kansas.

Haskell Indian Pow Wow — Lawrence. Haskell Junior College.

Kansas Polkatennial — Wichita. Three days of non-stop polka music and dance.

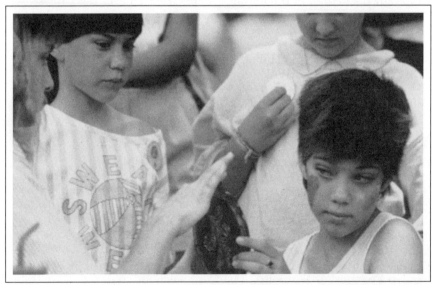

Photo courtesy of Twin Rivers Festival, Inc.

Face painting in KIDFEST at the Twin Rivers Festival in Emporia.

123

festivals

Mother's Day Walleye Tourney — Lovewell Lake. Jewell County.
Oregon Trail Festival — Westmoreland. Last Saturday in May.
River Bend Art Fair — Atchison. Art show and sale.
Square Fair — Garnett. An arts and crafts festival held annually in May on the Saturday before Mother's Day. Artists display, sell, and demonstrate their works at the Courthouse Square.
Wichita River Festival. The River Festival celebrates Wichita's historic, cultural, and civic roots. Activities include bike and bathtub races, parades, hot air balloon events and the festival is capped by the Wichita Symphony's 1812 Overture complete with cannons and fireworks over the river.

Summer

Heartland Park — Topeka. The Center of America's Motorsports features a variety of auto racing events.
The Woodlands — Kansas City. Fans can watch Thoroughbred and Quarter horse racing plus greyhound dog racing.
Wichita International Raceway. Drag racing is every Saturday night during the summer.

June

3-Dimensional Art Show — Lenexa. A national three-dimensional, outdoor art show.

Photo courtesy of Lindsborg Chamber of Commerce.
Young dancers preserve Swedish traditions during festivals in Lindsborg.

Beef Empire Days — Garden City. Celebrates the town's cattle industry heritage.
Butterfield Trail Ride, Dance & Rodeo — Russell Springs. Held the first weekend in June, this trail ride lets participants relive the historic past along the trail. A rodeo is held Sunday afternoon.
Crossroads Car Festival — Belleville. Features antique, custom, and hot-rod cars.
Heartland Festival — Paola. This annual festival is held the second Saturday of June.
Heritage Day — Hiawatha. Buggy rides and dining on homemade foods are just a fraction of the activities.
Kansas State Barbecue Championship — Lenexa. End of June. Attracts amateur and professional chefs from the Midwest to compete in nine categories.
Kansas State High School Rodeo Championships — Topeka. First or second weekend in June, Kansas Expocentre Livestock Arena. Exciting rodeo action from young athletes.
Midsummer's Day Festival (Midsommardag) — Lindsborg. This annual Swedish-American celebration, held the third Saturday of June, welcomes the return of summer. Celebrations center around the traditional May Pole. Swedish folk dancing, authentic arts and crafts and a Scandinavian smorgasbord are delightful highlights of this celebration.
Old Shawnee Days — Shawnee. First week in June.
Ottawa Quilters Guild Quilt Shoe. First weekend in June.
Sidewalk Sale — St. Mary's. Features a barbecue and craft sale. Held first Saturday in June.
Skunk Run Book Sale and Art Fair — Ottawa. Held the first Sunday in June in Ottawa's City Park.
Smoky Hill River Festival — Salina. Variety of food, arts and crafts, and entertainment highlight this large, annual festival.
Teddy Bear Fair — Topeka. The World Famous Topeka Zoo presents a fun day for participants and teddy bears alike, featuring contests, a parade and "Bear-Paw Readings" by Gypsies.
Territorial Days — Lecompton. Civil War re-enactments with participants wearing period clothing.
Wahshungah Days Arts and Crafts Fair — Council Grove. Annual fair featuring original arts and crafts.

July
"1876 Fourth of July Celebration" — Wichita. Old Cowtown Museum. Held the weekend before July 4.
After-Harvest Festival — Cuba. Held in mid-July, this event relates to the early Czech and Bohemian settlers who first settled this community.
Chautauqua Days — Ottawa. July 4th in Forest Park.

festivals

Comin' Home Days — Onaga. Activities include a barbecue, fireworks, and dance.
Courtland Fun Day. Held last weekend in July, the event features Swedish foods and crafts.
Dodge City Roundup PRCA Rodeo. The rodeo, held the last week in July and first weekend in August, is billed as Kansas' largest rodeo.
Downs Celebration — Downs. The event started in 1879 and features homemade crafts, food, and events.
Fiesta Mexicana — Topeka. A parade, authentic Mexican food, carnival, and dance are all part of this local tradition.
Fireworks Display — Fort Leavenworth. A display over the lake on July 4.
Fourth of July Celebration — Larned. Activities include a fun run, buffalo feed, and fireworks display.
Fourth of July Celebration — Wamego. Features the largest Fourth of July parade in Kansas.
Fourth of July Celebration — Wichita. An all-day event featuring a musical synchronized fireworks show at Cessna Stadium, Wichita State University.
Go 4th — Topeka. Held the weekend before July 4th, this celebration held on the Washburn University campus features crafts, exhibits, talent show, and fireworks the evening of the 4th.
Independence Days — Lawrence. Arts and crafts booths plus entertainment located in Bircham Park by the Kaw River.
Indian Pow-wow — Wichita. Traditional Indian dancing, both Gourd Dance and War Dancing.

Photo courtesy of Wichita Convention and Visitors Bureau.
Full dance regalia and rich heritage are found at the Pow-wow in Wichita.

International Aerobatics Contest — Ottawa. Held in mid-July at the Ottawa Municipal Airport.
July 3rd Parade and Celebration — Westmoreland. Features homemade ice cream.
Kansas River Valley Art Fair — Topeka. Gage Park. Pictures, carvings, crafts, weaving, and other arts are on display by local and regional artists.
Lenexa Community Days — Lenexa. The July 4th activities are held in Lenexa's Old Town and include a street fair with crafts, music, games, and food. Also included is a parade, Freedom Run, and a Miss Lenexa contest.
Main Street Event — Hutchinson. The Main Street Event is held annually on the weekend prior to July 4th. Activities include an "eat-in-the-street" barbecue, street dance and stage show.
Old Soldiers & Sailors Reunion — Erie. The event was started in 1871 and is usually held the second week of July. Features arts and crafts, 3-night rodeo, bean feed, games, dances, and River Run.
Pioneer Days — Haysville. July 4th.
Plains Theater Guild — Oakley. Third weekend of July.
Prairie Port Festival — El Dorado. Contests, sailboat regattas, arts, crafts, and entertainment are included in this festival held in July/August.
Prairiefest — Hutchinson. Held each year on the Fourth of July weekend. Musical entertainment, games, contests and food vendors highlight this jubilee held on the Kansas State Fairgrounds.
Quilt Show — Beloit. Hundreds of quilts are displayed at the annual show held in late July.
Summerfest — Dodge City. The Summerfest includes arts and crafts, steam engine display, and entertainment.
Sundown Salute — Junction City. A parade and patriotic ceremony plus food and music highlight the Sundown Salute.
Wheat Festival — Wellington. Sumner County is the leading county throughout the United States in hard winter wheat production. Events include a carnival, horseshoe tournament, dance, contests, dog show, antiques, parade, and entertainment.
Wilson Czech Festival. Authentic bratwurst and sauerkraut as well as Czech arts and crafts are highlights of this festival held the last Friday and Saturday of July in the Czech Capital of Kansas.

August

Allen County Rodeo — Iola. Seven rodeo events plus a specialty act are featured at this event.
Alton Summer Jubilee. This town in Osborne County holds the jubilee at the end of August.
City-wide Garage Sale — Haysville. Smart shoppers can find bargains.

Frontier Days — Haddam. Washington County. Activities re-create pioneer days and spirit.

Inter-State Fair and Rodeo — Coffeyville. Second full week in August. Includes the finest professional rodeo cowboys in the nation.

Kansas State Chili Cook Off — Chanute. A cook off for the best chili statewide.

Kansas State Fiddling & Picking Championship — Lawrence. Held in South Park.

McLouth Threshing Days. The first weekend in August. Features a parade of antique farm equipment and threshing demonstrations.

Miller High Life Midget Nationals — Belleville. Premier event of Dirt Track Racing in the nation.

National Baseball Congress — Wichita. The National Baseball Congress has its headquarters at Lawrence-Dumont Stadium in Wichita. The NBC originated in Wichita in 1931 and draws pro-quality, non-professional teams from all over the United States.

Old Settlers' Day Reunion — Mulvane. Features live music, crafts, parade.

Santa Fe Trail Bike and Motorcoach Tour. A seven-day tour for bicyclists and tour groups along the Santa Fe Trail from Olathe to Dodge City. The first days' activities take place in Topeka.

Scott County Free Fair and Beefiesta — Scott City. Activities include a barbecue and is intended as a salute to the beef feeding industry in the county. The fair is held during the second week in August. The Beefiesta is held on the final day of the fair and features a free beef barbecue. The Beefiesta was inaugurated as a salute to the beef feeding industry in the county.

Sunflower Festival — Colby. Third Saturday in August. Events include Field and Plant tours, games, crafts, and entertainment.

Wild Bill Hickok Rodeo and Central Kansas Free Fair — Abilene. The rodeo and fair events are held the third week of August.

"World's Greatest Home-Owned Carnival" and Decatur County Fair — Oberlin. Carnival activities including rides and entertainment.

September

Annual IPRA Sanctioned Rodeo — Argonia. Each autumn the participants come back for the junior rodeo.

Artist Alley — Chanute. Last Saturday in September. An annual art fair featuring original handcrafts, artwork and entertainment.

Autumnfest — Belle Plain. Usher in fall with Autumn Fest and the junior rodeo.

Bohemian Festival — Narka. Located in northeast Republic County, Narka is the site for this annual fall festival celebrating its Bohemian background.

Buffalo Bill Days — Leavenworth. Third week in September. This celebration honors Buffalo Bill and the pioneers who traveled on trails to the west. Visitors enjoy parades, balloon races, dances, and music.
Chautauqua — Beloit. Historic speeches and debates are re-enacted at the Chautauqua, which also features music, arts and crafts.
Cherokee Strip Land Rush Re-enactment — Caldwell. This is a nationally sanctioned bicycle race from Caldwell to Enid, Oklahoma.
Cider Days — Topeka. Old time arts and crafts and exhibits allow a look into the way of life in earlier pioneer days.
Cow Chip Throwing Contest — Russell Springs. Held on Labor Day weekend. Throwers of all ages compete.
Haskell Indian Pow Wow — Lawrence. Haskell Indian Junior College. Large Inter-tribal dance, Indian arts and crafts, plus traditional Indian foods.
Huff 'n' Puff Balloon Rally — Topeka. Each year at Billard Airport, this balloon rally features colorful balloons from across the Midwest.
Indian Peace Treaty Pageant — Medicine Lodge. Held the last weekend in September every three years. This pageant is a reenactment of historical events beginning with the Spanish conquistadores. Events include a colorful parade, ceremonial dancing, old-time melodramas, and the Kansas Championship Ranch Rodeo.
Johnson County Old Settler's Days — Olathe. A celebration of the early days of the county and events include a parade, stage shows, craft shows, carnival, games, and performances by local bands.
Kansas State Fair — Hutchinson. Begins the first Friday after Labor Day. Grandstand entertainment, 4-H exhibits, food, crafts, livestock, and exhibits.
Little Balkans Days — Pittsburg. Labor Day weekend. Activities include parades, street dances, games, food, crafts, a Little Balkins barbecue, music and contests.
Louisburg Cider Mill's Ciderfest Celebration. An annual autumn event highlighted by fresh apple cider.
Mexican Fiesta — Chanute. A celebration of Mexican Independence Day with Mexican dancing and food.
Mexican Independence Day Celebration — Wichita. Celebration of independence with music, food, games, and sports tournaments.
Mini-Sappa Festival — Oberlin. Last weekend in September. Relive the area's heritage and commemorate the Last Indian Raid in Kansas. Activities include the Antique Car, Thresher and Engine Show and a Pioneer Shootout as well as an ethnic foods dinner.
Oktoberfest — Chanute. Held the second and third weekends in September, this festival includes an annual bed race, an air show, and sports events.
Oktoberfest — Wichita. Sept/Oct. A three-day ethnic festival with German food, entertainment, polka dances, parade, and Volksmarch.
Old Settler's Day — Oakley. Held on Labor Day weekend.

Photo courtesy of The Renaissance of Kansas City.

Knights battle at the Renaissance Festival.

Old Settler's Day — Russell Springs. Annual event held on Labor Day weekend includes a parade. Also that weekend is the State Cow Chip Throwing Contest in Russell Springs. **Old Settler's Day —\Smith Center.** Lots of foods, barbecue, crafts, and events are on hand for this celebration. **Old Settler's Day Reunion — Mulvane.** Live music, arts and crafts, a vintage car show and parade highlight this event. **Old Shawnee Town Craft Fair — Shawnee.** Third Saturday in September at Old Shawnee Town. **Railroad Days — Topeka.** Labor Day weekend at Forbes Field. Celebration of Topeka's railroad heritage. Activities include arts and crafts, railroad memorabilia displays, and model train exhibits.

Renaissance Festival — Bonner Springs. An authentic re-creation of a 16th century village in the midst of a harvest celebration. More than 2,000 costumed participants take part and activities include jousting exhibitions, crafts, and stage entertainment. The festival opens Labor Day weekend and continues through six weekends.

Spinach Festival — Lenexa. In the 1930s, the Belgian farmers of Lenexa raised and sold more spinach than anywhere in the country. The Spinach Festival celebrates that heritage featuring Popeye memorabilia, arts and crafts, a sunflower seed spitting contest, and bubble gum blowing contest.

Stampede Rodeo — Oakley. Held the Saturday of Labor Day weekend.

Stay-a-Day Folk Festival — Westmoreland. Second Saturday in September.

Walnut Valley Festival — Winfield. Third weekend in September. Features folk, bluegrass, and country music contests.

Whimmydiddle — Scott City. Arts and crafts at the city park are
the highlight of the Whimmydiddle, held the last Saturday in
September.
Wichita Arts Festival. A weekend of dance, theater, music, and art
held each September.

October

Apple Festival — Topeka. First weekend in October at Ward-Meade
Park. A folk-life celebration of pioneer life in Kansas. Features crafts
and food.
Arkalalah Celebration — Arkansas City. Two day-event. Activities
include a crowning of Queen Alalah, a parade, biathlon, and crafts.
Arkalalah was started in the Depression as a means of lifting local spirit.
The name is a manufactured word using the "Ark" from Arkansas City
and "alalah," supposedly an Indian word for "Good Times."
Biblesta Parade — Humbolt. All of the floats in this one-of-a-kind
parade depict a scene from the bible. The floats are aligned in sequence
starting at the beginning of the bible. There is a variety of entertainment provided. The event is held the first Saturday in October.
Columbus Day Celebration — Topeka. A parade downtown
highlights this event.
Corn Show and Parade — Jewell. Second weekend of October.
Features many grains of the area plus crafts, barbecue, and talent show.
Dalton Defender Days — Coffeyville. A tribute to the four peace-
loving townsmen who lost their lives during the Dalton Raid.
Halloween Frolic — Hiawatha. This event has been held annually
since 1914. The tradition includes contests, parades, and a Halloween
Pageant with the winner advancing to the Miss Kansas Pageant.
Haysville Fall Festival. Annual event held in October. Activities
include entertainment.
Hidden Glen Arts Festival — Olathe. Cedar Creek. The two-day
event features artists, stage shows, and two performance stages.
International Food Fair — Oakley. Held the third weekend of
October.
Maple Leaf Festival — Baldwin City. Includes crafts and
entertainment with beautiful fall foliage as a backdrop.
Maple Leaf Festival and Maple Fun Run — Hiawatha. First
Saturday in October. Features arts and crafts with open booths around
the courthouse square and the colorful setting of maple trees.
Neewollah — Independence. Neewollah, or Halloween spelled
backwards, is the setting for a week-long schedule of events including a
parade, carnival, and Neewollah Queen coronation as well as concerts
and entertainment featuring popular entertainers.
Oktoberfest — Wamego. Held the first Saturday in October, this festival
features the ethnic flavor of the Nordic festival for which it is named.
Old Sedgwick County Fair — Wichita. Held the first weekend of

Photo courtesy of Wichita Convention and Visitors Bureau.
Actors re-enact the days of the "old West" in Wichita.

Sip'n Cider Days — Leavenworth. Events include entertainment, food, and handmade crafts and quilts.
State Cornhusking Contest — Oakley. First weekend of October. Participants challenge their skills at husking ears of corn.
Trail Days and Heritage Day — Abilene. Heritage craft demonstrations and living history exhibits are displayed. On the first Sunday in October guests can tour a selection of historic homes.
Wichita Asian Festival. Annual event in October. Traditional costume fashion shows, dances, skits, karate demonstrations, and Oriental food.

November

Christmas in the Country — Oxford. This event, held during Thanksgiving weekend, opens the holiday season. Activities include a tour of the decorated homes and arts and crafts.
Christmas Through the Windows of Cowtown — Wichita. Held during the week after Thanksgiving. Holiday decor, Victorian gifts, music and customs; held evenings under the lamps.
Festival of Carols — Topeka. A lighting ceremony of the holiday decorations on the Capitol grounds highlights this festive event held the Friday after Thanksgiving. Singing, ethnic dances, choirs, carols, hay rides, Santa Claus, and more enhance this event.
International Holiday Festival — Wichita. Arts and crafts show featuring international food and entertainment.

Tall Grass Prairie Arts and Crafts Fair — Olsburg. Third
Saturday in November. Event highlights local artists' work.
Veteran's Day Celebration — Chanute. The activities include a
celebration and parade held on Veteran's Day, Nov. 11.
Veteran's Day Parade — Kensington. Activities include a parade
and barbecue.

December

Christmas Card Lane — Chanute. The Christmas Card Lane is a
neighborhood elaborately decorated with Christmas lights. The lights
can be seen the day after Thanksgiving through New Year's Eve.
Christmas City of the High Plains — Wakeeney. Several tons of
Colorado greenery form this Christmas tree with 3,000 light bulbs to
illuminate it. Three miles of electrical wiring and 6,000 bulbs shine on
downtown Wakeeney at Christmas.
Christmas Luminaria — Belle Plaine and Caldwell. The
luminarias light up the Christmas spirit.
Christmas Open House — Westmoreland. Held the Saturday
before Christmas.
Christmas Parade — Larned. An annual holiday event.
Christmas Parade — Ottawa. First Saturday in December.
Christmas Tree Lane — Abilene. North Buckeye street between 3rd
and 14th Streets and 3rd Street from Buckeye to Mud Creek is
decorated for the season with a lighted Christmas tree in each yard.
Festival of Trees — Topeka. Decorated Christmas trees are
auctioned off. The trees are on display in the Kansas Expocentre
Ag Hall.
Haysville Community Library Christmas Bazaar — Haysville.
First Saturday in December.
Holiday Happenings — Topeka. Ward-Meade Park. Features turn-
of-the-century decorations and tours of the historic grounds. A
wonderful way to usher in the holiday season by taking a step back to
another time.
Holiday Home Tour — Wamego. Second weekend in December.
Jayhawk Bowl — Coffeyville. First Saturday in December. Enjoy
college football and the Coffeyville Christmas parade.
Potwin Lights — Topeka. Victorian-style homes are lit with
Christmas lights and decorations for the holiday season.
St. Lucia's Festival — Lindsborg. Held the second Saturday in
December. The arrival of St. Lucia signals the beginning of the
Christmas season in this community of Swedish heritage.
WIBW Holiday Basketball Tournament — Topeka. Washburn
University. One of the fastest growing small college tournaments in the
nation. It attracts top college teams from across the country.
Ye Olde Englishe Feaste — Ottawa. Held the first weekend in
December at Ottawa University.

kansas state fair

The Great Kansas Get-Together

On September 23 and 24 of 1873 a tradition began. The Reno County Agricultural Society hosted a fair which was held in a small wooden livery stable behind the town's only bank on the northwest corner of Sherman and Main. Total receipts were counted at $90. The town was Hutchinson, Kansas, and the fair would become known as the Kansas State Fair. Kansas is a land filled with proud traditions, and the Kansas State Fair is no exception.

Although accounts of the Fair's early history are sketchy and even clouded with mystery at times, records show the first fair was conducted at Leavenworth in 1863, just two years after Kansas had been granted statehood.

In 1919, tanks and field artillery used in World War I were displayed on the fairgrounds.

Following several different location sites and a heated legislative debate, the Kansas State Fair finally found a permanent home in Hutchinson in 1913. In that year the first official Kansas State Fair opened with the duty of promoting "industries of the state, especially the predominant industry of agriculture, and to foster better citizenship by promotion of the state's activities, institutions and youth work."

While that philosophy has not changed over the years, the Fair has often reflected the times. In 1919, tanks and field artillery used in World War I were displayed on the fairgrounds. When America again went to war in the 1940s, the Fair contributed to the effort by donating several buildings for manufacturing war materials and troop training.

German prisoners were housed in fair buildings, and in 1942 "Scrap Day" was created admitting adults to the Fair in exchange for 100 pounds of scrap metal.

Exhibits have conformed with the society's demand since the first fair featured entries in such categories as homemade shoes, quinces, and even currant and grape wines.

Entertainment has always been the highlight of the Fair, and until 1969 consisted mainly of variety shows. Today, however, the acrobats, animal acts, and dancing girls have been replaced by big-name celebrities, tractor pulls, and stock car races.

Even today, buried deep beneath the smell of corn dogs, popcorn, and diesel; hidden behind the mesmerizing lights and beckoning carnival barkers, there lies a kernel of the spirit of that first little fair that was held in a livery stable behind the town's only bank. The Fair has come a long way since its beginnings more than a century ago. But one thing is the same – for the people of Hutchinson and all of Kansas, the Fair is truly "the great Kansas get-together." ❑

KANSAS   hollywood comes to kansas

Film Industry Discovers Kansas

In the late 1980s, a variety of television and motion pictures were filmed in the state of Kansas. The growing film industry in Kansas has accounted for more than $20 million into the state's economy since 1987 as well as increased publicity for the state.

The expanding film industry in Kansas received a boost in 1982 when the television movie "The Day After" was filmed around the Lawrence area. The movie, which was about the effects of a nuclear war, helped establish Kansas as a prime location for future filmmaking ventures.

The Kansas Film Commission was established in 1982 by then-Governor John Carlin to help in the making of "The Day After." Since then, the commission has worked to attract filmmakers to the state as well as assist during the production phases.

One of the earlier productions filmed in Kansas was the motion picture "Paper Moon," starring Ryan O'Neal and Tatum O'Neal. More recent productions in 1989 were the television motion pictures "Where Pigeons Go to Die," starring Michael Landon and Art Carney, and "Cross of Fire," a mini-series filmed in northeast Kansas. The state was the site for filming of a motion picture entitled "Kansas," starring Andrew McCarthy and Matt Dillon.

The high production costs in the traditional Southern California filmmaking area account for just one of the reasons filmmakers are expanding to other areas. The geographic locations, natural resources, historic buildings, and historical sites in Kansas offer filmmakers many possibilities for production sites.

Listed below are works made in Kansas. ❐

The 34th Star (1976)	Moonlight Express
Ace Eli and Rodger of the Skies (1973)	Murder Ordained (1986)
Americana (1981)	Nice Girls Don't Explode (1986)
The Attic (1979)	Night Screams (1986)
Bad Company (1972)	Nursery Crymes (1981)
Carnival of Souls (1962)	Paper Moon (1973)
Cross of Fire (1989)	The Parade (1984)
Dark Before Dawn (1987)	Picnic (1955)
The Day After (1982)	Prime Cut (1972)
Fred Harvey and the American West	Reunion (1987)
Gypsy Moths (1969)	Rooster (1976)
Hambone and Hillie (1983)	Student Body (1981)
In Cold Blood (1967)	Twister (1988)
Kansas (1987)	Up the Academy (1980)
King Kung Fu (1973)	Wait 'til the Sun Shines,
The Leaning Tree (1969)	Nellie (1952)
Linda Lovelace for President (1976)	Where Pigeons Go to Die (1989)
Mary White (1977)	

Abilene Area Chamber of Commerce, P.O. Box 446, Abilene 67410.
Accessible Arts, Inc., 1100 State Ave., Kansas City, Kansas 66102.
Arts and Recreation Commission, City of Paola, USD #368, P.O. Box 409, Paola 66071.
Association of Kansas Theatre, 949 Parklane #332, Wichita 67218.
Averill, Thomas Fox. "Oz and Kansas Culture." Kansas Historical Society: **Kansas History**, Vol. 12, Spring 1989.
Barn Players, P.O. Box 12767, Shawnee Mission 66212.
Beef Empire Days, Box 1197, Garden City 67848.
Colby Area Chamber of Commerce, P.O. Box 572, Colby 67701.
Concordia Area Chamber of Commerce, 219 W. 6th, Concordia 66901.
Dodge City Convention and Visitors Bureau, P.O. Box 1474, Dodge City 67801.
El Dorado Chamber of Commerce, P.O. Box 509, El Dorado 67042.
Helen Hocker Performing Arts Center, Room 259 City Hall, Topeka 66603.
Iola Area Chamber of Commerce, P.O. Box 722, Iola 66749.
Kansas Arts Commission, Jayhawk Tower, 700 Jackson, Suite 1004, Topeka 66603-3714.
Kansas Committee for the Humanities, 112 W. 6th, Suite 210, Topeka 66603.
Kansas Film Commission, 400 W. 8th St., Suite 500, Topeka 66603-3957.
Kansas Grass Roots Arts, Attn: Jon Blumb, 835 1/2 Massachusetts, Lawrence 66044.
Kansas Museum of History, 6425 SW 6th, Topeka 66615.
Kansas Sculptors Association, 2030 Ousdahl, Lawrence 66044.
Kansas State Fair, 2000 N. Poplar, Hutchinson 67502.
The Lawrence Arts Center, 200 W. 9th, Lawrence 66044.
Lenexa Convention & Visitors Bureau, 11900 W. 87th Street Parkway, Lenexa 66215.
Liberal Convention & Tourism Bureau, P.O. Box 2257, Liberal 67905-2257.
Lindsborg Chamber of Commerce, P.O. Box 191, Lindsborg 67456.
Manhattan Convention and Visitors Bureau, 505 Poyntz Ave., P.O. Box 988, Manhattan 66502.
Nottage, James H. and Floyd R. Thomas, Jr. "There's No Place Like Home: Symbols and Images of Kansas." Kansas State Historical Society: **Kansas History**, Vol. 8, Autumn 1985.
The Renaissance Festival of Kansas City, 207 Westport Rd. #206, Kansas City, Mo. 64111.
Salina Arts & Humanities Commission, Box 2181, Salina 67402-2181.
Theater for Young America, 7204 W. 80th St., Overland Park 66204.
Twin Rivers Festival, Inc., P.O. Box 1707, Emporia 66801.
Very Special Arts Kansas, 124 S. Broadway, Wichita 67202.
Western Plains Art Association, Colby Community College, 1255 S. Range, Colby 67701.
Wichita Convention and Visitors Bureau, 100 S. Main, Wichita 67202.
William Inge Festival, P.O. Box 708, Independence 67301.

CHAPTER 6

BUSINESS

Labor Force • Manufacturing
Retail • Communication
Utilities • Transportation
Construction • Finance

Photo courtesy of Kansas State Board of Agriculture.

Labor Force
141

From 1940 through 1989, more Kansans were employed in service industries than any other single non-agriculture sector.

Georgia-Pacific
Feature
142-143

The Blue Rapids plant mines more than 2,000 tons of gypsum daily, and the gypsum deposits have a purity of 99%.

Manufacturing
144-145

Nineteen manufacturing plants employ more than 1,000 workers and an additional 36 plants employ between 500 and 999 workers.

Kansas Food
Products Feature
146-147

Popcorn, wheat bread, cheese, sorghum, summer sausage, and pizza are a sample of the products made in Kansas.

Retail
148

Automotive dealerships and food stores generated the most retail sales in 1989.

Communication
149

More than 57,000 Kansans are employed in the transportation, communications, and utilities industries.

Transportation
and Utilities
150

According to 1989 estimates, Kansas is fifth among nearby states in total number of registered vehicles.

Construction
151

In 1987, total Kansas construction receipts were over $4.2 billion, with more than $2.8 billion from new construction.

Finance
152

Kansas has 561 banks with 950 branches and total deposits of approximately $25 billion.

CHAPTER OPENER PHOTO: A sample of the many Kansas products included in the "From the Land of Kansas" promotion sponsored by the Kansas State Board of Agriculture.

L ocated in the center of the country, Kansas offers a strategic location for many businesses and industries serving national markets. The state has a favorable business climate and consistently ranks among the lowest in the nation for unemployment rates. Kansas also has a high worker productivity rate. Air, rail, and highway ground transportation link the state to the world and ensure companies can get their products to market rapidly. In addition, businesses and industries in Kansas have access to one of the nation's most sophisticated telecommunications networks, allowing for quick access to customers and information.

The state's labor force has undergone several transitions since the 1950s when the economy was based largely on agricultural and mining jobs. Since then, the number of employees in the agricultural sector has declined. Today a greater share of the work force is comprised of professional, clerical, and service workers. The number of women in the work force has steadily increased since 1940. As of 1980 more than 40% of the employed workers in the state were women.

Manufacturing industries have increasingly provided more jobs for the state. The largest concentration of manufacturing employment is in Sedgwick County. Wichita is the hub for a variety of industries, including the ever-important aviation industry that dominates the state's business climate. Kansas is the world leader in the production of general aviation aircraft. Other important manufacturing activities include the transportation equipment industry, food processing, and printing and publishing.

Johnson County, which is part of the Kansas City metropolitan area, is one of the most affluent counties in the nation. Overland Park, Kansas, is the site for a variety of beautifully landscaped business parks and some of the newest office developments in the Kansas City area. Several firms have their national headquarters in Johnson County. The area's rapid growth has had a significant impact on the business climate in Kansas.

Food products made in the state are beginning to be recognized nationally. Bloomingdale's, the trendy department store in New York City, chose Kansas foods as the theme for one of the store's promotions in May 1988. Forty-three Kansas food companies received national attention for their product lines.

In addition to the state's larger corporations, the smaller, entrepreneurial companies are equally vital to the state's economic future. Of all the firms in Kansas, 75% employ less than 10 workers.

From the board rooms of the large cities to the factories in the smaller towns, business in Kansas is steadily progressing and continually competing with other cities across the country. The state has always prided itself on hard work and productivity. Kansans are working toward a better tomorrow. ☐

Walking Tall — The Olathe Boot Company, Inc., in Olathe manufactures more than 25,000 pairs of western boots each year.

High Notes — The Player Piano Co., Inc., in Wichita has the largest selection of player piano parts and accessories in the world.

Volcanic Ash — Kansas Minerals, Inc., is a unique business for Kansas because it mines and processes volcanic ash. The business is seen at the one o'clock position on the north horizon 1 mile north of the US-36, KS-14-S junction.

Home of Salt Mines — Hutchinson is home to one of the world's largest salt mines and three of the largest salt evaporation plants.

Flying High — Clyde Cessna, Walter Beech, Lloyd Stearman, and less remembered flyers flexed their wings on Kansas plains and built Wichita into "the Air Capital of the World." All three major aircraft companies – Beech, Boeing, and Cessna – are located in Wichita. These three companies manufacture two-thirds of the general aviation aircraft produced in the world and employ nearly 36,000 people.

Coleman Headquarters — Wichita is also the headquarters for the Coleman Company, famous for their outdoor lantern and indoor and outdoor products.

Pizza Hut — The international restaurant chain Pizza Hut is based in Wichita, where it was founded in 1958.

A Piece of the Pattern — McCall Pattern Company's only manufacturing plant in the United States is located in Manhattan. Nearly 100 million sewing patterns are produced there each year and patterns are distributed to 86 countries.

Affluent County — Johnson County is one of the nation's most affluent suburban areas. In 1990, the Median Household Effective Buying Income for Johnson County was $40,400, which was 45% above the U.S. average of $27,900.

Changes in Labor Force

Since 1940, the distribution of employment among various job categories in Kansas has seen many changes. Professional, clerical and service workers make up a greater share of the work force today, while the share of farmers, farm laborers and private household workers have decreased significantly.

QUICK FACTS:
In 1989, more Kansans were employed in the trade industry than in any other industry; services was second and government third.

From 1969-89, total employment increased by 327,000 workers or 38%.

KANSAS EMPLOYMENT BY INDUSTRY

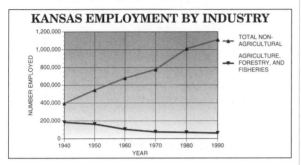

Source: Census of the Population, General Social and Economic Characteristics, U.S. Department of Commerce, Bureau of the Census.

Employment by Industry

From 1940 through 1989, more Kansans were employed in service industries than any other single non-agricultural sector. The most important service industries in Kansas, in terms of employees, are health services, followed by business services. These two service industries comprise about 53% of the total employment and about 61% of the annual payroll in the services sector of the economy.

Of all the firms in Kansas, 75% employ less than 10 workers.

In the state, 25% of the firms employ 85% of all the state's workers.

The only sector that has shown a significant decline in its share of employees is the agricultural sector.

KANSAS EMPLOYMENT BY SEX

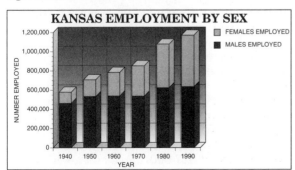

Approximately 1.3 million people are currently employed in Kansas, which is more than twice as many as in 1940. As of 1980, 42% of the employed workers were female, as compared to only 20% in 1940.

Source: U.S. Bureau of the Census.

georgia pacific

Photo by Diana J. Edwardson.

Gypsum Mining in Kansas

Kansas may be known as the wheat state, but there is another bountiful product that can be found in the state and is used in many everyday products. That product is a gypsum rock and is mined at Blue Rapids, Kansas.

The Georgia-Pacific Corporation has been mining gypsum at Blue Rapids since 1894. Due to the development of Tuttle Creek Reservoir in 1960, the old mine was closed and a new mine was started at its present location, ten miles south of Marysville. Everything from mining to product testing is done at the Blue Rapids plant.

Headquartered in Atlanta, Ga., Georgia-Pacific Corporation is a national manufacturer of building products, pulp, paper, and chemicals. Georgia-Pacific is one of the world's largest forest products companies, with almost 400 plants, mills, and offices throughout the United States. It manages gypsum reserves of 127 million tons and has sizable coal deposits. Gypsum is the only product mined at the Blue Rapids plant.

Although gypsum is used in many everyday products, it is still one of the most mysterious rocks known to man. The pyramids of Egypt, built from the 13th to the 15th centuries B.C., contain mortar made of hydraulic gypsum. The mortar remains hard and strong to this day. The Assyrians called gypsum "beautiful alabaster" and used it for sculpture. The ancient Greeks gave it the recognizable name of "Gypsos." Michelangelo painted many of his finest works on large panels covered with a thin layer of gypsum. Around 1775, gypsum was mined and calcined near Paris, France, thus the name plaster of Paris.

Benjamin Franklin was one of the first to introduce gypsum to this
country when he used ground raw gypsum, called land plaster, on his
farm to fertilize clover fields.

The Blue Rapids gypsum was formed over 200 million years
ago, when a vast sea dried up, leaving large mineral deposits
extending from Kansas to Texas. The Blue Rapids plant mines
more than 2,000 tons of gypsum daily. The "room and pillar" system
is used in mining this gypsum. A long entry is developed with side
entries turning off at intervals. From these side entries, rooms are
developed, usually paralleling the main entry. About three-fourths
of the available rock is removed from these side rooms and entries,
leaving one-fourth as pillars to support the roof. To remove the
gypsum, it is undercut, drilled and blasted. The result is a pile of
rock that is loaded into a mine shuttle car to a conveyor belt for
delivery to the crusher. The gypsum deposits at Blue Rapids have a
purity of about 99%, which is among the purest in the country.

Gypsum can be found in a wide variety of products. Most of the
gypsum mined is used in wallboards for homes. These gypsum
"boards" are formed by sandwiching a
core of wet plaster between two sheets
of heavy paper. When the core dries,
the sandwich becomes a strong, rigid,
fireproof building material.
Wallboard is manufactured on
continuous machines almost a quarter
of a mile in length. The quantity
produced is gigantic; enough for a
wall 90 feet high around the earth.

*The Blue Rapids
plant mines more
than 2,000 tons of
gypsum daily.*

China plates, cups, and saucers are formed in gypsum plaster molds,
as are most bathroom fixtures. Car windows are made of plate glass
which is held in a bed of gypsum for polishing. Dentists use a gypsum
dental plaster to cast bridges. Gypsum is even used as a conditioning
agent for water, in the brewing of beer, and as an agent to control the
tartness and clarity of wine.

Some other everyday products which contain gypsum are
toothpaste, blackboard chalk, lipstick, canned vegetables, seasoning
for spinach, match heads, and sidewalk cement. Hollywood even uses
gypsum to represent snow in movies whether for a white Christmas or
a raging blizzard. Hollywood also uses gypsum molds to make
spectacular movie and TV sets. On the other end of the glamour scale,
gypsum is mixed with manure in mushroom beds. For being a "rock
nobody knows," gypsum is certainly well used.

The gypsum mining business is strong in Kansas. Georgia-
Pacific has produced jobs and has been an asset to the Blue Rapids
area economically as well as the business climate for the state. ❏

manufacturing

KANSAS

QUICK FACTS:

Twelve counties in the state have manufacturing employment that exceeds 1,000 workers. The largest concentration of manufacturing employment is in Sedgwick County (Wichita) which is more than 1.8 times larger than its nearest competitors, Johnson County (Kansas City) and Wyandotte County (Kansas City). Lesser but important employment concentrations are in Shawnee County (Topeka).

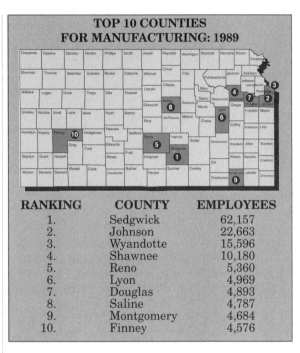

TOP 10 COUNTIES FOR MANUFACTURING: 1989

RANKING	COUNTY	EMPLOYEES
1.	Sedgwick	62,157
2.	Johnson	22,663
3.	Wyandotte	15,596
4.	Shawnee	10,180
5.	Reno	5,360
6.	Lyon	4,969
7.	Douglas	4,893
8.	Saline	4,787
9.	Montgomery	4,684
10.	Finney	4,576

Source: "1989 County Business Patterns," U.S. Bureau of the Census.

Climate for Manufacturing

The largest concentration of manufacturing is in Sedgwick County (Wichita).

One measure of the strength of a state's manufacturing climate is "value added," or in general terms, the difference between the value of the raw material and the value of the finished product. Value added per employee is also a measure of the productivity of the individual.

In 1987, Kansas was adding more value per employee to its manufacturing than any of its neighboring states, with the exception of Iowa, implying a high productivity level among Kansas employees.

Source: 1987 Census of Manufacturers, Geographic Area Series, U.S. Department of Commerce, Bureau of the Census.

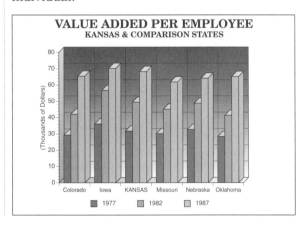

VALUE ADDED PER EMPLOYEE
KANSAS & COMPARISON STATES

(Thousands of Dollars)

Colorado   Iowa   KANSAS   Missouri   Nebraska   Oklahoma

■ 1977   ■ 1982   ▢ 1987

KANSAS
manufacturing

Manufacturing Employment

Between 1982-1987, total manufacturing employment has grown more than 10.8%. During the same period, significant employment growth was recorded in three industries: transportation equipment (37%); and printing and publishing (6.5%). Other important employment growth occurred in , chemicals (5.1%) and food preparation (17.7%). Major decreases in employment were recorded in rubber and plastics (-33.3%).

Major Manufacturers

Nineteen manufacturing plants in Kansas employ more than 1,000 workers and an additional 36 plants employ between 500 and 999 workers. These 55 plants are located in 25 communities with the largest concentrations in Wichita, Kansas City and Topeka. Other important concentrations of manufacturing employment are found in Salina, Emporia, and Olathe. The largest concentration of companies employing more than 1,000 workers are with transportation and food processing industries.

QUICK FACTS:

The Hesston Corporation, located in Hesston, is an international producer of farm equipment.

The Goodyear factory in Topeka, manufactures giant earthmover, heavy equipment, and truck tires.

Hallmark Cards has large production centers in Topeka, Lawrence, and Leavenworth.

The largest areas of manufacturing are in Wichita, Kansas City, and Topeka.

VALUE ADDED BY MANUFACTURER: 1987
(millions)

All Other Industries (2,551)

Transportation Equipment (3,440)

Stone, Clay, & Glass Products (380)

Fabricated Metal Products (349)

Electronic & Electric Equipment (448)

Chemicals & Allied Products (1,223)

Machinery, except Electrical (1,127)

Food & Kindred Products (1,807)

Printing & Publishing (1,485)

The production of transportation equipment is Kansas' major manufacturing activity. Transportation equipment together with non-electrical machinery manufacturing, printing, publishing, and food products comprise more than 60% of the total value added by manufacturers in the state. All major industry groups are represented in Kansas.

Source: 1987 Census of Manufacturers, Geographic Area Series, U.S. Bureau of the Census.

kansas food products

Photo Courtesy of Dillons

Land of Kansas Food Products

Kansas cooks know that taste-tantalizing, down-home good meals can be made from food products manufactured right in the state. From bakery products to barbecue sauce to popcorn, Kansas food products are a delightful and delicious treat for consumers.

Food products made in Kansas are starting to earn national recognition. Bloomingdale's, the trendy department store in New York City, featured Kansas foods as part of an in-store promotion in May 1988. Forty-three food companies from Kansas were invited to participate in the exhibition. Bloomingdale's shoppers got the chance to taste-test a variety of foods from Kansas as well as see food preparation demonstrations. In November 1988, the Bloomingdale's stores in Chicago also featured Kansas food products. The publicity from the promotions was a boost for the state's food processing companies, many of which are smaller sized and family owned.

The "Land of Kansas" trademark can be found on foods that are processed or produced in the Sunflower state. Nearly 300 companies are registered in the trademark program, which is sponsored by the Kansas State Board of Agriculture. "From the Land of Kansas" is a free marketing program available to any Kansas food company. Programs are offered throughout the year to make consumers more aware of locally produced foods.

"Celebrate! Kansas Food" is the promotion developed to urge retailers to highlight locally produced foods. Television and radio advertisements, in-store cooking demonstrations and taste-testing are a few of the activities that encourage consumers to buy food products made in Kansas.

kansas food products

Known as "the wheat state," Kansas produces a variety of flour and grain products. Amaranth, a grain grown in Kansas, is combined with wheat to make a high-fiber, nutritious flour. Whole wheat flour is used in bread and baked goods recipes. Sunflower bread is another healthy multi-grain product made in Kansas.

Sweet sorghum syrup has been produced in the country since colonial days. Sorghum is a sweet syrup used in cooking and baking. In addition, several companies market honey and honey products that can be eaten on breads or as topping for ice cream as well as used in recipes instead of sugar.

In southeast Kansas, along the banks of the Neosho River, are some of the best native pecans grown in North America. The native pecans are smaller in comparison to the larger papershell varieties. Soynuts are cholesterol-free, high in protein and fiber, and can be used as a topping for salads or eaten as a snack.

In May 1988, Bloomingdale's in New York City featured Kansas products.

For popcorn fans, Kansas-grown popcorn literally bursts with flavor. Several companies offer popcorn and popcorn seasonings ready to make at home, or buy a bag of already-popped corn. Top this tasty snack with butter, Cheddar cheese or spicy toppings to create your own snack treat.

Processed meats, including summer sausage and luncheon meats, as well as smoked meats like beef jerky are popular snack foods. Dairy products such as cheese, milk, ice cream, and eggs are also made in the state.

Barbecued steaks are a perfect option for summer picnics or backyard barbecues. The beef industry is especially important in Kansas. Many Kansas manufacturers offer a blend of barbecue sauces, ranging from mild to extra spicy, that are sure to please a variety of taste palettes.

Autumn is apple time in the Midwest, and a glass of hot or cold apple cider on a chilly day just hits the spot. Sweet and cinnamon-spicy apple butter is a delicious topping for breads, and nothing can beat mom's old-fashioned apple pie!

For a south-of-the-border taste, try some of the Mexican food products such as tortillas, chili powder, and salsa manufactured in the state. Also, Kansas manufacturers offer frozen pizza and Mexican foods. For a different taste, try eating a bierock or experiment with recipes using tofu.

For more information about Kansas products contact the Kansas State Board of Agriculture, Marketing Division, 901 S. Kansas, Topeka, Kansas 66612-1282. Phone: (913) 296-3736. ❏

BUSINESS

retail

QUICK FACTS:

Wholesale and retail trade establishments provide more than 200,000 jobs for Kansans, and an annual payroll of more than $2.8 billion.

The Garden City beet sugar factory shipped 18 million pounds of sugar beets during 1912.

Source: "County Business Patterns," 1989, U.S. Department of Commerce, Bureau of the Census.

ESTABLISHMENTS, EMPLOYEES, AND ANNUAL PAYROLL OF WHOLESALE AND RETAIL TRADE COMPANIES IN KANSAS: 1989

	Establishments	Employees	Annual Payroll ($ 000)
ALL INDUSTRIES	22,551	209,496	2,852,331
Wholesale	5,754	60,810	1,289,783
Durable Goods	3,362	34,549	771,510
Nondurable Goods	2,329	26,261	511,273
Retail	16,797	174,947	1,569,548
Building Materials & Garden Supplies	995	7,072	100,445
General Merchandise Stores	404	20,902	185,404
Food Stores	1,766	25,667	251,873
Automotive Dealers & Service Stations	1,300	13,925	255,824
Apparel & Accessory Stores	1,429	9,601	73,260
Furniture & Home Furnishings Stores	1,214	6,794	90,556
Eating & Drinking Places	4,186	61,638	333,666
Miscellaneous Retail	3,376	16,268	143,951

As the major retail center in the state, Wichita has nearly 50% more stores, and twice as many sales and employees as Lawrence and Topeka combined.

The retail establishments that generated the most sales in 1990 were automotive dealerships, with more than $3.8 billion in retail sales, and grocery stores, which accounted for more than $3.4 billion in sales. The volume of retail sales in Kansas in 1990 was $16.6 billion.

Source: Sales & Marketing Management's "Survey of Buying Power, Demographics USA, 1991."

Retail Sales Generated in Kansas

In 1990, the two types of retail establishments generating the most sales were food stores (grocery stores, etc.) and automotive dealerships. The Kansas City metropolitan area lead the state, accounting for over 78% of all retail sales, but this figure also includes sales from the Missouri portion of the Kansas City metropolitan statistical area.

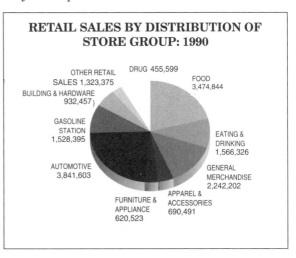

RETAIL SALES BY DISTRIBUTION OF STORE GROUP: 1990

OTHER RETAIL SALES 1,323,375
DRUG 455,599
FOOD 3,474,844
BUILDING & HARDWARE 932,457
GASOLINE STATION 1,528,395
EATING & DRINKING 1,566,326
AUTOMOTIVE 3,841,603
GENERAL MERCHANDISE 2,242,202
FURNITURE & APPLIANCE 620,523
APPAREL & ACCESSORIES 690,491

communication

*A lineman for
Southwestern Bell
Telephone feeds cable
for telephone service.*

Photo courtesy of
Southwestern Bell Telephone.

Employment

More than 57,028 Kansans are employed in the
transportation, communications, and utilities
industries. More than one-third work in
trucking and warehousing and about 25% in
communications. These two industries account
for more than 72% of the establishments in the
state's economic sector and more than 55% of
the annual payroll generated in this economic
sector.

Southwestern Bell
employs 4,636 people
statewide.

Source: "1989 County
Business Patterns," U.S.
Department of Commerce,
Bureau of the Census.

ESTABLISHMENTS, EMPLOYEES, AND ANNUAL PAYROLL OF TRANSPORTATION, COMMUNICATIONS, AND UTILITY COMPANIES IN KANSAS: 1989		
	Establishments	Employees	Annual Payroll ($ 000)
ALL INDUSTRIES	3,221	57,028	1,493,709
Local & Interurban Passenger Transit	114	2,859	22,692
Trucking & Warehousing	1,763	18,881	416,433
Water Transportation	11	44	609
Transportation by Air	84	3,539	89,579
Pipe Lines, Except Natural Gas	33	750	27,234
Transportation Services	289	2,485	44,707
Communication	567	14,290	406,919
Electric, Gas & Sanitary Services	309	10,326	336,244

QUICK FACTS:

In 1917, there was reported to be a car for every 13 people living in the state.

There are 124,068 miles of rural highway in Kansas.

In 1988 there was 576 Billion cubic feet of natural gas marketed in the state of Kansas with a value of $781 million.

In a comparison of nearby states, Kansas ranked in the middle for deaths resulting from motor vehicle accidents in 1989 with 426 deaths. Missouri had the highest death rate of 1,052.

Compared to its neighboring states, Kansas ranked fourth in gas utility customers and revenues, and fourth in sales.

Kansas has only one nuclear power plant — the Wolf Creek Generating Station located near Burlington in southeast Kansas. Wolf Creek provided a net power generation of almost 7 billion kiloWatts in 1986.

Source: Statistical Abstract of the United States, 1991, U.S. Department of Commerce, Bureau of the Census.

Motor Vehicle Registrations

While the number of vehicles registered in Kansas has increased more than 40% since 1970, its share of total U.S. vehicle registrations has declined slightly. According to 1989 estimates, Kansas is fifth among nearby states in total number of registered vehicles. In 1989, there were 2,237,000 motor vehicles registered in Kansas.

Number of Highway Miles

Kansas has more miles of rural highway (a total of 124,068 miles) than any of its neighboring states. The state has 8,897 miles of urban highways. Kansas has 8,923 miles of total primary federal-aid highway miles, and ranks second behind Iowa in comparison with its neighboring states.

Motor Vehicle Deaths

Since 1970, motor vehicle accident deaths in Kansas have declined by nearly 27%. In 1970, there were 684 deaths from motor vehicle accidents in Kansas. By 1990 that figure had decreased to 472 deaths.

Utilities

In 1989, there were 825,000 gas utility customers in Kansas. The recorded total sales were 141 trillion Btu. Total revenues in Kansas were $542 million.

NUCLEAR POWER PLANTS AND THEIR CAPACITIES IN KANSAS AND NEIGHBORING STATES: 1991

	NUMBER OF UNITS	NET SUMMER CAPABILITY (mil kW)	NET GENERATION (mil kWh)
U.S.	108	94.7	529,355
Colorado	1	0.2	8,380
% of U.S.	.9%	0.2%	1.6%
Iowa	1	0.5	40,196
% of U.S.	.9%	0.5%	7.6%
KANSAS	1	1.1	—
% of U.S.	.9%	1.2%	—
Missouri	1	1.1	10,926
% of U.S.	.9%	1.2%	2.1%
Nebraska	2	1.3	—
% of U.S.	1.9%	1.4%	—

Construction Costs

For all metropolitan areas in Kansas, the labor costs of construction are below the national average, ranging from 75% of the average in Wichita to 96% of the average in Kansas City. Likewise, materials costs are also below the national average, ranging from 81% of the average in Wichita to 91% of the average in Kansas City.

QUICK FACTS:

In 1987, the total Kansas construction receipts were over $4.2 billion, with more than $2.8 billion from new construction. Single family residences accounted for the largest segment of building activity in the state.

KANSAS CONSTRUCTION RECEIPTS: 1987
(Thousands of Dollars)

	TOTAL	NEW CONSTRUCTION	MAINTENANCE & REPAIR
TOTAL CONSTRUCTION	4,291,125	2,809,926	513,758
BUILDING CONSTRUCTION	2,908,206	1,967,320	339,665
Single Family Houses	890,121	639,785	123,596
Apartment Bldgs W/ Two or More Apts	125,555	98,898	8,542
Other Residential Buildings	60,536	41,238	8,173
Office Buildings	395,857	278,008	26,965
Farm Buildings	38,577	26,837	9,163
Industrial Buildings & Warehouses	442,130	280,492	67,336
Stores, Restaurants, Car Garages, etc.	420,715	286,021	37,632
Religious Buildings	128,851	101,443	8,080
Educational Buildings	160,635	86,083	21,640
Hospitals & Institutional Buildings	167,335	91,699	17,770
Amusement, Social, and Recreat'l Bldgs	19,455	11,159	4,362
Other Nonresidential Buildings	40,519	25,657	6,406
NONBUILDING CONSTRUCTION	1,247,165	842,605	174,093
Highways, Streets, & Related Facilities	521,115	330,310	82,287
Bridges, Tunnels, & Elevated Highways	145,045	113,960	8,097
Dam & Reservoir Construction	31,702	28,702	(D)
Parking areas including private driveways	41,241	28,669	4,040
Power & Communications Lines, Towers, etc.	78,308	42,400	8,091
Sewers, Water Mains, & Related Projects	141,806	107,812	18,913
Pipeline, Other than Sewer or Water	30,532	23,400	4,476
Sewage & Water Treatment Plants	49,983	28,569	2,201
Earthmoving, nonbuilding	27,090	19,785	1,529
Heavy Industrial Facilities	62,044	(D)	(D)
Other Nonbuilding Construction	118,920	19,139	10,175
Construction Work, n.s.k.	135,755	(NA)	(NA)

(D) - data withheld to avoid disclosure of individual firms

Source: Census of Construction, 1987, U.S. Bureau of the Census.

QUICK FACTS:

The Kansas City metropolitan area is the second largest railroad hub in the nation.

Employment

More than 58,000 Kansans are employed in the finance, insurance, and real estate sector of the economy. The banking industry is the largest employer, and real estate brokers and insurance carriers are also important. The annual payroll of the 5,515 establishments in this sector represents an injection of $1.1 billion annually to the Kansas economy.

ESTABLISHMENTS, EMPLOYEES, AND ANNUAL PAYROLL OF FINANCE, INSURANCE, AND REAL ESTATE COMPANIES IN KANSAS: 1989

	Establishments	Employees	Annual Payroll ($ 000)
ALL INDUSTRIES	5,515	58,080	1,313,900
Banking	841	19,507	396,718
Credit Agencies other than Banks	460	5,336	124,467
Security, Commodity Brokers & Services	231	1,275	50,964
Insurance Carriers	485	10,579	266,855
Insurance Agents, Brokers & Service	1,434	6,337	123,713
Real Estate	1,646	11,012	146,819
Holding & Other Investment Offices	230	3,486	124,522

Source: "1989 County Business Patterns," U.S. Bureau of the Census.

Kansas banks have total deposits of nearly $25 billion.

Source: Operating Banks and Branches Data Book, Federal Deposit Insurance Corporation, June 30, 1990.

Commercial Banking Industry

Kansas has 561 banks with 950 branches and total deposits of approximately $25 billion. While banking operations are concentrated in Wichita and Topeka, with 21.8% of the state's total bank deposits, more than 75% of the total bank deposits are distributed throughout the state in many smaller banks. Some Kansas assets are also included in the Kansas City, Mo., figures. Among its neighboring states, Kansas ranked first in 1989 in number of banks but third in total deposits. Wichita has the most banks and banking offices.

KANSAS INSURED BANKS AND DOMESTIC BRANCHES OF FOREIGN BANKS, AND THEIR DEPOSITS FOR METROPOLITAN STATISTICAL AREAS: JUNE 1990

METROPOLITAN STATISTICAL AREA	NUMBER OF BANKS	NUMBER OF BANKING OFFICES	TOTAL DEPOSITS ($ 000)
KANSAS	561	950	25,062,489
Lawrence	5	13	229,944
Topeka	12	54	1,522,237
Wichita	12	54	3,006,838

Atchison Area Chamber of Commerce, P.O. Box 126, Atchison 66002; (913) 367-2427.
Butler County Economic Development Board 18 S. Main St., P.O. Box 590, El Dorado 67042; (316) 321-2668.
Dodge City Area Chamber of Commerce, 4th & Spruce St., P.O. Box 939, Dodge City 67801; (316) 227-3119.
Economic Development Group, 431 Court, Clay Center 67432; (913) 632-5974.
Emporia Area Chamber of Commerce, 427 Commercial, P.O. Box 417, Emporia 66801; (316) 342-1600.
Garden City Area Chamber of Commerce, 201 E. Laurel, Garden City 67846; (316) 276-3264.
Georgia-Pacific Corporation, P.O. Box 187, Blue Rapids 66411.
Great Bend Chamber of Commerce, 1307 Williams, P.O. Box 400, Great Bend 67530; (316) 792-2401.
Goodland Area Chamber of Commerce, 104 W. 11th St., P.O. Box 628, Goodland 67735; (913) 899-7130.
Greater Hutchinson Convention and Visitors Bureau, 309 N. Main, Hutchinson 67501; (316) 662-3391.
Independence Chamber of Commerce, 322 N. Penn, P.O. Box 386, Independence 67301; (316) 331-1890.
Johnson County Community College, Business & Industry Institute, 12345 College at Quivira, Overland Park 66210; (913) 469-3845.
Junction City Area Chamber of Commerce, 425 N. Washington, P.O. Box 5A, Junction City 66441; (913) 762-2632.
Kansas City, Kansas Area Chamber of Commerce, 727 Minnesota Ave., P.O. Box 171337, Kansas City 66117; (913) 371-3070.
Kansas Corporation Commission, 4th Floor Docking State Office Building, Topeka 66612; (913) 296-3324.
Kansas Department of Commerce, Suite 500 Capitol Tower, 400 S.W. 8th, Topeka 66612; (913) 296-3481.
Kansas Department of Human Resources, 401 S.W. Topeka Blvd., Topeka 66603; (913) 296-5317.
Kansas Department of Transportation, 7th Floor, Docking State Office Building, Topeka 66612; (913) 296-3566.
Kansas Directory of Commerce, 1992, The Wichita Eagle and Beacon Publishing Co., 825 E. Douglas, Wichita 67202.
Kansas Inc., Suite 113, Capitol Tower, 400 S.W. 8th, Topeka 66603; (913) 296-1460.
Kansas State Board of Agriculture, 901 S. Kansas, Topeka 66612; (913) 296-3556.
Kansas State Chamber of Commerce, 500 Bank IV Tower, Topeka 66603; (913) 357-6321.
Kansas Technology Enterprise Corporation, 112 W. 6th, Suite 400, Topeka 66603; (913) 296-5272.
Lawrence Chamber of Commerce, 209 W. 8th St., P.O. Box 581, Lawrence 66044; (913) 4843-4411.
Leavenworth-Lansing Area Chamber of Commerce, 518 Shawnee St., P.O. Box 44, Leavenworth 66048; (913) 682-4113.
Lenexa Chamber of Commerce, 11900 W. 87th St. Pkwy., #115, P.O. Box 14244, Lenexa 66215; (913) 888-1414.
Lenexa Economic Development Council, 8700 Monrovia, Suite 300, P.O. Box 14244, Lenexa 66215; (913) 888-1826.
Liberal Area Chamber of Commerce, 505 N. Kansas, P.O. Box 676, Liberal 67905; (316) 624-3855.

Liberal Economic Development Department, 700 Terminal Ave. - Municipal
Airport, Liberal 67905; (316) 626-0156.
Mid-Kansas Economic Development Commission, 2015 Lakin, Great Bend 67530;
(316) 792-1375.
"Operating Banks and Branches Data Book," June 30, 1990, Federal Deposit Insurance
Corporation.
Ottawa Area Chamber of Commerce, 109 E. Second, P.O. Box Q, Ottawa 66067;
(913) 242-1000.
Overland Park Chamber of Commerce, 10975 Benson #350, P.O. Box 12125, Overland
Park 66212; (913) 491-3600.
South Central Kansas Economic Development District, Inc., River Park Place, Suite 580,
727 N. Waco, Wichita 67203; (316) 262-5246.
Survey of Buying Power: Demographics USA, 1991, by "Sales and Marketing
Management Magazine", Market Statistics, 633 Third Avenue, New York, NY
10164-0615.
Topeka Community & Economic Development Department, 820 Quincy, Suite
501, Topeka 66612; (913) 234-0072.
Topeka Chamber of Commerce, Division of Economic Development, 120 E. Sixth,
Three Townsite Plaza, Topeka 66603; (913) 234-2644.
U.S. Department of Commerce, Bureau of the Census,
— **1987 Census of Manufacturers,** Geographic Area Series;
— **1990 Census of Population,** Summary Tape File 3;
— **1989 County Business Patterns;**
— **Statistical Abstract of the United States, 1991**
WI/SE Partnership for Growth, Marketing & Business Development, 350 W. Douglas,
Wichita 67202; (316) 265-2095.
Wichita Area Chamber of Commerce, 350 W. Douglas, Wichita 67202; (316) 265-7771.

PLACES

KANSAS

PLACES

Dodge City Feature • Lindsborg
Feature • Lucas Feature • Wamego
Feature • Attractions

Photo courtesy of Lindsborg Chamber of Commerce.

Dodge City Days
159

As the buffalo hunters departed, the cattle drives began. Dodge City became known as the "Queen of the Cowtowns."

Swedish Tradition
160

The Messiah Festival with over 400 participants is held each year between Palm Sunday and Easter in Lindsborg.

Strange but True
161

Lucas is home to the strange and wonderful Garden of Eden. Listed on the National Register of Historic Places, it has been featured in *People* magazine and *Ripley's Believe It or Not.*

Dutch Mill
162

The Old Dutch Mill in Wamego grinds grain once more and visitors may purchase the Old Dutch Mill flour.

Attractions
163-181

The Davis Memorial in Hiawatha is just one of the many unusual and interesting attractions in the state.

CHAPTER OPENER PHOTO: *Mills like this once occupied streams and waterways across Kansas; now they are a rare sight. In Lindsborg, Kansas, the Old Mill Museum offers visitors a glimpse of how this mill was used and what life was like at the time.*

F rom the unusual to the breathtaking, it's here in Kansas. Kansas
achieved its reputation in the early years of its statehood from
the character of the towns and cities that dotted its plains. Over
the years Kansas has become known as a barren wasteland, the boom
and bust of the 1800s taking its toll on the state. Today this image is
far from accurate. The character of these original Kansas towns is still
evident.

In the heartland of America there are attractions tucked away in
towns and cities that offer pleasant surprises for both citizens and
visitors. Although the varying landscapes of Kansas are enough to
delight visitors, the attractions one will find in the state add to the
state's appeal. From the small towns of western Kansas to the
bustling districts of the cities, there are countless places to be
discovered throughout the state. Visitors can enjoy many interesting
sights while traveling the main thoroughfares of the state. However,
for a unique glimpse of Kansas, the small communities off the beaten
path are well worth the effort.

Kansas offers a wide variety of attractions from nature trails and
historic sites to such modern exhibits as the Cosmosphere and Space
Center in Hutchinson. The wild west comes alive in places like Dodge
City and Abilene where visitors can experience firsthand the atmosphere of a thriving cowtown. A town with Old World charm and strong
cultural heritage is Lindsborg, located in the south central section of
the state. For those interested in the unusual, Lucas offers the unique
Garden of Eden, which has become known worldwide as a folk art
wonder. In keeping its past alive, the small town of Wamego offers a
special attraction that is still being used today, the Old Dutch Mill.

To really experience Kansas, visitors should make a point of
traveling the backroads. Places such as Great Bend, Hiawatha,
Newton, and Liberal offer unique getaways that will leave visitors
with a glimpse of Americana.

Larger cities such as Kansas City, Topeka, and Wichita offer a
metropolitan blend of historical and contemporary attractions such as
parks, zoos, race tracks, and observatories.

Kansas has an extremely diverse collection of attractions, literally
something for everyone. For those looking toward nature, there are
state parks which offer camping and fishing and the opportunity to get
away from it all. Cheyenne Bottoms is a wildlife preserve known for
its numerous species of migrating waterfowl. Natural landmarks such
as Castle Rock and Rock City present a different look at Kansas'
landscape and its naturally sculpted rock formations.

Historical buildings and attractions can be found in every corner of
the state and these structures depict the pioneer heritage and growth
of many Kansas towns. Some of the most interesting attractions in the
country can be found in Kansas. From wild west to state of the art,
Kansas offers a striking blend of scenic wonders. ❐

High Strung | Cawker City is the site of the oldest pipe organ in Kansas, located in the Baptist Church. The World's Largest Ball of Twine, which weighs over 7 tons, is also located in Cawker City.

Holly-Woodson | In its heyday, the Woodson Hotel in Yates Center accommodated such notable guests as singing cowboy Gene Autry and Buffalo Bill and his Medicine Show.

A Lofty Record | The St. John's Catholic Church in Beloit was built in 1901 and is believed to be the first church in the United States featuring flying buttresses. It is on the National Registry of Historic Places.

The Mouse Struck One | The Old Town Clock, located in downtown Hiawatha, is the only such clock between Indianapolis and Denver on U.S. Hwy. 36.

School Days | Yates Center has had 100 graduating classes as of 1989.

Tagged | Kansas won the award for Most Beautiful License Plate for the "wheat plate" in 1981.

Countdown | Pittsburg has the distinction of being the home of all the microfilm census data collected from 1900 through 1980 housed at the Census Bureau.

'Tis the Season | Potwin Place in Topeka is an area of historical Victorian homes. Each Christmas the homeowners put up ornate decorations for an old-fashioned holiday season.

High Water | The limestone water tower in Paradise was built in 1936.

Shirley Not | Cloud County was originally named Shirley County but was changed in 1867 to Cloud County. Citizens of "Shirley" protested the name as it was also the name of a well-known "lady of the evening" in the Junction City area at the time.

Historic Kansas Cowtown

Dodge City may be remembered as one of the wildest towns in the west. Founded in 1872 the town got its reputation from early buffalo hunters, cowboys and travelers who eagerly participated in all the activities a young cowtown could offer.

For five years, Dodge was known as the Buffalo Capital. Two-thirds of the town's population were buffalo hunters. A hunter could easily make more than $100 a day. But soon the market was flooded with hides, and buffalo carcasses littered the Plains. During hard times, farmers gathered the buffalo bones and sold them for $6 to $8 a ton.

As the buffalo hunters departed, the cattle drives began. Dodge City became known as the "Queen of the Cowtowns." Dodge's cattle era was the longest of any of the cowtowns. When the cowboys reached Dodge, they had been on the trail for two or three months. They collected their pay, which was $30 to $40 a month, and set out to spend it all on a good time.

Photo courtesy of Dodge City Convention and Visitors Bureau.

Historic Front Street - Dodge City, Kansas

Dodge was inhabited by such top-notch lawmen and gunfighters as Wyatt Earp; Bat, Ed and Jim Masterson; Doc Holliday; Bill Tilghman; Clay Allison; Ben and Billy Thompson; and Luke Short.

One of the most famous attractions at Dodge City is Boot Hill. In 1872, two cowboys camped on a hillside, had a gunfight, and one was killed. The dead man, friendless and unknown, was wrapped in a blanket by townsmen and buried where he fell, with his boots on. Due to Dodge's wild reputation it became the perfect subject matter for movies. The television series "Gunsmoke" and the 1939 movie "Dodge City" starring Errol Flynn and Olivia de Havilland were both about the wild west days of the town.

Dodge City today offers a wonderful opportunity to look at how the "Old West" really functioned. There are live demonstrations as well as gunfights and the famous Long Branch Variety Show. Some points of interest are: Front Street, Boot Hill Museum, Old Santa Fe Trail Monument, Cowboy statue on Boot Hill, The Home of Stone, and more. *For more information call (316) 227-2176.* ❑

lindsborg

Holding on to Tradition

In 1868 a group of immigrants left Sweden to make a new home in America's heartland. Here they settled in the Smoky Hill River Valley where they established the community of Lindsborg.

A well-known symbol of Swedish tradition is the Dala Horse (Dalahast). Long winter evenings with little to do, coupled with the availability of wood scraps, bred the development of the Dala Horse. The Dala Horse epitomizes one of the only "living" Swedish traditions.

Several Swedish celebrations are held throughout the year for visitors to participate in at Lindsborg. Midsummer's Day Festival is the celebration welcoming the return of summer on the third Saturday of June. The Svensk Hyllningsfest is a three-day biennial tribute to the Swedish pioneers celebrated in October of odd-numbered years. The St.

Photo courtesy of Lindsborg Chamber of Commerce.

Painting a Dala Horse - Lindsborg, Kansas

Lucia Festival ushers in the Christmas season with live Christmas music and the crowning of St. Lucia on the second Saturday in December. The Messiah Festival is held each year between Palm Sunday and Easter. For over 100 years, the nationally known 400-voice Bethany College Oratorio Society has performed classical pieces.

Lindsborg is home to two distinguished folk dancing groups The Lindsborg Swedish Folk Dancers and The Lindsborg Folkdanslag Dancers. Both wear traditional Swedish folk costumes many of which are family heirlooms.

Also located at Lindsborg is Bethany College, which was founded by Swedish pioneers. The college has a century of tradition in academic excellence and notable pursuits in the fine arts.

Main Street in Lindsborg offers a wide variety of unique shopping experiences. Stroll downtown and you'll find an outstanding selection of Scandinavian imports, original arts and crafts and full service shopping accented by the colorful personality of Old World storefronts and charm.

For more information about Lindsborg, Kansas, contact: Lindsborg Chamber of Commerce, 104 East Lincoln, P.O. Box 191, Lindsborg, 67456-0191. Phone: (913) 227-3706. ❑

Next Best Thing to Paradise

Many times, special places are found off the beaten path. One such place can be found in Lucas, Kan., in Russell County. Founded in 1887, Lucas is located just 16 miles north of I-70 at the Junction of K-18 and K-232, where visitors can discover a wonderful surprise. Lucas is a small town of 600 and is proud of its heritage.

Lucas is home to the strange and wonderful Garden of Eden. Listed on the National Register of Historic Places, it has been featured in *People* magazine and in *Ripley's Believe It or Not.* Created by S.P. Dinsmoor, this has become one of the most unusual attractions in Kansas. In 1907, at age 64, he began construction of the Stone Log Cabin Home. Mr. Dinsmoor built his home of native limestone and cut each stone in the shape of logs in a log cabin. He quarried the stone and hauled it by wagon to the site. Over the next 22 years, in the yard surrounding the house, Mr. Dinsmoor constructed the Garden of Eden, containing among other things, trees, flower beds, human figures, animals, and more. All these things are sculpted in cement, and by 1927 he had used over 113 tons or about 2,273 sacks of cement.

Photo by Jon Blumb.

The Garden of Eden - Lucas, Kansas

Mr. Dinsmoor even had live animals on display ranging from coyotes to an eagle. To the east of the Cabin Home, Mr. Dinsmoor built a 40-foot high mausoleum. He also built his own coffin using cement. Mr. Dinsmoor continued working on the Garden of Eden until his death in 1932.

Today visitors can tour the house and grounds. The house has been preserved, including all the furnishings Mr. Dinsmoor made for the home, and looks just as it did when the Dinsmoor family lived there. The Garden of Eden has become a haven for artists and is known nationwide as a folk art masterpiece. Visitors from all over the country and overseas have flocked to The Garden of Eden to see this unique creation.

The Garden of Eden is open daily March through November. For more information call (913) 525-6395. ❏

Wamego
KANSAS

Original Mill Once Again Grinds Grain

Wamego, located on the banks of the Kansas River, was originally a child of the Kansas Pacific Railroad and today offers a unique blend of progressive spirit and hometown tradition.

The most famous attraction in Wamego is the Old Dutch Mill. A Dutch immigrant, John Schonhoff, began constructing the mill in the early 1870s on his farm. The mill was 40 feet high and 25 feet in diameter at the base. It was completed in 1879. The family-operated mill did custom grinding of feed and flour for a few years. In the late 1880s the Schonhoffs ceased operating the mill.

The next owner of the property was Ed Regnier. In 1924, A.M. Bittmann and Forest Leach, had the idea of moving the mill to the city park. On June 6, the mill was taken down one stone at a time. The mill's reconstruction was completed on Aug. 14, 1925. Since then the mill has stood as an attraction in the Wamego City Park and until 1988 had not been functioning. On July 1, 1988, the mill was put back in service and now grinds grain once more and visitors may purchase the Old Dutch Mill flour.

Other attractions in Wamego include the White Chapel School built in 1882, Log Cabin, and a 120-year-old stone jail originally located in Louisville, Kan. These historic structures can be found in Wamego's city park.

Photo courtesy of Wamego Chamber of Commerce.

The Old Dutch Mill - Wamego, Kansas

Several special events take place in the town throughout the year. In April the Tulip Festival is celebrated. There are Dutch-style crafts, foods, entertainment and thousands of tulips. The Fourth of July celebration features a parade, community picnic, antique car show, a four-day carnival and a giant fireworks display. Wamego's Oktoberfest is held the first Saturday of each October. The day-long event features crafts and ethnic foods.

For more information contact: Wamego Chamber of Commerce P.O. Box 34, Wamego, Kansas 66547. Phone: (913) 456-7849. ❏

KANSAS

Abilene

Antique Doll Museum. Collection of bisque, china, wooden, and tin dolls on display.
C.W. Parker Carousel. Complete handcarved working carousel manufactured in Abilene at the turn of the century by the C.W. Parker Amusement Co. This national landmark is powered by its original steam engine.
Eisenhower Center. The Center's library and museum depict the military and civilian careers of Dwight D. Eisenhower. Also on display is the home where President Eisenhower lived as a boy, and the burial site in The Place of Meditation.
The Kirby House. The restored Thomas Kirby mansion, built in 1885, includes a fine historic restaurant.
Lebold-Vahsholtz Mansion. Twenty-three room Victorian mansion built in 1881 by C.H. Lebold, early Abilene banker. Listed on the National Register of Historic Places. Tours available.
Seelye Mansion. The mansion was built in 1905 by Dr. A.B. Seelye, patent medicine entrepreneur. The 25-room Georgian style mansion includes eleven bedrooms, a bowling alley, ballroom, and captain's walk.

Argonia

The Historic Salter House. This was the home of the first woman mayor in the world, Susanna Madora Salter. The Salter House, which was constructed in 1883, has been restored. The adjacent nine-room brick museum in the old Mayfield church holds antiques and artifacts of the area. Listed on the National Registry of Historic Places.

Ashland

Big Basin and Little Basin. The geographic sink holes lie a few miles west of Ashland.
St. Jacobs Well. The well is a mysterious wonder that is considered by many people to be bottomless. The pool is 125 feet across and its depth has never been determined, despite numerous attempts.

QUICK FACTS:

Abilene was one of the famous names of the early West and was the first cattle boom town. It was the end of the famous Texas Cattle Trail and the western terminus of the railroad in the days of the overland cattle drives.

The Rawlins County Museum in Atwood includes a 28-foot mural painted by Rudolph Wendelin, creator of Smokey the Bear. The mural depicts pioneering history.

In September 1901, Abilene was quarantined because of smallpox.

Burlington is the headquarters for the Country Critter animal puppets company. Almost 1,000 puppets are made each day.

Butler County, located in the southcentral part of the state, contains the most square miles of any county in Kansas.

163

attractions

Atchison

Amelia Earhart Birthplace. Constructed in 1861, this is the birthplace of Amelia Earhart and is undergoing restoration.

International Forest of Friendship. This forest is dedicated to those contributing to all facets of the advancement of aviation. There are trees from the 50 states, U.S. territories and 33 countries. A special grove includes a tree from George Washington's Mt. Vernon estate.

Athol

Home on the Range Cabin. Dr. Brewster Higley wrote the words to "Home on the Range," the state song of Kansas, in this cabin. The present cabin is a restoration of the Brewster home.

Baldwin

Midland Historical Railway. A renovated diesel-engine which pulls vintage railroad cars offers a six-mile round trip from the Baldwin Depot. The 1906 depot has welcomed Presidents Taft and Teddy Roosevelt.

Parmenter Hall. Baker University. This was the first building located on the campus proper. Construction began in 1881 and was completed with a $100 donation from Abraham Lincoln. This building is still in use by the University.

Beeler

George Washington Carver Memorial. The monument marks the northeast corner of Carver's former homestead. Carver was a scientist/benefactor who rose from slavery to fame.

Belle Plaine

Belle Plaine Arboretum. This 20-acre park is the only mature arboretum between the Mississippi River and the Rocky Mountains and features flowers, shrubs, trees, and grasses from around the world. During the last full weekend in April, the community hosts "Tulip Time," when 30,000 tulips are in bloom.

Bonner Springs

Agriculture Hall of Fame and National Farmers Memorial. The hall is a shrine to America's rich history of agriculture. Thousands of relics including a barbed wire collection, farm implements, antique cars and trucks, and tools are on display. The National Farmers Memorial features three large, high-relief bronze panels weighing 1½ tons each.

Beloit

Mitchell County Courthouse. The courthouse was built in 1901 at the cost of $38,310. The Richardsonian-Romanesque limestone building features ornate fireplaces and granite pillars.

Cawker City

Oldest Pipe Organ in Kansas. The pipe organ can be seen at the Baptist Church. **World's Largest Ball of Twine.** The twine is housed in an octagonal building and the ball of twine weighs over 7 tons.

Coffeyville

The Brown Mansion. This restored three story mansion was built in 1904 by W.P. Brown, an early natural gas and oil developer. The mansion has the family's original furnishings and features Tiffany glass.

Photo courtesy of Coffeyville Convention & Visitors Bureau.

QUICK FACTS:

Humbolt was the home of the Vegetarian Colony. It was established in the spring of 1856 by a group of almost 100 easterners who were attracted by promoters' advertisements. They experienced endless hardships. Stoves, utensils, and farm implements were inadequate; food was scarce; and clouds of mosquitoes made life unbearable. The colony lasted less than a year.

The first trading post in Kansas, Four Houses, was established within Bonner Springs in 1812.

Visitors to Coffeyville can walk over the actual threshold as did the Dalton Gang to rob the First National Bank on Oct. 5, 1892. Members of the Dalton Gang were killed during the famous Dalton Raid on that day.

The steamer "City of Erie," which carried 60 passengers on river excursions, was built in Chanute in 1899.

One of the beautiful attractions in Kansas, the Brown Mansion in Coffeyville, features original furnishings and Tiffany glass.

165

attractions

QUICK FACTS:

Conway Springs is best known for its mineral springs. Water from Conway Springs is bottled and sold to hospitals, businesses, and homes across the region.

The Harvey County area boasts one of the largest Mennonite populations in the United States.

The hot and cold water towers in Pratt were built between 1900 and 1910. Few towns in the country have their own hot and cold water towers.

The Nazareth Convent and Academy in Concordia, Kansas, is a splendid example of Gothic architecture.

An estimated 850,000 buffalo hides were shipped from Dodge City from 1872-1874.

Columbus

Clock Tower. This 1919 Seth Thomas Clock is believed to be the only one of its kind now operating. It was originally placed in the tower of the 1889 courthouse and is now on display in its new 40-foot tower.

Concordia

Brown Grand Opera House. The opera house has an original painting of Napoleon on the drop curtain that was revealed in 1907 during the opening night. Today the opera house serves as a stage for cultural plays and concerts.

Photo courtesy of Concordia Chamber of Commerce.

Nazareth Convent and Academy. The structure was built in 1906 and served as Motherhouse for the Sisters of St. Joseph, not only in Kansas, but for seven other states and one foreign country, Brazil. The four-storied limestone and red brick structure is of Gothic style throughout. National Register of Historic Places. Tours by appointment.

Dodge City

Boot Hill Museum and Front Street. Attractions include the Long Branch Saloon, original Boot Hill Cemetery, Fort Dodge Jail, one-room schoolhouse, a melodrama and medicine show, stagecoach rides, gunfights, and western chuckwagon dinner.

Cattle Feedlot Overlook. Visitors get a view of the cattle industry today in one of the largest operations in southwest Kansas.
The Coronado Cross and Park. A 38-foot cross marks the site where Francisco Vasques de Coronado, a Spanish explorer, crossed the Arkansas River in search of the fabled cities of gold in 1541. The cross was erected in June 1975.
Cowboy Statue on Boot Hill. Dodge City's oldest monument is a tribute to the early day cowboy. The inscription reads: "On the ashes of my campfire this city is built."
Dodge City Zoo. A children's zoo contains animals of North America and a petting farm.
El Capitan. A bronze statue by Jasper D'Ambrosi commemorating the 1870s Texas cattle drives to Dodge City. The statue in Dodge City faces south, and an identical statue in Abilene, Texas, faces north. The two statues symbolize the beginning and end of the long-horned cattle drives.
Home of Stone. Listed on the National Register of Historic Sites. The native limestone home was begun in 1879 by bootmaker John Mueller.

El Dorado

Teter Nature Trail. Located at El Dorado Lake, the trail is three-quarters of a mile long and winds through eight acres of land known as the Butler County Historical Society Wilderness Area. Visitors can see native grasses, large timber trees, a pawpaw patch, and many types of vines.

Elkhart

Cimarron National Grasslands. The U.S. Forest Service maintains a healthy ecosystem here suitable for grassland agriculture, public recreation, and wildlife habitat. Tourists can go on a self-guided automobile tour.

QUICK FACTS:

El Capitan in Dodge City commemorates the 1870s cattle drives.

Photo courtesy of Dodge City Convention & Visitors Bureau.

The Murdock House in El Dorado, now a private residence, was the longtime home of Thomas Benton Murdock, publisher of the El Dorado Republican. The house was a frequent meeting place for such literary figures as William Allen White and Edna Ferber.

PLACES
attractions
KANSAS

QUICK FACTS:

Emporia was named after a historic Greek market center on the African Coast of the Mediterranean Sea.

Fort Riley was originally called Camp Center because it was believed to be near the geographical center of the country. On June 27, 1853, it was renamed Fort Riley in honor of Major General Bennet Riley who led the first protective military escort along the Santa Fe Trail.

Beginning in 1905, the Erie Manufacturing Company built the then-newly patented Atlas windmills.

Garden City was so named because of the beautiful garden of Mrs. William D. Fulton, one of the town's founders.

Ellis

Walter P. Chrysler Boyhood Home. Look into the early life during the 1800s of Chrysler Corporation's founder.

Emporia

Emporia State University Campus. Points of interest include the Peterson Planetarium and Ross Natural History Reservation, which may be viewed by appointment. Also visit the Eppink Art Gallery, a one-room school, and the Schmidt Natural History Museum.
Emporia Zoo. The zoo is located in Soden's Grove Park and houses nearly 400 specimens of birds, mammals, and reptiles.
Soden's Grove Bridge. The rainbow arch style bridge, which was built in 1923, spans the Cottonwood River at the site of Soden's Mill.
William Allen White Memorial Drive. Visitors can see the William Allen White Home, the William Allen White Elementary School, the William Allen White Library, the White Memorial Park, the Emporia Gazette, and the William Allen White bust and memorial.

Eskridge

Ludwigshof Winery. This winery features apple, cherry, strawberry, and eldeberry fruit wines. The winery is open Wednesday through Sunday, May through October, for tastings.

Fairway

Shawnee Methodist Mission. The Mission was established in 1830 by Rev. Thomas Johnson. The starting points of the Oregon and Santa Fe Trails passed through the center of the Mission complex.

Garden City

Finney County Wildlife Area. Prairie animals including deer, coyotes, foxes, badgers, quail, and 60 head of buffalo roam freely here.
Lee Richardson Zoo. Features more than 675 animals and birds. Cars are allowed to drive through the zoo area and paths are marked for pedestrians.

168

Windsor Hotel. "The Waldorf of the Prairies" was built in 1886 and its famous guests include Buffalo Bill Cody and Lillian Russell.

Great Bend

Brit Spaugh Park and Zoo. The park includes 46 acres and features a variety of recreational activities, and more than 100 different mammals and birds inhabit the 12 acre zoo.

Cheyenne Bottoms. Numerous species of wildlife including the whooping cranes, bald eagles and peregrine falcons stop by this important waterfowl area in the Flyaway. The name "Cheyenne Bottoms" was said to follow a ferocious battle for hunting grounds between the Cheyenne Indians and the Pawnees in 1825.

Quivira National Wildlife Refuge. Sand dunes, cottonwood trees, and natural grasses harbor around 500,000 birds during spring migrations. Bald eagles, cranes, and geese are just some of the birds that can be seen.

Greensburg

The Pallasite Meteorite. Also on display at the Celestial Museum at the Big Well in Greensburg is the largest meteorite of its kind to survive entry into Earth's atmosphere. The meteorite is half iron and half stone and weighs 1,000 pounds.

World's Largest Hand-Dug Well. The well, which was completed in 1887, is 32 feet in diameter and 109 feet deep. It is cased with a wall of native stone to prevent caving in.

Halstead

The Warkentin Farmstead. The original house, barn, and silo was built by Bernhard Warkentin, who was instrumental in convincing Mennonites to come to Kansas.

Hays

1870s Log Cabin. See the frugal living conditions of one of Kansas' earliest pioneer families.

QUICK FACTS:

For years, Woodson County has been called "The Hay Capital of the World" because of the huge haying operations in the Yates Center, Vernon, Rose and Batesville areas. The rich grasslands need no irrigation and provide excellent grazing for the abundant livestock.

Albert Henley, a mechanic, made the first barbed wire in Kansas when he started a factory in Lawrence. By 1882, he was operating nine machines that made 10,000 pounds of wire a day. Barbed wire changed the frontier and helped small farmers gain a foothold in the Great Plains.

Half-way Park in Kinsley has a sign saying that San Francisco is 1,526 miles west and New York is 1,526 miles east.

attractions

QUICK FACTS:

The original town site of Hiawatha was staked out on February 17, 1857. In 1870, Hiawatha was named after the Indian brave in Longfellow's poem, "Song of Hiawatha."

One of the most unusual and haunting attractions in Kansas is the Davis Memorial at Hiawatha.

Calamity Jane's Wildest House in the West. Learn about the wild era in which Buffalo Bill Cody and Wild Bill Hickok lived in Hays. **Missouri-Pacific Depot.** Glimpse into the daily routine of a train depot.

Hesston

Dyck Arboretum of the Plains. A 25-acre Kansas arboretum. Features both formal demonstration areas and natural settings of prairie plants, flowers, and trees. **Hesston College Bird, Rock, and Mineral Display.** The display houses over 300 birds indigenous to Kansas and an extensive rock and mineral display. **Wheat Bin.** For a tour of this authentic Kansas wheat milling operation and farmstead visit the Wheat Bin and see how Kansas hard winter wheat is ground into whole wheat flour as the Mennonite forefathers did.

Hiawatha

The Davis Memorial. This memorial is one of the nation's most unusual tombs. When Sarah Davis of Hiawatha died in 1930, her husband, John M. Davis, decided to have a memorial erected. The memorial is made of marble and granite and cost an estimated $100,000. The statuary is eleven life-sized figures depicting the Davises at various stages of their marriage. The memorial was featured on *Ripley's Believe It or Not.*

Hutchinson

Amish Community. Southeast of Hutchinson. Visitors are welcome at the gift shops, bakery, and buggy shop.

Photo courtesy of The Topeka Capital-Journal.

Kansas Cosmosphere and Space Center. A space exhibition center that chronicles the U.S. space program. Visitors can see actual moon rock brought back by the Apollo 11 astronauts. A planetarium and Omnimax movie projection theater are also open for viewing.

Independence

Little House on the Prairie. The house is a reproduction of the cabin made famous by the Laura Ingalls Wilder children's books.
Ralph Mitchell Zoo. Features birds and mammals. The park includes a merry-go-round, playground and miniature train.
William Inge Collection. At Independence Community College. Records, tapes, and books from the private collection of Pulitzer-winning playwright William Inge. He wrote **Picnic** and **Splendor in the Grass.**

Iola

General Funston Home. Funston's military career highlights included earning the rank of brigadier general in the U.S. Army for his courageous acts in the Philippines in 1901.

Kanopolis

Faris Caves. The caves are carved out of a Dakota sandstone bluff and were built as a residence, but have also served as a blacksmith shop and schoolhouse. Indian writings are still visible on the walls.

Kansas City

Granada Theater. Concerts, silent films and special events provide countless hours of entertainment at this renovated theater. It houses the only theater organ in the Kansas City area.
John Brown Statue. This life-sized statue was the first full memorial to the martyred abolitionist.
Rosedale Memorial Arch. Modeled after the Arc de Triomphe in Paris, the Arch is dedicated to men who gave their lives in service for our country.

QUICK FACTS:

The Wolcott Building located at 201 N. Main in Hutchinson was completed in 1938. When it was built, it had concealed connections for a new invention: television. The Wolcott Building was the first office building in the state to be air conditioned at the time of construction.

Buffalo bones were used to mark off the early streets of Hutchinson.

Holton was named for E.D. Holton, a Milwaukee abolitionist who promoted an expedition to Kansas in 1856 to help ensure another free state for the Union.

Junction City in Geary County was named because it lies at the junction of the Republican and Smoky Rivers.

PLACES
attractions

KANSAS

QUICK FACTS:

Prairie Dog State Park is located on Keith Sebelius Reservoir in Norton County. An old sod house in the park is restored and furnished with articles of the homestead era.

The Woodlands Racetrack. The first racing complex anywhere to offer greyhound and horse racing at separate facilities, with a track for each type. It also offers both Thoroughbred and Quarter horse racing in the same day. Greyhound season is from May to September. Thoroughbred & Quarter horse racing from August to November.

Photo by Vernon Leat.

Dog racing is just one kind of racing visitors will see at The Woodlands in Kansas City.

Lawrence's city seal shows a phoenix rising from ashes and proclaiming "From ashes to Immortality."

Lawrence

Campanile Bell Tower. A World War II memorial with a 53-bell carillon.

Haskell Indian Junior College. This college began in 1884 and has a national reputation for educating American Indian and Alaska native youth.

Old West Lawrence. This is the location of some of the city's finest 19th century homes. Architecture syles range from Victorian to Italianate to Stone vernacular.

University of Kansas. The 1,000-acre University sits atop Mount Oread. Many of the buildings are constructed of native limestone and the campus overlooks the Kansas and Wakarusa River valleys.

172

QUICK FACTS:

The oldest newspaper in Kansas, so far as continuous publication, is the Leavenworth Times established in March 1857.

Photo by Paul Beaver, The Topeka Capital-Journal.

Watson Library on the University of Kansas Campus is one of the many buildings on Mount Oread. The KU campus encompasses some 1,000 acres.

Leavenworth

Immanuel Chapel. The chapel was built in 1893 and was featured in *Ripley's Believe It or Not* for being the only church at that time to conduct Protestant and Catholic services simultaneously. This church features architecture reminiscent of the early European cathedrals.

The Rookery. Fort Leavenworth on the Main Parade. This home was built in 1832 and is the oldest continuously occupied residence in Kansas. General Douglas MacArthur lived here in the early 1900s. The home also served as the temporary home of the first territorial governor.

Liberal

Dorothy's House. Built between 1907 and 1909, about the same time Frank Baum wrote the story **The Wizard of Oz**. Dorothy's House includes the original model house used in the filming of the 1939 movie "Wizard of Oz," plus an exact reproduction of Dorothy's room, complete with her red slippers and Toto's bed. "The Wizard of Oz" movie is shown daily.

Samson of the Cimarron. It is the largest bridge of its kind in the world. Built in 1938 at a cost of $1.5 million, this 1,269 foot giant spans the the meandering Cimarron River.

In 1906, the first cellhouse of the Leavenworth Federal Penitentiary was opened. Among the famous criminals incarcerated there were Al Capone, Pretty Boy Floyd, and the Birdman of Alcatraz.

Alma in Wabaunsee County was named for a city in Germany from which many of its settlers originated.

During the Christmas season, Russell is known as the "Plaza of the Plains" with over 100 blocks of lights and decorations.

QUICK FACTS:

The first rural telephone line in Kansas was established in Riley County in 1879. Its lines were strung on barbed wire fences for several miles.

Able, the first monkey in space, was born at the Ralph Mitchell Zoo in Independence.

Swedish shops and a unique atmosphere await visitors in Lindsborg, Kansas.

A 500,000 year-old elephant tusk is on display at the Edwards County Historical Museum in Kinsley.

Sam Dinsmoor, creator of the Garden of Eden in Lucas, laid the first cement street paving in town at the intersection in front of his home. The rest of the streets remained dirt.

Lindsborg

Bethany College. The famous Messiah Festival is presented annually the week before Easter. Presser Hall Auditorium features one of the largest pipe organs in the country.

Photo courtesy of Lindsborg Chamber of Commerce.

Downtown Shops. A variety of shops with storefronts designed with native Swedish folk art. Swedish crafts, food, and gifts are available, and guests can see many artists' studios.

Louisburg

Louisburg Cider Mill. The mill is housed in a 120-year-old barn. Visitors can watch the milling process, which is done on an old-fashioned rack and cloth fruit press, as well as sample freshly milled apple cider.

Lucas

Garden of Eden. The man-made "Garden of Eden" was started in 1907 by 64-year-old, Civil War veteran S.P. Dinsmoor. Twenty-two years, native limestone, and over 113 tons of cement went into the construction of this display of art, the Stone Log cabin, and his unusual mausoleum. Featured in *People* magazine and *Ripley's Believe It or Not.*

Manhattan

Kansas State University. The main campus is located in Manhattan. Kansas State University was established in 1863 and was the nation's original land-grant university.

Konza Prairie Research Center. Kansas State University has preserved 8,616 acres of tallgrass prairie and uses the area for study. "Konza" is one of over 100 spellings for the American Indian tribe that lived here in the 1700s; another is "Kansas."

Sunset Zoological Park. The Sunset Zoo began in 1933 and today houses more than 200 animals. The zoo began when the local railroad donated a 52-acre tract of land and two burros.

Medicine Lodge

Carry Nation Home. This residence of out-spoken temperance leader Carry Nation is furnished with many of her personal belongings.

Minneapolis

Rock City. A National Natural Landmark. Rock City features Dakota sandstone concretions that do not appear in such size and number anywhere else in the world. At least 200 concretions occur in three groups, and some of the boulders are 27-feet in diameter. Pictures of the formations appeared in geology textbooks as far back as the 1870s.

Neodesha

Norman No. One Oil Well. The Birthplace of the Mid-Continent Oil Field. From this discovery well the field spread first west, then south to the Gulf of Mexico. The well has been designated a National Historic Landmark. Artifacts from the original construction and a working scale model of Norman #1 can be seen.

QUICK FACTS:

Photo courtesy of Kansas Department of Commerce.

This covered bridge, which is located on private property near McPherson, provides a glimpse of Americana.

Ninety-nine bottles of beer were found in an old wall in the basement of the Gilley store in Minneapolis.

In 1906 the Smith Automobile Company in Topeka contracted with a New York firm to build 130 cars.

attractions

New Cambria

Iron Mound. Located near New Cambria in Saline County. An apparent "mountain" with an elevation of 1,497 feet is visible from I-70 to the south and is capped with greenhorn limestone. The site is the eastern-most extent of outcropping for the Cretaceous limestone in Kansas.

Newton

The Bernhard Warkentin House. Home of Bernhard and Wilhemina Warkentin. With his help, 5,000 Mennonites were settled in Kansas between 1874 and 1884, and the Mennonites brought with them Turkey Red hard winter wheat. His letters encouraged thousands of other Mennonites to settle in Kansas. The house is an example of Victorian period architecture and is furnished with 80% of the original Warkentin family possessions. It is listed on the National Register of Historical Places and the Kansas Register of Historic Places.

500 Main Place. National Register of Historic Places. This building is a fine example of architecture of the American Renaissance. One-foot thick walls support this structure of limestone, granite, marble, and brass.

Granary. Visitors can tour this unique Kansas cottage industry that supplies wheat to wheat weavers throughout America. Learn how the craft originated. Wheat weaving souvenirs are available for purchase.

Newton Station. This railroad station was modeled after Shakespeare's house at Stratford on Avon. It was one of the most important stations on the Santa Fe line. In 1931, Fred Harvey located his Harvey House Restaurant in the station and the second story was a hotel and dormitory for the Harvey Girls.

Norton

Adobe House. Prairie Dog State Park. This adobe house was constructed of mud and straw in the 1890s and is the only adobe house in Kansas still in its original location.

Oakley

Prairie Dog Town. The prairie zoo shows western Kansas wildlife as well as exotic animals. Wildlife displays including deer, donkeys, horses, goats, sheep, raccoons and prairie dogs as well as buffalo, live rattlesnakes and Texas Longhorn cattle. Closed winter months. Tourists are given food to feed tame deer, sheep, goats, prairie dogs, raccoons, foxes and coyotes. Experience seeing native Kansas animals in their natural habitat.

Olathe

Olathe Memorial Cemetery. Many of the pioneers to the area are buried in this cemetery, which also includes a Civil War Circle.
Prairie Center. The center features a natural history lesson on Olathe's tallgrass prairie. A self-guided nature trail gives an overview of the center.

Oswego

Littletown Well. Historic markers at the site give the background of this well.
The Log Cabin. A popular attraction in Oswego and a lesson in history.

Ottawa

Historic Downtown. The Downtown Ottawa Historic District is a block of commercial structures built between 1872 and 1900 of late Victorian styling and Renaissance. The facades have been almost completely unaltered. The block was placed on The National Register of Historic Places on June 29, 1972.

Oxford

Oxford Grist Mill. The over century-old grist mill still processes grain with the power of the rambling Arkansas River.

Pittsburg

Kelce Planetarium. Pittsburg State University. The planetarium is a service and educational facility instructing in sky simulation and space exploration.

QUICK FACTS:

Big Brutus, located outside of Pittsburg, was the world's second-largest electric mining shovel when it was built, and is the only one of its kind. Big Brutus weighs 11 million pounds, or 5,500 tons, and was able to scoop up 150 tons of rock and dirt in a single bite of its giant bucket, enough to fill three railroad cars. It took four cables, each 3 1/2 inches thick, and the thrust of eight 500 horsepower motors to lift the bucket. It is open to the public for viewing.

Osage was named after the Shawnee Indian word meaning "beautiful."

Franklin County is considered to be the Dairy Capital of Kansas.

Just outside the city of Marysville stands the Bronze Pony Express Horse Rider statue. Sculpted by Dr. Richard Bergen of Salina, the work of art comes to life as it appears to thunder along the trail. It was dedicated in 1985 on the 125th anniversary of the Pony Express.

QUICK FACTS:

Legendary Notre Dame football coach Knute Rockne died in a plane crash March 31, 1931, when the plane carrying Rockne and seven other men crashed in the Flint Hills area in Kansas. The plane had left Kansas City and was bound for Wichita. The Rockne Memorial, which bears the names of the victims, is located on private property south of Cottonwood Falls in Chase County. A public memorial was built in 1965 at the Mattfield Green service area along the Kansas Turnpike.

The National Collegiate Athletic Association (NCAA) has its headquarters in Overland Park, Kansas.

The Carnegie Library building in Stockton was constructed in 1916.

The late Gary Ormsby set the fastest speed (296 mph) and the quickest time (4.88 seconds) in drag racing history at Heartland Park in Topeka in 1990.

Quinter

Castle Rock. A chalk spire 70 feet high. Castle Rock is a natural landmark. Several important fossil discoveries have been made here. It is an example of some of the more unusual natural landmarks in Kansas.

Republic County

Republican Waterfowl Management Unit (Jamestown Salt Marsh). Many migratory waterfowl birds gather here. During the migrating months the area provides protection and food for thousands of birds.

Salina

Coronado Heights. A structure sitting on the hill designates the point furthest north in Kansas that Coronado was believed to have traveled in 1541 during his search for the mythical kingdom of Quivira.

Scott City

El Cuartelejo. An archeological site that was occupied by the Taos and Picurie Indians from 1650-1720. It was the northernmost Indian pueblo in the Americas and was also the first white settlement in Kansas.

Shawnee

Old Shawnee Town. A re-creation of a pioneer town featuring a collection of buildings from 1840-1880. Among the attractions are the first jail in Kansas, built in 1844, a farmhouse, a one-room school, and a century-old barn.

Shawnee Mission

Shawnee Methodist Mission. The Mission, established in 1830, was one of the earliest Indian missions in pre-territorial Kansas. Three of the original structures remain where the first territorial legislature met in 1855.

Smith Center

Geographic Center Marker. This location has been officially established as the exact geographic center of the 48 contiguous states.

Topeka

Carousel in the Park. Take a ride on a newly restored antique Herschell-Spillman carousel. The carousel, built in 1908, is one of only 200 remaining intact today.

Cedar Crest Governor's Mansion. The mansion, built in 1928, has been home to the First Family of Kansas. Tours available.

Heartland Park. Professional motorsport racing brings a variety of automotive and motorcycle racing to Topeka.

Reinisch Rose Garden. Thousands of different varieties are in the rose garden, which is one of the most extensive rose gardens in the world. Blooming season is June through October.

State Capitol. Construction on the five-story State Capitol was started in 1866 and completed in 1903. The east and west wings of the building feature murals painted by John Steuart Curry.

Topeka Zoo. Exhibits include the Lion's Pride, a tropical rain forest, and a unique Discovering Apes exhibit.

Ward-Meade Park and Botanical Gardens. The buildings on the grounds include the family house, a one-room country schoolhouse and a pioneer cabin. The gardens feature a variety of flowers, trees and shrubs.

Traer

Elephant Rock. A natural landmark that served as a guide to pioneers on cattle drives across the Western Plains.

Troy

"Tall Oak" Indian Monument. This monument by artist Peter Toth is 67 inches in diameter 27 feet high. He chose the site because of the rich Indian lore.

QUICK FACTS:

The mast spar from "Old Ironsides" can be seen on the east lawn of Topeka High School.

On June 8, 1966, Topeka was hit by one of the most destructive tornadoes ever to strike an American city.

One of the intricately restored horses on the carousel at Gage Park is the Kansas horse, a favorite with riders. The carousel also has a chicken, pig, zebra and other beautifully restored animals to ride.

Photo by Diana J. Edwardson.

179

QUICK FACTS:

The Republic Valley Cattle Feeders Association located near Scandia is the largest feedlot in north central Kansas, capable of feeding more than 25,000 head of cattle at one time. The area contained within its fences is almost one mile.

The Trading Post Complex in Pleasanton has restored buildings and artifacts from the turbulent "Bleeding Kansas" days.

Oakley is known as the "Crossroads of the High Plains."

In 1868, William Cody and William Constock competed in a buffalo shooting contest near what is now Oakley. Cody won and thus earned the name "Buffalo Bill."

Victoria

Cathedral of the Plains. Known as St. Fidelis Church, this remarkable church has a Romanesque structure made of native limestone and was completed in 1911 by industrious German-Russian immigrant settlers.

Wakefield

Kansas Landscape Arboretum. Over 193 species of trees and shrubs and a beautiful flower garden are featured at the arboretum.

Wamego

The Beecher Bible and Rifle Church. The church was built in 1862 by abolitionist settlers and was used to store rifles in cartons marked "bibles" during proslavery/anti-slavery conflict.
Ditto-Leach House. The Leach House was built to resemble an Italian villa by one of Wamego's most prosperous early residents. The house has been restored to its regal splendor. Tours available during community events.
Fields of Fair Vineyard. Opened in 1989 it is the first commercial vineyard in Kansas since the days of Prohibition. Kansas' first licensed vineyard presently cultivates five varieties of French hybrid grapes on 15 acres in the Black Jack Hills. A tasting room is open to the public.
Old Dutch Mill. The mill was built of native limestone in 1879 and is the only authentic Dutch mill in Kansas. It was originally located 12 miles north of Wamego.
Walter Chrysler Home. The birthplace of Walter P. Chrysler, founder of the Chrysler Corporation. Mr. Chrysler was born in Wamego in 1875.

Wichita

Botanica. Visitors can see beautiful plants and flowers year-round. It also provides an excellent place for study.
Lake Afton Public Observatory. Visitors can view the wonders of the cosmos through the 16-inch telescope at the observatory.

QUICK FACTS:

In 1985, more than $2 billion in revenue was generated from travel and tourism in the state of Kansas.

Photo courtesy of Wichita Convention &Visitors Bureau.

The Omnisphere in Wichita is one of the most popular attractions in Kansas. It offers an excellent space education program.

Omnisphere and Science Center. Visitors to the Omnisphere can gaze deep into space at the planetarium shows. It also offers hands-on physical science laboratory.

The Pyradomes. The most architecturally unique campus in the world. Eight geodesic domes designed by H. Buckminster Fuller and a 60-foot pyramid. The Pyradomes are located on more than 90 acres and are the home of The Olive W. Garvey Center for the Improvement of Human Functioning, a nonprofit medical health facility.

Sedgwick County Zoo and Botanical Garden. This zoo features compatible animals that are grouped on terrain where they would live normally rather than caged exhibits. Also features a rain forest and a darkened herpetarium where night is switched for day.

Winfield

Spring Hill Farm. The Spring Hill Farm was originally homesteaded in 1872. Fresh foods and vegetables are available for visitors to pick.

Yates Center

Courthouse Square Historic District. This is the only courthouse square in Kansas on the National Register of Historic Places. The buildings were constructed between 1883 and 1928.

The first nighttime football game in Kansas was between Fairmount College and Cooper College, now Sterling College.

The 120-foot Campanile on the University of Kansas campus in Lawrence was built of native Kansas limestone. It contains a 53-bell carillon cast by the John Taylor Company of Loughborough, England, in 1950-1951. The largest of the bells weighs seven tons and the smallest only 10 pounds.

sources

Abilene Convention and Visitors Bureau, P.O. Box 146, Abilene 67410.
Chanute Chamber of Commerce, P.O. Box 747, Chanute 66721.
Coffeyville Convention & Visitors Bureau, Box 457, Coffeyville 67337.
Colby Area Chamber of Commerce, P.O. Box 572, Colby 67701.
Concordia Chamber of Commerce, 219 W. 6th, Concordia 66901.
Dodge City Convention and Visitors Bureau, P.O. Box 1474, Dodge City 67801.
Doniphan County Chamber of Commerce, P.O. Box 231, Troy 66087.
El Dorado Chamber of Commerce, P.O. Box 509, El Dorado 67042.
Emporia/Lyon County Convention and Visitors Bureau, P.O. Box 417, Emporia 66801.
Fredonia Chamber of Commerce, P.O. Box 449, Fredonia 66736.
Garden City Area Chamber of Commerce, 201 E. Laurel, Garden City 67846.
Garnett Area Chamber of Commerce, 134 E. 5th, Garnett 66032.
Great Bend Chamber of Commerce, P.O. Box 400, Great Bend 67530.
Haysville Chamber of Commerce, P.O. Box 372, Haysville 67060.
Herington Chamber of Commerce, 106 N. Broadway, Herington 67449.
Hiawatha Chamber of Commerce, 110 N. 7th, Hiawatha 66434.
Hutchinson Convention/Visitors Bureau, 309 N. Main, Hutchinson 67501.
Iola Area Chamber of Commerce, Box 722, Iola 65749.
Junction City Convention and Visitors Bureau, P.O Box 1976, Junction City 66441.
Kansas Department of Commerce, Travel and Tourism Division, 400 SW 8th,
    Topeka 66603.
Kansas Department of Wildlife and Parks, Room 502, 900 Jackson St.,
    Topeka 66612.
Larned Chamber of Commerce, P.O. Box 240, Larned 67550.
Leavenworth Convention and Visitors Bureau, P.O. Box 44, Leavenworth 66048.
Liberal Convention and Tourism Bureau, P.O. Box 2257, Liberal 67905-2257.
Lindsborg Chamber of Commerce, P.O. Box 191, Lindsborg 67456-0191.
Lucas Chamber of Commerce, P.O. Box 186, Lucas 67648.
Minneapolis Chamber of Commerce, 213 W. 2nd, Minneapolis 67647.
Neodesha Chamber of Commerce, P.O. Box 266, Neodesha 66757.
Newton Convention and Tourism Bureau, P.O. Box 353, Newton 67114.
Oakley Chamber of Commerce, P.O. Box 548, Oakley 67748.
Oberlin Convention and Visitors Bureau, 132 S. Penn, Oberlin 66749.
Ottawa Area Chamber of Commerce, 109 E. 2nd, Box Q, Ottawa 66067.
Pittsburg Area Chamber of Commerce, P.O. Box 1115, Pittsburg 66762.
Salina Area Chamber of Commerce, P.O. Box 586, Salina 67402.
Scott City Chamber of Commerce, Scott City 67871.
Topeka Convention and Visitors Bureau, 3 Townsite Plaza, 120 E. 6th St.,
    Topeka 66603.
Wamego Chamber of Commerce, P.O. Box 34, Wamego 66547.
Wellington Area Chamber of Commerce, 207 S. Washington, Wellington 67152.
Wichita Convention and Visitors Bureau, 100 S. Main, Suite 100, Wichita 67202.
Woodson County Chamber of Commerce, P.O. Box 211, Yates Center 66783.

CHAPTER 8

LAND

KANSAS

LAND

Agriculture • Rock Formations
Geography • State Parks • Forests
Wildlife • Minerals & Mining
Water • Energy • Climate

Photo by John Schlageck, Kansas Farm Bureau.

overview

Agriculture **187-189**	In 1990, Kansas ranked first nationally in production of wheat, and sorghum for grain, and fourth in the production of sunflowers.
Rock Formations **190-191**	Monument Rocks was the first national landmark to be designated in Kansas by the National Parks Service.
Geography **192**	Near Lebanon in Smith County, Kansas, is the location of the geographic center of the 48 contiguous states.
State Parks **193**	The first state park in Kansas was at Kanapolis Reservoir, which was started in 1958.
Forests **194-195**	Kansas has 681,000 acres of forest land, of which 108,000 acres are within the National Forest System.
Hunting & Fishing **Feature** **196-197**	Pheasant hunting in Kansas is a big attraction, and hunters from all over the Midwest flock to Kansas each fall primarily in pursuit of the state's large pheasant population.
Wildlife **198**	Hundreds of bald eagles migrate from Canada to Kansas during the winter.
Minerals & Mining **199**	Principal minerals produced in Kansas in 1989 were Portland cement, crushed stone, and salt.
Water **200-201**	Kansas' per capita water consumption totals approximately 2,310 gallons per day.
Energy **202**	Among neighboring states, Kansas is second only to Oklahoma in the production of crude oil.
Climate **203**	The average annual temperature is 55 degrees Fahrenheit.

introduction

T he Kansas landscape offers a beautiful variety of rolling hills, reservoirs, unspoiled prairies, and green meadows. For the first-time visitor, the state may present a delightful surprise! Kansas offers a myriad of hunting and fishing opportunities, or for those who want to get away from it all the beauty and tranquility of nature abounds in Kansas.

In the summer, the fields turn golden when the wheat harvest gets underway. The rich Kansas soil produces many cultivated crops. Wheat is the state's biggest cash crop, but corn and soybeans are also important crops. As a leader in agricultural production, Kansas is referred to as the "Breadbasket of the Nation."

While many people may think of Kansas as strictly an agriculture state, the landscape provides numerous opportunities for boating, fishing, camping, and hunting. Wildlife enthusiasts are in for a real treat when they visit Cheyenne Bottoms wildlife management area. More than 300 species of waterfowl and shorebirds have been observed at the Cheyenne Bottoms migration point, located near Great Bend in western Kansas.

The state's reservoirs, ponds, and streams offer an array of fishing opportunities. Crappie, bass, walleye, bluegill, gar, and catfish are abundant. For hunters, large flocks of pheasant, quail, prairie chicken, and turkey are popular game birds.

Kansas may have the reputation as being just a flat area, but the landscape is quite varied. The Flint Hills section in the heart of the state is one of the most distinctive regions in the Midwest. The Flint Hills are one of the few open ranges left in the nation and the grassy meadows are some of the world's richest grazing lands. Bluestem grasses and wildflowers are abundant. The area is named for the chert or flint rock that covers the bluestem slopes.

The northwestern part of the state includes one of the most extensive beds of pre-historic ocean fossils. Unusual-shaped, spiraling rock formations provide picturesque photo opportunities. The southwest region contains the largest share of minerals and natural resources to be found in the state.

The northeastern region of the state is hilly with slopes gently sweeping the landscape. In this corner of the state are remains of glaciers that moved into Kansas about a million years ago, leaving behind silt, clay, and large, red, quartzite boulders. In addition, the southeast portion of the state has more trees and rivers than other sections.

The high plains of Kansas stretch for miles — as far as the eye can see in some places. The spectacular sunsets across the prairie provide a splash of color that visitors and native Kansans don't soon forget.

Since the days of the early settlers, Kansans have appreciated the beauty and value of its precious resource — the land. ❏

Pass the Salt | Salt is the most abundant mineral in the state. In recent years Kansas has ranked 6th in tonnage and 5th in value of salt produced in the United States.

Wheat Bin | In an average year, Kansas grows, stores, and grinds more wheat into flour than any other state.

Largest Flock | Kansas has the largest flock of prairie chickens on the North American continent.

Don't Fence Me In | It has been estimated that Kansas has between 30,000 to 40,000 miles of stone fence posts. Largest concentrations are in Ness and Hodgeman Counties.

Top Ten | Kansas ranks among the top ten mineral-producing states in the nation.

300 Million Years | The oldest part of the Kansas landscape is in the southeastern part of the state. The rocks at the surface were deposited more than 300 million years ago.

Up, Up, and Away | The natural gas called helium was first discovered near Dexter. Kansas leads the nation in production of helium.

Onshore Reserves | The Hugoton natural gas field was discovered in the 1920s and is among the biggest onshore natural gas reserves in the world, producing billions of cubic feet of natural gas annually. Counties in southwest Kansas generally lead the state in gas production.

Say It Again | The Arkansas River is pronounced "Ar-KAN-sas" by residents.

Whooping Cranes Call | Every spring, Cheyenne Bottoms near Great Bend is one of only two locations in America to host 75% of all migrating shore birds. In the fall whooping cranes call at this federally listed critical habitat. Only 156 whooping cranes are in the wild and of that number about 134 whoopers migrate through Kansas.

KANSAS

Land Dedicated to Farm Use

As of 1990, 47.9 million acres of the total Kansas land area was in farms, with more than 31.3 million acres of farmland as cropland. Total land in farms has decreased slightly since 1950, while cropland acres have risen modestly during the same period.

QUICK FACTS:

Kansas is among the national leaders in wheat production. It would take a train stretching from western Kansas to the Atlantic Ocean to contain all the wheat grown in Kansas in a single year.

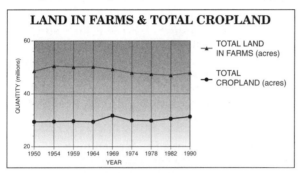

LAND IN FARMS & TOTAL CROPLAND

TOTAL LAND IN FARMS (acres)

TOTAL CROPLAND (acres)

*Source: **Kansas Farm Facts, 1990**; 1990 Census of Agriculture, Bureau of the Census.*

Size and Number of Farms

The number of farms in Kansas has decreased by 60% since 1935 (the highest year), and the average size of farms has increased by 300% since 1860. In 1860, there were 10,000 farms with an average size of 171 acres for a total of 1.8 million acres. In 1990, the average size of farms was 694 acres, with a total number of farms of 69,000.

In 1990 there were nearly 21 million acres harvested on Kansas farms.

Kansas has more than 5.7 million cattle and is among the nation's leading producers of red meat.

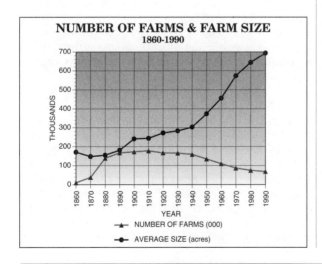

NUMBER OF FARMS & FARM SIZE
1860-1990

NUMBER OF FARMS (000)

AVERAGE SIZE (acres)

While the number of farms in Kansas has declined since the early 1900s, the average size of the farms has increased.

*Source: **Kansas Farm Facts, 1990**; Census of Agriculture, U.S. Bureau of the Census.*

Farm Income and Expenses

In 1989, Kansas farms netted just over $1 billion in income. This resulted from nearly $7.7 billion in cash receipts from marketings and other income, less approximately $6.5 billion in farm production expenses.

Major Crops Produced in Kansas

Wheat leads Kansas' agricultural products in acres planted, harvested, production, and value. The production of wheat, sorghum grain, corn, and hay represent the major crop growing activities in Kansas. These four crops comprise about 88% of the total value of crop production in the state.

Value of Agriculture Crops

In 1990, the total value of Kansas farm products was more than $2.7 billion. Wheat accounted for more than 43% of the total, followed by corn, which represented nearly 15.5% of the total. Other major crops are hay, soybeans and sorghum.

VALUE OF KANSAS CROP PRODUCTION
1990

CROP	VALUE ($000)	PRODUCTION (000)	PRICE ($000)	UNIT(1)
Wheat	1,180,000	472,000	$2.50	bu
Sorghum Grain	373,296	184,800	$2.02	bu
Corn Grain	424,125	188,500	$2.25	bu
Soybeans	262,080	46,800	$5.60	bu
Hay	402,600	6,100	$66.00	ton
Oats	8,580	6,600	$1.30	bu
Barley	1,571	924	$1.70	bu
Rye	202	130	$1.55	bu
Cotton	212	0.7	$302.86	bale
Dry Edible Beans	9,975	665	$15.00	cwt
Apples	1,461	8,000	$0.18	lb
Peaches	23	100	$0.23	lb
Sunflowers	8,057	81,880	$.09	lb
TOTAL	2,728,879	na	na	

na - data not applicable
(1) bu=bushel   cwt=hundred weight

KANSAS agriculture

National Ranking

The importance of Kansas agriculture to the Kansas and U.S. economies is evidenced by its ranking among all states in production of crops and livestock. In 1990, Kansas ranked first nationally in production of wheat and sorghum for grain, fourth in sunflowers, and fourth in the production of non-alfalfa hay. In livestock production, Kansas ranked first in cattle slaughtered, and third in cattle and calves on farms. Kansas ranked sixth in farm exports.

Highs and Lows in Crop Production

In the history of Kansas agriculture, 1986 was a bumper crop year, with record yields in corn, sorghum, and soybeans. The most recent low point in production was 1936, with low yields recorded for soybeans and sorghum.

Cash Receipts from Livestock and Poultry Raised in Kansas

More than 5.7 million cattle and 1.5 million hogs were on Kansas farms in 1990. Cash receipts from cattle production were $4.3 billion and $320 million from hog production. Among poultry, the number of chickens produced had a cash receipt value of $515,000. The number of chickens marketed exceeds that of turkeys sold. However, in terms of value of production, turkeys are the dominant poultry.

Food Products Manufacturing

Of all food-related manufacturing, meat products have historically created the biggest impact, both in terms of jobs and the value of shipments. Overall, between 1967 and 1987, the greatest percentage gain in value of shipments has been in the beverage products industry, while the largest numerical increase in value of shipments has been in the meat processing industry. In 1987, there were 25,300 Kansans employed in the food manufacturing industry, and total shipments were $9 billion.

QUICK FACTS:

Kansas ranks second in cropland acres, second in prime farmland (as defined by USDA), third in land in farms, third in motor trucks on farms, and fourth in combines on farms.

Kansas has several large haying operations. The rich grasslands provide excellent grazing for livestock.

Photo by John Schlageck, Kansas Farm Bureau.

LAND

rock formations

KANSAS

Monument Rocks

Monument Rocks, or the Kansas Pyramids as some people call them, are unusually shaped chalk rock formations that rise abruptly from the valley of the Smoky Hill River. The formations rise to heights of 60 feet and can be seen from a distance. One of the best-known formations resembles an Indian Chief and is called "Old Chief Smoky."

The wind-carved and water-eroded formations are sediment remains of ancient marine life up to 200 million years old. Geologists have determined that from 80 to 100 million years ago much of western Kansas was covered by a sea. Today, the area from south of Quinter to west of Russell Springs is the largest cretaceous fossil bed in the United States. Numerous petrified sharks' teeth, which are a delight for collectors, have been found in the area.

Monument Rocks was the first national landmark to be designated in Kansas by the National Park Service. Monument Rocks are located 21 miles south of Oakley on US-83, east on a county road for six miles, then two miles south.

Cedar Bluff State Park

Cedar Bluff State Park gives visitors a sweeping view of the Smoky Hill River valley as it winds through prehistoric chalk beds. More than 200 species of vertebrate and invertebrate fossils have been found there. The state park is located on the north and south shores of Trego County's Cedar Bluff Reservoir near Ellis.

Castle Rock, a unique land formation, is a 70-foot-high chalk spire that is visible for miles. The chalk bluffs are some of the most scenic parts of Kansas. This natural landmark has been the site for several important fossil discoveries. Castle Rock was named by an Army lieutenant who discovered it while surveying the Butterfield Trail.

190

Mushroom Rock State Park

Mushroom Rock State Park, located about 10 miles east of Ellsworth, consists of about five acres of prairie containing unique rock foundations. The Dakota sandstone formations are in the shape of mushrooms. Mushroom Rock State Park and the surrounding area was a major landmark during the 1800s. Wild Bill Hickock, John C. Fremont, and Kit Carson are just some of the more notable persons who visited the area. Mushroom Rock was also a meeting place for Indians and white traders.

Rock City

Rock City is a group of Dakota sandstone concretions that are unique because they do not appear in that size and number anywhere else in the world. The odd-shaped rocks, some of which are 27 feet in diameter, occur in three distinct groups. While some of the rocks are entirely exposed, others are partly embedded in the Dakota limestone.

The rock formations have been the source of debate for many years. One article published in the American Journal of Science in 1901 described the rocks as "Titanic marbles." Rock City was proclaimed a National Natural Landmark on May 29, 1977. Rock City is located just southwest of Minneapolis.

QUICK FACTS:

Mushroom Rock State Park is maintained as a satellite park by nearby Kanopolis State Park officials.

Sandstone, which is formed out of small grains of sand that are naturally cemented together, is found throughout Kansas and comes in a variety of colors from bright yellow to dark brown.

Chalk Bluffs in Gove County are just one of the diverse rock formations found in Kansas.

Photo courtesy of Kansas Department of Commerce.

LAND

geography

KANSAS

QUICK FACTS:

Kansas is a 208 by 411 mile rectangle that is located in the center of the United States.

The landscape rises from less than 700 feet above sea level in the southeast corner of the state to more than 4,000 feet at its western border. The state has a total of 82,264 square miles.

Kansas ranks 14th among the states in geographic size.

Geographic Center of the Continental United States

Near Lebanon in Smith County, Kansas, is the location of the geographic center of the 48 contiguous states. Located north of US-36 on KS-281, the center lies 1 mile west of KS-281 and KS-191 junction near Lebanon. This point is exactly halfway between San Francisco and Boston.

Geodetic Center of the United States

The marker for the geodetic center of the United States is located at the Osborne rest area, Highways 281 & 24. A bronze disk marks the geodetic center of the United States. The site is the controlling point for all North American land surveys and is a reference point for all property lines and city, county, state, and international boundaries tied to the triangulation network of the United States, Canada and Mexico. The area is listed on the National Register of Historic Places.

Highest and Lowest Elevation

At 4,039 feet above sea level, Mount Sunflower is the highest point in Kansas, located ten miles north and four miles west of Weskan in Wallace County. The Verdigris River in Montgomery County is the lowest elevation in the state at 680 feet above sea level.

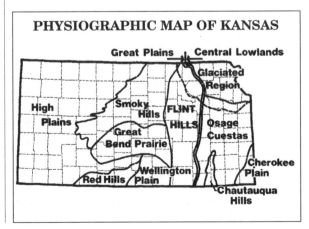

PHYSIOGRAPHIC MAP OF KANSAS

Great Plains Central Lowlands
Glaciated Region
High Plains
Smoky Hills FLINT
Great Bend Prairie HILLS Osage Cuestas
Wellington Plain
Red Hills Cherokee Plain
Chautauqua Hills

Source: Stephen M. Perry, "The Flint Hills of Kansas," Kansas Department of Economic Development.

192

KANSAS STATE PARKS

State Park	No. of Acres	No. of Areas
Cedar Bluff	1,715	2
Cheney	2,495	2
Clinton	1,455	1
Crawford	439	1
El Dorado	3,800	4
Elk City	857	1
Fall River	917	2
Glen Elder	1,250	1
Hillsdale	1,475	3
Kanopolis	1,585	2
Lovewell	1,126	2
Meade	443	1
Melvern	1,785	1
Milford	1,084	1
Mushroom Rock	5	1
Perry	1,597	2
Pomona	490	1
Prairie Dog	1,578	2
Sand Hills	960	1
Scott	1,120	1
Toronto	1,075	3
Tuttle Creek	1,156	4
Webster	880	2
Wilson	927	2

QUICK FACTS:

The first state park in Kansas was at Kanapolis Reservoir, which was started in 1958.

Kansas has 24 state parks offering a variety of boating, fishing, and recreational activities.

Toronto State Park and Fall River are surrounded by oak and pine covered hills in an area once inhabited by prehistoric Indians, as demonstrated by the local cave petroglyphs.

Source: Kansas Department of Wildlife and Parks.

KANSAS STATE PARKS

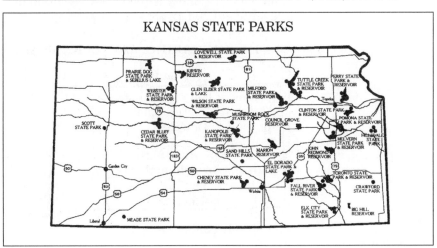

forests

QUICK FACTS:

Laura Ingalls Wilder wrote in her diary about her travels in Kansas: "Soon croosed Little Elm Creek and Big Elm Creek and drove through beautiful woods of elm, oak, ash, hickory, butternut, and walnut. Wild plums, grapes, and currants are abundant, and briars and wild flowers of all kinds. A rich sight."

Source: U.S. Forest Service, as cited in Agricultural Statistics, 1987, U.S. Department of Agriculture.

The Flint Hills, located in the east-central part of the state, is an area about 50 miles wide and is the only extensive, unplowed tract of bluestem or true prairie remaining in the United States.

National Forest System

Kansas has 626,000 acres of forest land, of which 108,000 acres are within the National Forest System.

NATIONAL FOREST SYSTEM, NATIONAL FOREST SYSTEM LANDS (1) AND OTHER LANDS WITHIN UNIT BOUNDARIES, IN KANSAS AND NEIGHBOR STATES
(Sept. 30, 1986)

	GROSS AREA WITHIN BOUNDARIES (000 acres)	NATIONAL FOREST SYSTEM LANDS (000 acres)	OTHER LANDS WITHIN UNIT BOUNDARIES (000 acres)	1982 TOTAL FOREST LAND (000 acres)
Colorado	16,030	14,446	1,584	4,030
Iowa	0	0	0	1,756
KANSAS	**117**	**108**	**9**	**626**
Missouri	3,082	1,471	1,610	10,986
Nebraska	442	352	90	732
Oklahoma	461	296	166	6,539

(1) National Forest System Lands-a nationally significant system of Federally owned units of forest, range, and related land consisting of national forests, purchase units, national grasslands, and other lands, waters, and interest in lands which are administered by the Forest Service or designated for administration through the Forest Service. National Forests-units formally established and permanently set aside and reserved for national forest purposes.

Lumber/Wood Product Manufacturing

As of 1982, lumber and wood product manufacturing accounted for only about 3,200 employees statewide, producing shipments of slightly more than $253 million. While employment has grown more than 200% since 1967, the value of shipments has increased more than 11 times.

The largest industry within this sector in terms of both employment and shipments is the wood building and mobile home industry, with 1,500 employees and a total value of $164.5 million in shipments. Also important are the millwork and plywood industry.

Forest Cover

Nearly 76% of all the forest cover in Kansas is comprised of oak-hickory, which accounts for 472,900 acres of land. The next largest tree group, the elm-ash-cottonwood group, comprises only about 12%, with 76,500 acres.

FOREST COVER TYPES IN KANSAS

TREE TYPE	KANSAS (000 acres)
Loblolly-shortleaf pine	2.1
Oak-pine	2.5
Oak-hickory	472.9
Oak-gum-cypress	55.6
Elm-ash-cottonwood	76.5
Nonstocked	10.9
Hardwoods	5.7
Total	626.2

Note: According to Soil Conservation Service, data has not been checked for errors. Numbers should be used only in relative comparisons of acres and types, and not as absolute numbers in and of themselves.

A One Tree National Forest

The Louis Vieux Elm is the largest living American Elm in the United States. At last measure the elm tree stood 99 feet high, 23 feet in circumference and its branches spread 133 feet. The largest living elm tree has been certified by the National Register of Big Trees of the American Forestry Association. The elm is estimated to be 270 years old. The tree is named after Louis Vieux who operated an Oregon Trail toll ferry on the Vermillion River a few yards from the tree. Nearby is a pioneer cemetery which contains the ornate headstones of Vieux, his family, and other pioneers who died along the Oregon Trail.

To find the Louis Vieux Elm, from the intersection of U.S. Highway 24 and K-99 at Wamego, drive four miles east, across the Vermillion River, then turn north on the Onaga Road and go three miles. Turn back west and travel approximately one-half mile.

QUICK FACTS:

The pawpaw tree, which can be found in Kansas, offers shade in the summertime. The Plains Indians cherished the pawpaw, calling it "assimin." They ate its fruit, which tastes somewhat like a banana, and used its tough and fiberous bark for making cloth and cord.

Source: U.S. Department of Agriculture, Soil Conservation Service, "1982 National Resources Inventory."

Hiawatha is known as the "City of Beautiful Maples." The colorful maples create a spectacular fall foliage display.

Pheasant Hunting Popular in Kansas

Kansas has an abundance of fish and game that is a hunter's delight. Pheasant, quail, and prairie chicken are predominant game birds, but the state also has a variety of turkey, dove, and geese.

Pheasant hunting in Kansas is a big attraction, and hunters from all over the Midwest flock to Kansas each fall primarily in pursuit of the state's large pheasant population. Norton is known to hunters all over North America as "The Pheasant Capital of the World." According to Kansas Department of Wildlife and Parks officials, approximately 30,000 non-resident licenses are sold each year and another 180,000 resident hunting licenses are issued annually.

Pheasants are not native to Kansas. The brilliantly-colored game birds were introduced to the state in the early 1900s. In the late 1950s, the pheasant hunting season was expanded to a 20-day season. Now the season always begins on the second Saturday in November and ends January 31. Other game birds are also popular for hunters. Wild turkey hunting has increased in popularity in the state. There are two seasons for turkey hunting — spring and fall — with the spring season being the most popular.

Besides pheasant hunting, Kansas has some of the best quail hunting in the nation.

Beside pheasant hunting, Kansas has some of the best quail hunting in the nation and consistently ranks in the top three states every year for number of quail taken by hunters. While Kansas has more prairie chickens than anywhere else in the nation, the prairie chickens are not as avidly pursued by hunters.

Dove hunting is increasing in popularity as well. Kansas has the largest number of breeding population of doves in the country. The state's dove hunting season is annually in September and lasts two weeks.

Although deer hunting is fairly recent in the state — the first deer season was in 1965 — the popularity has steadily increased and is now a top attraction for residents. Deer licenses are restricted for Kansas residents only, and approximately 70,000 permits are issued each year. Deer hunting is divided into firearm, archery, and black powder permit categories. An average of 30,000 deer are harvested annually by firearms hunters and 4,000 by archery hunters.

The archery deer hunting season is the longest, starting Oct. 1 and ending Dec. 31. Archery season is closed during firearm season, which lasts for 10 days in early December. In 1989, Kansas introduced a special deer season in September for muzzle loaders and that special season is expected to be continued.

hunting & fishing

Fishing enthusiasts can find numerous reservoirs, ponds, and streams in Kansas that offer a variety of fishing opportunities. Walleye fishing is perhaps the most popular, although Kansas also offers some of the best crappie fishing in the country. White bass and striped bass are popular choices for winter ice fishing. Approximately 200,000 resident fishing licenses are issued annually by the state.

Hunting and fishing provides a strong economic impact for Kansas in addition to attracting visitors into the state. Millions of dollars are generated into Kansas' economy by out of state visitors who come to Kansas primarily to hunt.

For more information about hunting, fishing, and wildlife in Kansas, contact: Kansas Department of Wildlife and Parks, Route 2, Box 54A, Pratt, Kansas 67124. Phone: (316) 672-5911. ❏

Photo courtesy of The Topeka Capital-Journal.

LAND
wildlife

QUICK FACTS:

Photo courtesy of The Topeka Capital-Journal.

The red-tailed hawk is an example of a wildlife species that can be found throughout the state.

Source: Kansas Department of Natural Resources, Fish & Wildlife Division.

The Maxwell Game Refuge near McPherson has a large herd of bison (buffalo) that roam more than 2,000 acres. Other game areas include Flint Hills National Wildlife Refuge near Burlington and Kirwin National Refuge.

THREATENED/ENDANGERED SPECIES IN KANSAS

Birds
- Bald eagle
- Eskimo curlew
- Least tern
- Peregrine falcon
- Piping plover
- Snowy plover
- White-faced ibis
- Whooping crane

Mammals
- Black-footed ferret
- Eastern spotted skunk
- Gray Myotis

Amphibians
- Cave salamander
- Central newt
- Dark-sided salamander
- Eastern narrowmouth toad
- Graybelly salamander
- Green frog
- Grotto salamander
- Northern crawfish frog
- Northern spring peeper
- Strecker's chorus frog
- Western green toad

Reptiles
- Broadhead skink
- Checkered garter snake
- Eastern hognose snake
- Kansas glossy snake
- New Mexico blind snake
- Northern redbelly snake
- Texas longnose snake
- Texas night snake
- Western earth snake

Fish
- Arkansas darter
- Arkansas river shiner
- Chestnut lamprey
- Flathead chub
- Hornyhead chub
- Neosho madtom
- Pallid sturgeon
- Redspot chub
- Sicklefin chub
- Silverband shiner
- Speckled chub

Invertebrates
- Amphibious snail
- Heel-splitter mussel
- Scott riffle beetle

Endangered Species

The Kansas Department of Natural Resources lists 102 species of wildlife that are in need of conservation. Of this number, 16 species are classified as endangered and 29 species are threatened. The 45 endangered and threatened species encompass amphibians, fish, reptiles, birds, mammals, and invertebrates.

Hundreds of bald eagles migrate from Canada to Kansas during the winter. Bald eagles soar high on their 6-8 foot wing span and cruise 20-40 miles per hour. They can dive at a speed in excess of 100 miles per hour.

Production of Fuel Minerals

In 1965, Kansas produced nearly 800 billion cubic feet of natural gas, more than 16 million barrels of natural gas liquids, and 104.7 million barrels of petroleum. By 1988, production of natural gas was about 576 billion cubic feet, and production of petroleum was 59 million barrels.

Non-Fuel Mining and Mineral Products

The total value of non-fuel mineral production in Kansas was $318 million in 1989. Portland cement, salt, and crushed stone represent nearly 70% of the total value. Among its neighboring states, Kansas is second in the production of sand and gravel and is third in the production of Portland cement.

Mining and the State's Economy

Mining industries account for nearly 15,800 jobs in Kansas, and provide an annual payroll of nearly $355 million. The oil and gas extraction industry represents 81% of the employment and 72% of the payroll of total mining industries.

Minerals Produced in Kansas

Principal minerals produced in Kansas in 1988 were Portland cement, crushed stone, and salt. Production of these minerals has increased since 1965.

QUICK FACTS:

Kansas' national ranking for production:
1st: Helium
5th: Natural gas
8th: Petroleum

By 1910, coal mines employed some 7,000 men in Pittsburg, named after the sister city, Pittsburgh, Pa., for industry.

According to the Kansas Geological Survey, there was salt beneath at least 7,500 square miles of the state's area.

Limestone has been used extensively in buildings and early day fence posts. It is also the basis for a large cement manufacturing industry.

Photo courtesy of Kansas Department of Commerce, Travel and Tourism Division.

QUICK FACTS:

Although Kansas is often considered a dry state, it has five river systems, and over 50,000 streams that are large enough to be named.

The Glen Elder State Park is located west of Beloit on the Solomon River. The reservoir inundated Waconda Springs which was a mineral pool and the site of Kansas' only health spa. It was here that Margaret Hill McCarter wrote some of her well-loved tales of Kansas.

Waterfalls dot the Kansas landscape, especially in the eastern section. Some springs in Kansas were well-known stops along the Santa Fe Trail in the 1800s, like Alcove Springs near the town of Blue Rapids. Several grave markers still stand in the area.

Irrigation by far constitutes the heaviest use of Kansas' water resources, coming primarily from ground water sources.

Source: *Statistical Abstract of the United States, 1990, Table 355.*

Water Consumption

Kansas' per capita water consumption totals 2,310 gallons per day. Compared to neighboring states, only Nebraska (6,250 gallons per day) and Colorado (with 4,190 gallons) use more water per day than Kansas on a per capita basis. Most of Kansas' water use comes from ground water sources, and most is used for irrigation.

Irrigation and Water Use

In 1990, Kansans used more than 5.67 billion gallons of water. The principal use of the state's water resources is for irrigation, coming primarily from ground water resources.

In 1990, more than 4.7 billion gallons of water was used for irrigation, constituting 83% of the state's overall water use. Thousands of acres of Kansas farmland are irrigated by modern irrigation systems supported by wells, federal and state reservoirs and farm ponds.

The heaviest use of surface water is also used for irrigation, but surface water resources account for only 15.3% of all water used in Kansas. Public supply water use represented 6.3% of the total, with 360 million gallons used.

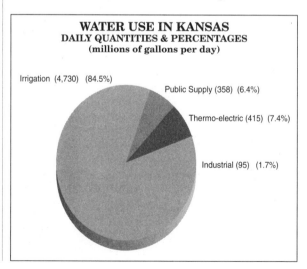

WATER USE IN KANSAS
DAILY QUANTITIES & PERCENTAGES
(millions of gallons per day)

Irrigation (4,730) (84.5%)

Public Supply (358) (6.4%)

Thermo-electric (415) (7.4%)

Industrial (95) (1.7%)

Quality of Surface Water

Overall, the surface water quality in Kansas is good, but declining slightly. On average, 80% of all Kansas lakes support all uses, while slightly fewer streams support all uses. The notable exception is contact recreation, which only 46% of Kansas streams support.

Primary Water Sources

Kansas has 232 lakes and reservoirs, comprising approximately 33,000 acres of water surface area. Added to this are 19,791 miles of rivers and streams, and 34,245 acres of wetland areas.

Major River Basins

Kansas has 12 river basins with a total of nearly 20,000 stream miles between them. The largest of these major river basins in the state is the Kansas-Lower Republican basin, with more than 56,000 acres of lakes, more than 1,200 acres of wetlands, and covering more than 3,600 stream miles. The Marais des Cygnes and Neosho are also major river basins in the state.

QUICK FACTS:

Water was scarce on the plains in 1888 and it was often sold in sparing amounts. Not so on the Rogers ranch. Water was free. Often travelers would respond "That's mighty liberal of you." And that is how the town of Liberal got its name.

The 113-year old Oxford grist mill in Sumner County still processes grain with the power of the Arkansas River. The mill has been the subject for many artists.

Source: "Kansas Water Quality Assessment 1986-1987, Section 1: State Background Information," Kansas Department of Health and Environment.

KANSAS RIVER BASINS				
BASIN	**TOTAL NO. OF LAKES**	**TOTAL LAKE ACREAGE**	**TOTAL STREAM MILEAGE**	**WETLAND ACREAGE**
Cimarron	6	693	987	0
Kansas-Lower Republican	44	56,260	3,635	1,265
Lower Arkansas	25	10,872	2,253	13,491
Marais des Cygnes	44	20,849	1,621	2,810
Missouri	11	711	717	0
Neosho	38	22,958	2,623	10,240
Smoky Hill-Saline	16	16,106	2,254	0
Solomon	8	21,331	1,141	1,750
Upper Arkansas	6	182	1,250	4,700
Upper Republican	4	2,553	915	0
Verdigris	23	12,788	1,654	0
Walnut	7	9,895	741	0
TOTALS	232	175,189	19,791	34,256

Since 1960, Kansas has recorded a decrease in the production of hydropower, crude oil, and natural gas, and wide fluctuations in coal production.

Kansas coal is mainly bituminous and is found in the eastern third of the state.

Kansas has produced oil since the 1860s and regularly ranks among the leading states in the nation in terms of oil production and exploration.

Source: U.S. Statistical Abstract, 1991, Table 1,233.

The Hugoton Gas Field in the southwest part of the state is one of the world's largest deposits of natural gas. During 1980, the Hugoton Gas Field accounted for 60% of the state's gas production.

Source: U.S. Statistical Abstract, 1991, Table 1,233.

Energy Sources

Kansas' energy needs are supplied primarily by petroleum and natural gas. Kansas has the highest per capita energy consumption among its neighboring states. In 1988, Kansas had a total energy consumption of 1,057 trillion Btu. and a per capita energy consumption of 423 million Btu.

Crude Oil Production

Among neighboring states, Kansas is second only to Oklahoma in the production of crude oil. Crude oil production levels have generally declined throughout the region, and Kansas' levels have dropped more than 21.3% since 1985. In 1985, Kansas produced 75 million barrels of crude oil, compared to 59 million barrels in 1988.

KANSAS CRUDE OIL PRODUCTION (1)
KANSAS & NEIGHBORING STATES: 1985-1988

	1985	1987	1988
Colorado	30	29	33
KANSAS	**75**	**61**	**59**
Nebraska	7	6	6
Oklahoma	163	134	129

(1) Million barrels per year

Natural Gas Production

Kansas is second only to Oklahoma among neighboring states in the production of natural gas. Natural gas production in Kansas has decreased by nearly 12.3% between 1985 and 1988.

KANSAS NATURAL GAS PRODUCTION (1)
KANSAS & NEIGHBORING STATES: 1985-1988

	1985	1987	1988
Colorado	178	165	192
KANSAS	**513**	**457**	**576**
Nebraska	2	1	(z)
Oklahoma	1,936	2,005	2,107

(1) Million barrels per year
(z) Less than 500 million cubic feet

Tornadoes

A record high of 116 tornadoes was set in 1991. As a result, there were 19 deaths, which was the second highest figure on record since 1978. On April 26 alone there were 350 injuries. In 1991, a total of 54 tornadoes occurred in six days. The cost of damage from that stormy year was $330 million statewide.

Precipitation and Temperature

Rainfall in Kansas was nearly 2 inches above normal in 1990 statewide, with the greatest variance, more than 4 inches, occurring in the southeast area. Typically, the rainiest month in Kansas is June, with an average of slightly more than 4 inches. In terms of temperatures, the state had an average year overall, with the greatest variance occurring in January, which was nearly 6 degrees warmer than normal. The average annual temperature is 55 degrees Fahrenheit.

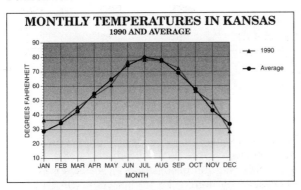

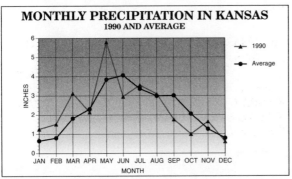

QUICK FACTS:

The largest hailstone documented by the National Weather Service fell on Coffeyville on Sept. 3, 1970. The hailstone measured 17½ inches around and weighed over one and a half pounds.

The coldest recorded temperature in Kansas was 40 degrees below zero which was recorded in Lebanon on February 13, 1905.

The highest recorded temperature in Kansas was 121 degrees on July 24, 1936 in Fredonia.

Kansas is a windy state. With an average wind speed of 14 m.p.h., Dodge City is one of the windiest cities in the United States.

The average yearly precipitation statewide is 26.95 inches. The average annual temperature in Kansas is 55 degrees Fahrenheit.

Source: Kansas Farm Facts, 1990.

Buchanan, Rex. **Kansas Geology: An Introduction to Landscapes, Rocks, Minerals and Fossils.** Lawrence, Kansas: The University Press of Kansas, 1984.

Buchanan, Rex C. and James R. McCauley. **Roadside Kansas: A Traveler's Guide to Its Geology and Landmarks.** Lawrence, Kansas: The University Press of Kansas, 1987.

Frazier, Ian and Straus Farrar. **Great Plains.** New York: Straus, Giroux, 1989.

Howes, Charles C. **This Place Called Kansas.** Norman, Oklahoma: University of Oklahoma Press, 1984.

Kansas Department of Commerce, Tourism Division, 400 W. 8th St., Topeka 66603.

Kansas Department of Health and Environment, Forbes Field Building 740, Topeka 66620.

Kansas Department of Wildlife and Parks, Route 2, Box 54A, Pratt 67124.

Kansas Farm Facts, 1991, Kansas State Board of Agriculture, U.S. Department of Agriculture, P.O. Box 3534, Topeka 66601-3534.

Kansas Geological Survey, 1930 Constant Ave., Campus West, University of Kansas, Lawrence 66046.

Kansas Secretary of State, Publications Division, Capitol Building, 2nd floor, Topeka 66612.

Minneapolis Area Chamber of Commerce, 213 W. 2nd, Minneapolis 67467.

Muilenburg, Grace and Ada Swineford. **Land of the Post Rock: Its Origins, History, and People.** Lawrence, Kansas: The Regents Press of Kansas, 1975.

Oakley Chamber of Commerce, P.O. Box 548, Oakley 67748.

Perry, Stephen M. **"The Flint Hills of Kansas."** Kansas Department of Economic Development.

Pittsburg Area Chamber of Commerce, P.O. Box 1115, Pittsburg 66762.

Statistical Abstract of the United States, U.S. Department of Commerce, Bureau of the Census.

Wamego Area Chamber of Commerce, P.O. Box 34, Wamego 66547.

Wilder, Laura Ingalls. **On the Way Home.** New York: Harper & Row, 1962.

index

Abilene 34, 50, 118, 163
Agriculture 187-189
  Crops produced 188
  Food products manufacturing 189
  Highs and lows in production..189
  Irrigation and water use.........200
  Livestock and poultry 189
  National ranking 189
  Value of commodities 188
Allen, Dr. Forrest C. "Phog".....103
Alley, Kirstie 97
Alma 34
American Indian tribes 85
Anthony 34
Arbuckle, "Fatty" 97
Area Codes 5
Argonia 163
Arkansas City 34
Art museums 118-119
Arts in Kansas 111-117
Ashland 34, 50, 163-164
Asner, Edward 97
Atchison 34, 164
Athol 164
Attorney General 62-63
Atwood 35
Automobile factories (early).......14

Baldwin 35, 164
Banking 152
  Deposits.....................................152
  Employment...............................152
Barnes, Debra 105
Battle of Mine Creek 25, 28
Beaumont, Hugh 97
Becknell, William 24
Beeler 164
Belle Plaine 15, 164
Belleville 35
Beloit 35, 165
Bender, Kate 17
Birth rates 88
Black settlement, first...............49
Bloch, Henry 101
Bonner Springs 35, 111, 165
Brinkley, John R. Romulus 101

Brookville 50
Browder, Earl R. 94
***Brown v. Board of Education of
  Topeka*** 74
Brown, John 9, 27, 94
Bryant, Deborah 105
Budget, state 71
  General Fund budget................71
  Revenues/expenditures..............71
  Tax collections..........................71
Bunker Hill 50
Burns, Carla 97

Caldwell 35
Capper, Arthur.............................96
Carey Salt Mine 16
Carlson, Frank.............................94
Carver, George Washington 101
Cawker City....................35, 50, 165
Chamberlain, Wilt 103
Chanute 35
Cheney 36
Cherryvale 36
Chisholm Trail 31
Chrysler, Walter P. 101
Cimarron 51
Civil War
  Battle of Mine Creek 25, 28
  Kansas troops............................25
Clark, Clifford..............................94
Cline, Nellie 101
Clyde 36
Cody, William "Buffalo Bill" 15, 94
Coffeyville.............................36, 165
Colbert, Jim 103
Colby.......................................36, 111
Coldwater 36
Columbus 36, 166
Communications industry 149
Concordia 36, 166
Congressional delegation...........59
Congressional districts..............59
Construction 151
  Costs 151
  Revenues 151
Corbett, Thomas R. Boston........94

index

Coronado, Francisco
  Vasquez de..........................23, 27
Cottonwood Falls........................36
Council Grove.................37, 48, 51
Counties
  County map................................11
  County seats...............................10
Court of Appeals..........................69
Crime rate....................................88
Crops
  High and low yields.................189
  Major crops produced..............188
  National ranking......................189
  Value of production.................188
Crumbine, Dr. Samuel J. 102
Cunningham, Glenn.................103
Curry, John Steuart..............9, 100
Curtis, Charles...........................95
Czech folk art...........................120

Dalton Gang..............................94
Death
  Leading causes of......................89
  Motor vehicle...........................150
  Rates...88
Defense spending........................57
Delphos.......................................48
Dickey, Lynn.............................103
District courts.............................69
Divorce rates..............................90
Dodge City..16, 37, 48, 118, 159, 166
Dodge, Maj. Richard Irving.......17
Dole, Robert...............................95
Douglas County.........................14

Earhart, Amelia......................102
Earp, Wyatt.................................94
Earthquake, largest...................15
Education..............................72-77
  A.C.T. scores..............................75
  College degrees conferred...........77
  College enrollment.....................76
  Education facilities.....................74
  Graduate programs....................77
  High school dropout rate...........73
  High school graduates...............73

Private school enrollment..........72
Public school enrollment...........72
Public school system.................74
Regents' institutions..................75
S.A.T. scores..............................75
Student-teacher ratios..............72
Teachers' salaries......................72
Undergraduate programs..........76
Eisenhower, Dwight D. 95
El Dorado.....................37, 119, 167
Elevation
  Highest......................................192
  Lowest.......................................192
Elkhart.......................................167
Ellis.....................................37, 168
Ellsworth.............................37, 118
Employment.................................91
  Banking....................................152
  Federal government...................57
  Income, average.........................91
  Labor force, changes in...........141
  Manufacturing..........................145
  Unemployment rates.................91
Emporia........................17, 37, 168
Emporia State University..........75
Energy
  Crude oil production................202
  Natural gas production............202
  Nuclear power...........................150
  Sources of.................................202
  Utilities....................................150
Engle, Joe..................................102
Ethnic populations.....................87
Eureka.................................37, 168
Evans, Ron.................................102

Fair, state.................................134
Fairway.....................................168
Farms
  Crop production........................188
  Farm land.................................187
  Income and expenses...............188
  Size and number......................187
Federal government
  Aid (per capita)...........................57
  Courts serving Kansas...............69

Federal employees 57
Federal dollars spent in Kansas 57
Federal offices 58
Federal taxes paid 57
Military installations.................58
Felton, Peter F., Jr. 100
Festivals..............................121-133
Films made in Kansas 135
Fitzwater, Marlin 95
Florence 38
Food products....................146-147
Forests...............................194-195
Forest cover.............................195
Louis Vieux Elm.......................195
Lumber manufacturing 194
National Forest System...........194
Fort Hays State University........75
Forts...33
Fort Larned...............................33
Fort Leavenworth 33
Fort Riley 33
Fort Scott..................................33
Fort Larned 33
Fort Leavenworth.................33, 58
Fort Riley 33, 48, 58
Fort Scott 33
Fossils 17
Fredonia...................................119
Funston, Gen. Frederick 104

Gage, Robert Merrell 100
Garden City.................38, 168-169
Garfield 38
Geodetic center of the United
States.....................................192
Geographic center of the United
States....................................192
Geography 192
Physiographic regions map 192
State ranking in size.................192
Georgia-Pacific....................142-143
Girard 38
Goessel.....................................38
Goodland 38, 48, 118
Goss, Col. Nathaniel S. 94
Gove 38

Governor
Duties 60
Length of term 60
Grasshopper infestation............16
Grassland of the Great Plains..17
Gray, Georgia Neese Clark........95
Great Bend.........................38, 169
Greene, Zula Bennington 99
Greensburg...............................169
Grisnik, Marijana.....................100

Haldeman-Julius, Emanuel 99
Halsey, Jim...............................101
Halstead 38, 169
Hanover.....................................38
Harlow, Jean 97
Hart, Gary.................................95
Hawley, Steve 102
Hays..............................39, 48, 170
Hazlett, Robert H. 101
Herington...................................39
Hesston.....................................170
Hiawatha...................................170
Hibbs, Ben.................................96
Hickock, James Butler "Wild Bill"
....94
Highland 39
Highways
Map..13
Miles, number of.......................150
Hill City.....................................39
Hillsboro....................................39
History, Kansas
Admitted to Union...........5, 23, 27
Attractions, historical............48-49
Chronology.............................27-30
Forts 33
Kansas history, essay 23-26
Museums, historical.............34-47
Restaurants, historical.........50-51
Trails 31-32
Holton.......................................39
Hopper, Dennis 97
Households/housing 92-93
Household characteristics 93
Household size 92

Median size of housing 92
Total number 92
Urban and rural households 92
Value of households 93
Hugoton......................................39
Hunting and fishing 196-197
Hutchinson 39, 118, 171

Independence 39, 111, 171
Ingalls, John J. 95
Inge, William 99
Iola..171

Jayhawker 14
Jetmore 39
Johnson, Don 97
Johnson, Martin 97
Johnson, Osa 97
Johnson, Walter "Big Train" 103
Judicial branch of government
....68-69
Court of Appeals 69
District Courts 69
Supreme Court, state 68
Judicial Center 63
Jump, Gordon 97
Junction City 40

Kanopolis 40, 171
Kansas City, Kan......40, 49, 112, 171
Kansas College of Technology...75
Kansas Day 6, 66
Kansas-Nebraska Act 27
Kansas State University..75, 76, 77
Kansas Supreme Court 68
Karpis, Alvin "Creepy"................94
Kassebaum, Nancy Landon........95
Keaton, Buster 97
Kelly, Emmett..............................98
Kenton, Stan................................98
Kersting, Kathleen......................98
Kinsley..40
Kurtis, William "Bill".................96

La Crosse 40
Labor force 141

Changes in labor force 141
Employment by industry..........141
Manufacturing 144
Lair, Mary Alice 95
Lakin..40
Landon, Alf 96
Larned 40
Lawrence....15, 41, 51, 112, 118, 172
Layton, Elizabeth "Grandma"..100
Leavenworth 41, 173
Lecompton 41, 49
Legislative Coordinating Council
....66
Legislature 64-67
How bills become laws...........64-66
Legislative Coord. Council 66
Organization 64
Qualifications and election.........64
Lenexa....................................41, 113
Lewis, Meriwether and William
   Clark 23
Liberal 41, 173
Lieutenant Governor 61
Life expectancy 88
Lincoln..41
Lincoln, Abraham 14
Lindsborg.......................................
.......42, 51, 118, 124, 155, 160, 174
Livestock
Cash receipts from 189
National ranking 189
Local Government 70
Incorporated cities 70
Local jurisdictions......................70
Sources of revenue 70
Lock, Don 103
Logan 42, 114
Longren, Alvin 102
Loo, Miriam 101
Lopes, Davy 103
Louis Vieux Elm tree 195
Louisburg...................................174
Love, Mike....................................98
Lucas 161, 174
Lyons 42
Lytle, Lutie 101

Macksville 42
Manhattan.........42, 51, 114, 175
Manufacturing.........144-145
  Employment.........145
  Food products.........189
  Lumber/wood.........194
  Major manufacturers.........145
  Products.........145
  Top counties for.........144
  Value added.........144
Maps
  Kansas counties.........11
  Kansas highways.........13
  Physiographic regions.........192
  Trails.........31
Marquette.........42
Marriage
  Average age for.........90
  Rates.........90
Marysville.........42, 48, 51
Masters, Edgar Lee.........99
Masterson, William "Bat".........94
May, Rudy.........103
McCarter, Margaret Hill.........99
McConnell Air Force Base.........58
McCormack, Jesse.........101
McDaniel, Hattie.........98
McFarland, Kay.........96
McPherson.........42
Meade.........43
Medicine Lodge.........43, 175
Mehringer, Pete.........103
Menninger, Dr. C.F..........102
Mileage chart.........12
Miles, Vera.........98
Minerals and mining.........199
  Economic impact of.........199
  Minerals produced.........199
  National ranking for.........199
  Non-fuel mining.........199
  Production of fuel minerals.........199
Minneapolis.........43, 175
Miss Americas.........105
Moore, Bruce.........100
Motor vehicle registrations.........150
Mount Sunflower.........5, 192

Mulvane.........43
Museums
  Art museums.........118-119
  Historical.........34-47
Naismith, Dr. James.........103
Nation, Carry.........94
Neodesha.........43, 175
New Cambria.........176
Newspaper, first.........16
Newton.........43, 51, 176
Nicodemus.........49
Niven, Lawrence Van Cott.........99
Norton.........43, 176
Nuclear power.........150
O'Loughlin, Kathryn.........96
Oakley.........43, 177
Oberlin.........43-44
Olathe.........44, 177
Oregon Trail.........32
Osawatomie.........44
Osborne.........44
Oswego.........44, 119, 177
Ottawa.........44, 177
Overland Park.........16, 114-115
Oxford.........177
Paola.........115
Parker, Charlie "Yardbird".........98
Parks, Gordon.........98
Parks, Larry.........98
Pawnee Rock.........49
Peabody.........44
Peterson, Col. Frank E., Jr..........105
Phillipsburg.........44
Pitts, ZaSu.........98
Pittsburg.........44, 118, 177
Pittsburg State University.........75
Pleasanton.........49
Population.........83-86
  Age.........84
  American Indian tribes.........85
  Density.........83
  Ethnic populations.........87
  Largest communities.........86

Migration trends 85
Racial composition 85
Smallest communities 86
Trends...84
Urban and Rural......................84
Pony Express route 32
Pratt 45
Precipitation, annual...............203

Quantrill, William 25
Quinter 178

Ramey, Samuel.......................98
Reed, Clyde M. 96
Reid, Albert T. 100
Regents, State Board of.............75
Religious affiliations.................87
Remington, Frederick..............100
Renko, Steve.............................103
Republic 45
Republic County 178
Restaurants, historical.........50-51
Retail sales 148
Riggins, John 103
River basins...............................201
Riverton 51
Rock formations.................190-191
 Castle Rock 190
 Monument Rocks 190
 Mushroom Rock State Park 191
 Rock City................................191
Rogers, Gen. Bernard W..........105
Rogers, Charles "Buddy"...........98
Ross, Edmund G. 96
Runyon, Damon.........................100
Russell 45
Russell, Bill................................104
Russell Springs...........................45
Ryun, Jim...................................104

St. Marys..............................46
Salina 45, 115-116, 118, 178
Salter, Susanna Madora.............96
Sandzen, Sven Birger...............100
Santa Fe Trail 32
Sayers, Gale...............................104

Scandia...45
Schreffler, Marilyn......................98
Scott City 178
Secretary of State 61
Sedgwick.......................................45
Shawnee 45, 178
Shawnee Mission.......................178
Sheldon, Charles M....................100
Smith Center.......................51, 178
Smith, Dean 104
Smith, Marilyn...........................104
Smoky Hill Trail 14, 32
Stafford..46
State Capitol 9, 16, 60, 67
State Government
 Budget 71
 Executive branch..................60-63
 Judicial branch 68-70
 Legislative branch................64-67
 Tax collections...........................71
State parks.................................193
State symbols 6-9
 Animal..8
 Banner..6
 Bird...7
 Flag...6
 Flower...7
 Insect 8
 March 7
 Motto 6
 Nickname 6
 Reptile..8
 Seal 6
 Song 7
 State name (meaning) 6
 Tree...8
Stone, Dee Wallace......................98
Stone, Milburn 98
Stout, Rex...................................100
Sublette 46
Supreme Court, state.................68
Sutherland, Earl.......................102
Swayze, John Cameron 97

Talley, Marion 99
Taylor, Lucy Hobbs 102

Temperature, average 203
Territorial Period.........................24
Thompson, Bradbury 100
Time zones 5
Tinker, Joe 104
Tombaugh, Clyde.........................102
Topeka 46, 116-117, 118, 179
Tornadoes 203
Torrez, Mike 104
Traer...179
Trails in Kansas....................31-32
  Chisholm Trail 31
  Lewis and Clark route...............31
  Oregon Trail..............................32
  Pony Express route....................32
  Santa Fe Trail 32
  Smoky Hill Trail 32
Transportation industry 150
Troy 179

Ulysses 46
Unemployment rates...................91
University of Kansas .17, 75, 76, 77
Utilities..150

Valley Falls...................................46
Vance, Vivian...............................98
Victoria..180
Vital statistics 87-90
  Birth rates..................................88
  Causes of death..........................89
  Crime rate 88
  Death rates.................................88
  Divorce rates 90
  Ethnic populations.....................87
  Life expectancy 88
  Marriage rates 90
  Religious affiliations..................87
Voter Requirements....................59

Waggoner, Lyle............................98
Wakeeney 46
Wakefield.....................................180
Wallace...46
Walt, Gen. Lewis 105
Walton 46

Wamego.....................46, 49, 162, 180
Washburn University 77
Washington 47
Water...................................200-201
  Consumption 200
  Irrigation and water use 200
  River basins 201
  Sources of 201
  Surface water...........................210
Watson, Tom................................104
Weather 203
  Precipitation.............................203
  Temperature.............................203
  Tornadoes 203
Welch, Gen. Larry D..................105
Wellington 47
Wendelin, Rudolph 101
Wheat
  Introduction of Turkey Red 26
  Production 188
White, William Allen 97
Wholesale trade 148
Wichita ...47, 117, 118, 119, 126, 180
Wichita State University 75, 76, 77
Wildlife
  Endangered species 198
  Hunting and fishing 196-197
Wilkie, Wendell 96
Willard, Jess 104
Winfield 181
Woodard, Lynette 104

Yates Center 47, 181